THERE WILL BE

WAR

VOLUME III

THERE WILL BE

WAR

VOLUME III

CREATED BY
JERRY POURNELLE

CASTALIA HOUSE

There Will Be War Vol. III
Edited by Jerry Pournelle

Published by Castalia House
Tampere, Finland
www.castaliahouse.com

Associate Editor: John F. Carr
Cover Art: Lars Braad Andersen

ISBN: 978-952-7303-17-7

The stories and articles were first published and copyrighted as follows:

DETERRENT OR DEFENSE? by Jerry Pournelle was written especially for the 1984 edition. Published by arrangement with the author and the author's agent, Blassingame, McCauley, and Wood. Copyright © 1984 by J. E. Pournelle.

THE SPECTRE GENERAL by Theodore Cogswell was first published in the June 1952 issue of *Astounding Science Fiction*. It is reprinted by permission of the author. Copyright © 1952 by Street and Smith Publications.

THIS EARTH OF HOURS by James Blish was previously published in the June 1959 issue of *Fantasy & Science Fiction*. Published by arrangement with the author's estate. Copyright © 1959 by Mercury Press.

007: "IT IS ENOUGH, IVAN. GO HOME!" by Reginald Bretnor first appeared in the October 1983 issue of *Survival Tomorrow*. It is presented here by special arrangement with the author. Copyright © 1983 by Personal Survival Center.

THE TOOLS OF WAR by Roland J. Green and Clyde R. Jones appeared for the first time in the 1984 edition. Published with the permission of the authors. Copyright © 1984 by Roland J. Green and Clyde R. Jones.

ACT OF MERCY by D. C. Poyer first appeared in *Unearth Magazine*. Published by permission of the author. Copyright © 1984 by D. C. Poyer.

The editor gratefully acknowledges that research for the non-fiction essays, including "The Defense of Europe" by Stefan Possony, was supported in part by grants from the Vaughn Foundation, and The L-5 Society. Responsibility for opinions expressed herein rests solely with the authors.

Dedication

For the non-commissioned officers of the armed forces of the United States: with thanks.

CONTENTS

Introduction: Deterrent or Defense?

Thus be it ever when free men shall stand
Between their loved homes and the war's desolation...

—"The Star Spangled Banner", Verse 4

Frederick the Great said that "neither the peasants in the fields, nor the burghers in the towns, should know or care when the state was at war." The U.S. ideal is given in the "military's verse" to "The Star Spangled Banner". Allowing for differences in attitude—in Frederick's day, his conquests, though less successful than today's Soviets', were less berated in rhetoric—both intend that armies *defend* their nations.

There had always been exceptions, of course. Coastal towns were vulnerable to raids or bombardment from the earliest days of naval war. Even so, defenses were possible: Witness Fort McHenry, where "The Star Spangled Banner" was written. For the most part, civilian populations were relatively safe until their national army had been defeated.

There grew up conventions, rules and laws of war. Most, like the convention that undefended cities could be declared "open" and thus spared bombardment, were designed to protect the helpless. War might be barbaric, but some elements of civility might be preserved.

The airplane changed that. The British threw away the open city convention for wide area bombardment. Their high-altitude night attacks by Bomber Command had an average miss distance of six miles. RAF bombardiers were told to dump their bombs anywhere they liked;

they'd at least kill some Germans. The Luftwaffe retaliated. World War II became a war against the helpless, culminating in Dresden and Cologne and the indiscriminate fire raids on Tokyo.

Even then there was defense. The RAF, Luftwaffe and Imperial Navy set new standards for heroism as they literally placed themselves between their homes and war's desolation. Bombers got through; but not all got through, and not all went home. Imperfect defense was better than no defense.

Nuclear weapons and the ICBM dealt the final blow to defense. The atom bomb, and later the hydrogen bomb, was so destructive that no more than a handful could devastate a nation's economy. World War II showed that a few bombers always got through—and there was no defense at all against the ICBM.

For a few years after the Soviets obtained nuclear weapons, the United States continued with the notion of defense. There are still abandoned missile sites around Los Angeles and other cities. Eventually, however, it was decided that the cost was too high and the effect too low. Interceptor aircraft would suffice to defend against conventional bombs; nothing would help against a nuclear attack. For the first time in our history, we admitted that we could not defend ourselves. We adopted a doctrine of pure deterrence.

There always was an element of deterrence in our national policy. To deter someone is to prevent him from acting, through either fear or doubt. If you seek to deter an attacker, one of the best deterrents is good defenses; if the attack is likely to fail, it's not rational to try it.

Unfortunately, the United States found itself forced to a strategic doctrine of pure deterence at a time when civilian intellectuals dominated strategic thought. Deterrence is a very soft concept. Defenses involve hardware and capabilities. One may have doubts about the adequacy of a defensive system vs. a particular attack, but at least there is an objective event under debate: Can Sea Cat prevent a Mirage aircraft from successfully attacking a ship? Deterrence, however, is a mental event. Only an attacker knows whether or not he has been deterred. The deterrer can only make guesses based on certain assumptions.

One of the assumptions is that deterrence is possible, i.e., that the potential enemy is sufficiently rational; that he knows the consequences of the forbidden action and cares enough to avoid them. You cannot deter the utterly mad or those who no longer care about the future.

Second, deterrence must be public. A secret defensive weapon may be decisive in actual combat; a secret deterrent weapon is utterly useless.

Third, deterrence may be based on pure bluff; alas, far too many cheese-paring officials seized on this aspect as a way to save money. Weapons need not work—indeed, one need not have any weapons at all—so long as the enemy believes you have workable weapons.

There followed any number of brilliant theoretical essays on deterrence. They had subject matters such as "The Rationality of Irrationality." I recall reading with quiet approval the statement that, "After all, if the other chap is rational and really believes you, then your threat that if he doesn't give you the last piece of toast, you'll blow your brains out all over his new suit will work." All you had to do was convince the other guy you were crazy enough to do it.

We didn't notice at first, but the defense of Europe became almost exactly analogous to that. In fact, it's worse. We now tell the Soviet leaders that if they attack Europe, we'll commit suicide by killing their helpless civilians while sparing their weapons and their leaders.

European defense has now resulted in stationing six U.S. divisions in the path of a hundred Soviet divisions. There is a slim possibility that the U.S. forces in Europe can stop a mobilized Soviet army; it is very unlikely they can do so without employing nuclear weapons. Do we then suppose that the Soviets do not know this? Are they not likely to open the attack by preemptive strikes against our theater nuclear forces? That attack will itself devastate much of Europe.

The Europeans know this, and many therefore oppose introduction of U.S. theater nuclear forces (TNF) to their territory.

It is all made more absurd by opposition to Enhanced Radiation Weapons, sometimes known as "neutron weapons." These can kill exposed personnel while sparing both buildings and their sheltered inhabitants. Such weapons are not magic, but they would be extremely useful in defending against massed armor armies. When we seek to deploy them, we are told that this is inhuman; that we seek to kill the Europeans while sparing their buildings.

"No incineration without representation," the European Peace Movement shouts; yet when we seek to bring home our army, we are accused of "isolationist selfishness" by the very governments that seek to prevent our deploying the weapons that might give our armies a chance in a European war.

In fact, the logic of MAD, of Mutual Assured Deterrence, robs us of credibility. We cannot defend Europe without threatening nuclear strikes against the Soviet Union—which is to invite Soviet retaliation against the U.S. We have arrived at a doctrine which, in the words of Henry Kissinger, "is one that exposes the United States to the devastation of her own territory for people who will not run that risk in defense of themselves."

Deterrence has not yet failed, but the balance of terror is delicate indeed and becomes increasingly more so as the U.S. Strategic Offensive Forces (SOF) grow obsolete and vulnerable.

Deterrence seeks to prevent war; but employing a strategy of pure deterrence pins our hopes not on technology, where we are strong, but on psychology and diplomacy—not fields in which we have had notable past successes.

We've gone farther. Mutual Assured Destruction—MAD, the strategic doctrine adopted by McNamara and continued to this day—has rigid logical requirements. Part of the justification for the Interstate Highway System—the largest and most expensive building program in human history—was that under each approach ramp we would build a fall-out shelter. After the system was proposed, we adopted MAD. The logic of MAD—never accepted by the Soviets—states that civil defenses are an act of aggression.

If we protect our citizens, we must believe the Soviets would attack them; if they're properly deterred, they won't attack except in response to our attack; therefore we must be planning to attack.

Note also that we must as a matter of public policy believe they are deterred; if we express any doubts, then rationally we must attack first.

On the other hand, pure deterrence promised considerable savings. The incremental costs of building fall-out shelters as part of the Interstate Highway System were not high, but there could be real savings on weapons systems. Since both sides were "like small boys standing in a pool of gasoline," there would be no need to collect matches. If the Soviets kill us, we'll kill them back; all we need, then, is enough to kill them with. Strategy was reduced to an engineering problem: If we have the capability to kill enough Russian civilians, all will be well.

Accordingly, the U.S. installed the Minuteman system and quit. Since the Soviets were assumed to be rational, and therefore to think like U.S. university professors turned military theorists, they would understand this unambiguous signal. No one wants to feel inferior in this modern world; therefore the Soviets might build a few more weapons systems than we have; but once they'd caught up, it would be silly for them to go on collecting matches...

The theory was brilliant, but apparently one or another of the assumptions was wrong. When the Soviets "caught up," they didn't halt. They didn't even slow down. They kept four separate assembly lines going three shifts a day, turning out ICBMs as quickly as possible, to the detriment of their civilian economy.

They do it still.

Deterrence certainly hasn't deterred them from building weapons.

Perhaps, though, this is all to the good? These weapons they build; surely they're a mere waste of precious resources. There's nothing they can do with them—

Now understand, there's no doubt that if the Soviet Union were ruled by Harvard professors, they'd be utterly deterred, not only from attacking the U.S. but also from adventures in Europe and Afghanistan. Alas, there's some evidence that they're not.

There's a second problem with deterrence.

It's immoral.

Free men standing between their loved homes and the war's desolation is compatible with Judeo-Christian tradition and the Thomistic doctrine of Just War. Setting fire to the enemy's women and children isn't. Yet if we don't threaten to bum Russian schoolgirls, how can we honor our pledge to Europe? Without credible threats, we are thrown upon the good will of a gang of aged homicidal maniacs who have conclusively proven that they care very little for their own civilians and nothing at all for anyone else's. Lest you doubt that, closely examine Andropov's role in the 1956 Hungarian uprising.

The dilemma is intolerable, and utterly divides the West.

Assured Destruction vs. Assured Survival

In 1969, Stefan T. Possony and I published *The Strategy of Technology*. We argued strongly for a policy of "Assured Survival" in opposition to the McNamara policy of MAD. Assured Survival was defined as a strategy that sought to ensure the survival of the United States, not merely to assure the destruction of the Soviet Union.

There were many approaches to Assured Survival. One was Civil Defense: If deterrence failed, some of our citizens might yet survive. Another was construction of defensive systems, first to protect our missiles, then to protect our cities. The defenses would not be perfect, but they would at least provide some protection.

Defense is, of course, a form of deterrence. Indeed, without some kind of defense, MAD itself becomes difficult; for MAD requires "invulnerable" second-strike weapons. If the enemy can destroy one's retaliatory weapons, then deterrence is not mutual.

Weapons may be made "invulnerable" through their basing, or through doctrine. Alas, the experts are agreed: There is no basing scheme that will guarantee the survival of the Strategic Offensive Forces (SOF) past the end of this decade. Survival of the SOF must increasingly depend on active measures.

The threats to the SOF are very real. Our strategic deterrent is based on the Triad principle: three independent kinds of offensive forces. Alas, all three are vulnerable.

The air leg of the triad depends on the B-52: a once glorious airplane, but old, older than most of her crew. The B-52 has been described as "a mass of parts flying in loose formation."

Adding air-launched cruise missiles helps a little, but not enough; the B-52 plus standoff missiles still must penetrate the Soviet defense systems. Unlike us, the Soviets believe in air defenses, and they have a lot of them.

Cruise missiles are nothing more than pilotless aircraft. They have range limits, and they are vulnerable to air defenses. They must operate in a nuclear environment; unlike the ICBM, they do not rise above the atmosphere but must fly through whatever is left after nuclear detonations. Worse though: They cannot survive a first strike. Whatever the value of cruise missiles, they are soft; they must launch on warning of attack or they will not be launched at all.

The ground leg of the triad is Minuteman. There are 1,000 Minuteman missiles. The location of each is known to inches: It is perfectly legal to buy copies of U.S. Geodetic Survey maps and use surveyors' transits to mark silo locations on them. Since Soviet missile accuracy is now well below 1,000 feet, the single-shot probability that one of their warheads will kill a Minuteman missile is something like 0.99. They have some 12,000 warheads they can target against the United States.

The wet leg of the triad depends entirely on staying hidden, but the oceans are increasingly less opaque. "Synthetic aperture radar" experiments made the news in 1982: A radar flown on the Shuttle was able to see through the sands of the Sahara and map ancient watercourses. Old irrigation canals in Yucatan, long hidden by dense jungle, were found—and whales were seen some fifty meters below the surface of the oceans.

The Soviets routinely fly naval observation radar satellites with nuclear-powered 100-kilowatt power supplies. We don't know precisely what they see with them: We have yet to fly a 10-kilowatt power supply for our observation satellites. We do know what we see with our lower power. All three legs of our SOF triad are vulnerable. It is difficult to believe they could survive a sophisticated first strike in the later years of this decade. If we cannot rely on passive measures such as basing, we must turn to active protection. There are two classes of active measures.

One, defensive systems, is here recommended. The alternative is one or another form of offensive protection: preventative war, preemptive strike or launch on early warning.

Launch on warning requires warning systems. There must also be control. In the event of an attack against Washington by submarine-based missiles, the warning time is twelve minutes or less. In the event of a smuggled weapon detonating in, say, the Soviet Embassy, there is no warning to national command at all.

Launch on warning requires, then, a decision mechanism that can function within the fifteen or so minutes that will elapse between confirmation of a massive attack on the missile forces and the detonation of the attacking weapons. Given human frailties, the pressure to computerize this decision process will be very great.

We will be forced toward the world of "War Games"; a silly picture, yet one that held some realities.

A world with both sides poised to launch on warning is not a stable world.

In 1969, Stefan Possony and I tried to convince the incoming administration to adopt Assured Survival. Alas, we failed.

However, there always was considerable opposition to MAD. After the election of 1980, there was another concerted attempt to persuade the White House that Assured Survival is preferable. Many experts—Edward Teller and Lowell Wood at Lawrence Livermore; Max Hunter and his "Gang of Four," who made alliance with Senator Wallop; General Daniel O. Graham and Project High Frontier—argued that MAD was bankrupt.

Eventually someone got through. On March 23, 1980, the president made an historic speech.

He said: "I have become more and more deeply convinced that the human spirit must be capable of rising above dealing with other nations and human beings by threatening their existence."

He proposed that "we embark on a program to counter the awesome Soviet missile threat with measures that are defensive… What if free people could live secure in the knowledge that their security did not rest upon the threat of instant U.S. retaliation to deter a Soviet attack, that we could intercept and destroy strategic ballistic missiles before they reached our own soil or that of our allies?

"I know that this is a formidable technical task, one that may not be accomplished before the end of this century. Yet current technology has attained a level of sophistication where it's reasonable for us to begin this effort… There will be failures and setbacks, just as there will be successes and breakthroughs… but isn't it worth every investment necessary to free the world from the threat of nuclear war? We know it is…

"My fellow Americans, tonight we're launching an effort which holds the promise of changing the course of human history."

The response was rapid: A number of Congress creatures giggled "Star Wars" and dubbed the president "Darth Vader."

However, when *The New York Times* took a poll, even though its questions were as "neutral" as the *Times's* polls usually are, the American people responded to "Star Wars" by saying, eight to three, "Damn right, and about time, too."

The Treaty of Tarzana

On the weekend of July 29, 1983, we held in Tarzana, California, the third meeting of the Citizens' Advisory Council on National Space Policy.

The Council is composed of some fifty top scientific, managerial and political leaders of the pro-space movement and aerospace community.

One purpose of our meeting was to examine the new policy of Assured Survival and to suggest candidate systems that might be used in this historic endeavor.

We looked at problems as well. They're formidable. For all that, we concluded something startling: We could have, by 1990, a defensive system sufficient to render it impossible for the Soviet Union to eliminate the U.S. strategic deterrent forces.

True: On that time scale, we still rely on deterrence; but from that moment on, we rely less and less heavily on deterrence and more and more on defense.

The Council proposes an interlocked system of defenses, some based in space, some on the ground. Ballistic non-nuclear "shotgun satellites," space-based laser battle stations, very powerful ground-based lasers with mirrors in space and nuclear-pumped "pop-up" lasers would combine to meet a variety of threats against the U.S. and our allies. Each system performs one or another task well; in addition, some of these systems can protect each other. None of this is easy or cheap. The problems with defense are formidable. As an example, space-based components are vulnerable, both in peacetime and to wave attacks when the war begins. Vulnerabilities can be overcome. One method is simple: Harden the satellites. The simplest method for hardening is to surround them with mass. An excellent source of mass is green cheese—i.e., lunar materials. The first shovelful of green cheese is terribly expensive, almost as expensive as fifty MX missiles; after that, green cheese gets cheaper, and it's being used for *defense*, which harms no one.

We also get experience in space operations and a scientific base on the Moon. The new technologies developed might well pay for the entire defense program: After all, the microcomputer industry was developed in response to the need for on-board computers for Minuteman missiles.

The harder the defense system, the more difficult it is to knock out; ideally, one hardens defensive satellites to the point that it requires a nuclear strike to destroy them. The enemy cannot start a war without taking out the defensive satellites. The result is a great increase in the complexity of any first strike—meaning a great increase in the stability of the balance of terror. In addition, a nuclear attack against our defensive satellites is an unambiguous act of war, greatly increasing our warning times.

All this and more is discussed in *The Report of the Citizens' Advisory Council,* which can be obtained for $10.00 from the L-5 Society, 1060 E. Elm St., Tucson, Arizona 85719. Note that the Society sponsors the Council but the Council's conclusions remain the responsibility of the Council.

The full report contains papers on strategy, economics and diplomacy. It also contains excellent unclassified descriptions of strategic defense systems.

One obstacle to deployment of defensive systems was selecting the system to deploy. A number of strategic experts agreed that we should begin deployment of strategic defenses, but each advocated a favorite system. Because each saw the situation as a zero-sum game in which deployment of one system meant suppression of the others, the different groups tended to speak harshly of each other.

Leading spokespeople for each major group were present at the Council meeting. The following open letter to the president was unanimously endorsed by those present. It represents a remarkable consensus among the most talented and best-informed group I have ever worked with.

Because the meeting was held in Tarzana, its joint statement has become known as "The Treaty of Tarzana."

---

30 July 1983

Dear Mr. President:

It has become a common, but erroneous, American dictum that an offense always overwhelms a defense. Yet Stalingrad and the Battle of

Britain, to name two examples within memory, proved that a good defense can defeat a vigorous offense. We believe that a stable peace is best assured by a balance of offense and defense; and that *even a modestly effective defense* can powerfully deter a first strike by any aggressor.

We believe that several systems, both kinetic and directed energy systems, should be developed concurrently for a spectrum of strategic defenses. After years of neglect of strategic defense, we find it imperative that several avenues be pursued concurrently. We must not have a triad of offense and a monad of defense.

While we agree that point defenses by kinetic energy weapons serve an immediate need and should be developed, we believe the nation should vigorously investigate the uses of space for strategic defense.

We believe it is imperative that we first address four candidate systems which provide a significant military capability, i.e., to deny assurance of first-strike success by any aggressor by 1990:

- Multiple satellite using kinetic energy kill.
- Ground-based lasers and mirrors in space.
- Space-based lasers.
- Nuclear explosive-driven beam technologies collectively known as third generation systems.
- Ground-based point defense systems.

We also urge greatly accelerated research on the many other candidate systems, including particle-beam weapons, which offer promise on the longer term.

Implicit in the adoption of our recommendations are the requirements to state openly and unequivocally our intent to adopt a balanced offensive-defensive national strategy and to assess the spectrum of threats and technical risks associated with actual deployment.

Daniel O. Graham, Lt. Gen., USA (Ret.)
Maxwell Hunter, Ph.D.
Francis X. Kane, Ph.D., Col., USAF (Ret.)

Stewart Meyer, Maj. Gen., USA (Ret.)
Dennis A. Reilly, Ph.D.
Lowell W. Wood, Ph.D.

SYSTEMS ASSESSMENT GROUP
CITIZENS' ADVISORY COUNCIL ON
NATIONAL SPACE POLICY

———————————

(The report of the Systems Assessment Group was unanimously approved by the entire Council, some fifty experts in military and space technology.)

The systems proposed are not cheap, but defense is not cheap; and even a small war is expensive. What is it worth to save even one American city? And none of these systems threaten the life of a single Russian schoolgirl.

Let the president and Congress know your views; for if we cannot build support for this, offensive systems will eat the budget and we will have another generation living under the balance of terror.

The choice is ours.

Hollywood, California
November, 1983

THE SPECTRE GENERAL

Theodore Cogswell

Editor's Introduction

I first met Ted Cogswell at the Chicago World Science Fiction Convention in 1962. I met the late H. Beam Piper at that same convention. One magnificent night was spent in Robert A. Heinlein's suite. (In those days, Mr. Heinlein was the only science fiction writer who made enough money to afford a suite.) Beam Piper, Ted Cogswell, Jay Kay Klein, about four others whose names and faces I cannot remember, and I devoured the night by consuming mass quantities of bourbon and singing magnificent old songs.

One of the songs was from the Spanish Civil War. Ted Cogswell taught it to us. He'd been there as a volunteer in the International Brigade.

I met Ted off and on over the years after that. Like many science fiction people, we don't see each other often, but we developed a friendship that wouldn't have been much closer if we lived next door to each other.

When I was president of the Science Fiction Writers of America (SFWA), I asked Ted to edit the SFWA *Forum*, which is our "private" official publication. In my judgment he was the best editor *Forum* ever had; while Ted was editor, the *Forum* was the first thing one read when it came in the mail. Alas, Ted has an, uh, interesting sense of humor, and absolutely no reverence for traditions or causes—even those he supports. There was no trouble while I remained president, but after my retirement, one group within SFWA thought Ted was insufficiently sympathetic to their cause. Storms and strife broke out. Ted resigned—and the *Forum* has never been that interesting since. Alas.

I was invited to Ted's wedding, which was held in San Miguel de Allende, Old Mexico. I suppose it's as well that I couldn't attend. Ted's bride, George Rae, has a strong temper; and through a number of misadventures, Ted and George spent their wedding night in a Mexican jail. They were rescued from durance vile by the efforts of another writer, Mack Reynolds, or rather by Jeanette Reynolds, Mack's wife, who thoroughly understands the local politics.

"The Spectre General" is Ted Cogswell's best-known story. When I first read it, I was in military service. I found it oddly disturbing, and I have never forgotten it. The story is, of course, a satire; but it is also a serious and thought-provoking work, incorporating a number of historical and military truths.

Empire, Commonwealth, Protectorate, Republic, Anarchy, Dictatorship, Timocracy, Tyranny, Monarchy; the tragic cycles of man's efforts turn through endless ages, as we seek the ideal government. Some abandon the search. Others turn cynical or succumb to the worship of power. Some are overcome with despair. Others simply say to hell with it.

Yet, through all ages of ages, there are those to whom duty and virtue are irresistible calls.

I

"Sergeant Dixon!" Kurt stiffened. He knew *that* voice. Dropping the handles of the wooden plow, he gave a quick "rest" to the private and a polite "by your leave, sir" to the lieutenant who were yoked together in double harness. They both sank gratefully to the ground as Kurt advanced to meet the approaching officer.

Marcus Harris, the commander of the 427th Light Maintenance Battalion of the Imperial Space Marines, was an imposing figure. The three silver eagle feathers of a full colonel rose proudly from his war bonnet and the bright red of the flaming comet insignia of the Space Marines that was painted on his chest stood out sharply against his sun-blackened, leathery skin. As Kurt snapped to attention before him and saluted, the colonel surveyed the fresh-turned earth with an experienced eye.

"You plow a straight furrow, soldier!" His voice was hard and metallic, but it seemed to Kurt that there was a concealed glimmer of approval in his flinty eyes. Dixon flushed with pleasure and drew back his broad shoulders a little farther.

The commander's eyes flicked down to the battle-ax that rested snugly in its leather holster at Kurt's side. "You keep a clean sidearm, too."

Kurt uttered a silent prayer of thanksgiving that he had worked over his weapon before reveille that morning until there was a satin gloss to its redwood handle and the sheen of black glass to its obsidian head.

"In fact," said Colonel Harris, "you'd be officer material if—" His voice trailed off.

"If what?" asked Kurt eagerly.

"If," said the colonel with a note of paternal fondness in his voice that sent cold chills dancing down Kurt's spine, "you weren't the most completely unmanageable, undisciplined, overmuscled and underbrained knucklehead I've ever had the misfortune to have in my command. This last little unauthorized jaunt of yours indicates to me that you have as much right to sergeant's stripes as I have to have kittens. Report to me at ten tomorrow! I personally guarantee that when I'm through with you—if you live that long—you'll have a bare forehead!"

Colonel Harris spun on one heel and stalked back across the dusty plateau toward the walled garrison that stood at one end. Kurt stared after him for a moment and then turned and let his eyes slip across the wide belt of lush green jungle that surrounded the high plateau. To the north rose a great range of snow-capped mountains and his heart filled with longing as he thought of the strange and beautiful thing he had found behind them. Finally he plodded slowly back to the plow, his shoulders stooped and his head sagging. With an effort he recalled himself to the business at hand.

"Up on your aching feet, soldier!" he barked to the reclining private. "If you please, sir!" he said to the lieutenant. His calloused hands grasped the worn plow handles.

"Giddiup!" The two men strained against their collars and with a creak of harness, the wooden plow started to move slowly across the arid plateau.

II

Conrad Krogson, Supreme Commander of War Base Three of Sector Seven of the Galactic Protectorate, stood at quaking attention before the visiscreen of his space communicator. It was an unusual position for the commander. He was accustomed to having people quake while *he* talked.

"The Lord Protector's got another hot tip that General Carr is still alive!" said the sector commander. "He's yelling for blood, and if it's a choice between yours and mine, you know who will do the donating!"

"But, sir," quavered Krogson to the figure on the screen, "I can't do anything more than I am doing. I've had double security checks running since the last time there was an alert, and they haven't turned up a thing. And I'm so shorthanded now that if I pull another random purge, I won't have enough techs left to work the base."

"That's your problem, not mine," said the sector commander coldly. "All I know is that rumors have gotten to the Protector that an organized underground is being built up and that Carr is behind it. The Protector wants action now. If he doesn't get it, heads are going to roll!"

"I'll do what I can, sir," promised Krogson.

"I'm sure you will," said the sector commander viciously, "because I'm giving you exactly ten days to produce something that is big enough to take the heat off me. If you don't, I'll break you, Krogson. If I'm sent to the mines, you'll be sweating right alongside me. That's a promise!"

Krogson's face blanched.

"Any questions?" snapped the sector commander.

"Yes," said Krogson.

"Well, don't bother me with them. I've got troubles of my own!" The screen went dark.

Krogson slumped into his chair and sat staring dully at the blank screen. Finally he roused himself with an effort and let out a bellow that rattled the windows of his dusty office.

"Schninkle! Get in here!"

A gnomelike little figure scuttled in through the door and bobbed obsequiously before him.

"Yes, commander?"

"Switch on your think tank," said Krogson. "The Lord Protector has the shakes again and the heat's on!"

"What is it this time?" asked Schninkle.

"General Carr!" said the commander gloomily, "the ex-Number Two."

"I thought he'd been liquidated."

"So did I," said Krogson, "but he must have slipped out some way. The Protector thinks he's started up an underground."

"He'd be a fool if he didn't," said the little man. "The Lord Protector isn't as young as he once was and his grip is getting a little shaky."

"Maybe so, but he's still strong enough to get us before General Carr gets him. The sector commander just passed the buck down to me. We produce or else!"

"We?" said Schninkle unhappily.

"Of course," snapped Krogson, "we're in this together. Now let's get to work! If you were Carr, where would be the logical place for you to hide out?"

"Well," said Schninkle thoughtfully, "if I were as smart as Carr is supposed to be, I'd find myself a hideout right on Prime Base. Everything's so fouled up there that they'd never find me."

"That's out for us," said Krogson. "We can't go rooting around in the Lord Protector's own back yard. What would Carr's next best bet be?"

Schninkle thought for a moment. "He might go out to one of the deserted systems," he said slowly. "There must be half a hundred stars in our own base area that haven't been visited since the old empire broke up. Our ships don't get around the way they used to and the chances are mighty slim that anybody would stumble on to him accidentally."

"It's a possibility," said the commander thoughtfully, "a bare possibility." His right fist slapped into his left palm in a gesture of sudden resolution. "But by the Planets! at least it's something! Alert all section heads for a staff meeting in half an hour. I want every scout out on a quick check of every system in our area!"

"Beg pardon, commander," said Schninkle, "but half our light ships are red-lined for essential maintenance and the other half should be. Anyway, it would take months to check every possible hideout in this area even if we used the whole fleet."

"I know," said Krogson, "but we'll have to do what we can with what we have. At least I'll be able to report to sector that we're doing *something!* Tell Astrogation to set up a series of search patterns. We won't have to check every planet. A single quick sweep through each system will do the trick. Even Carr can't run a base without power. Where there's power, there's radiation, and radiation can be detected a long way off. Put all electronic techs on double shifts and have all detection gear doubled-checked."

"Can't do that either," said Schninkle. "There aren't more than a dozen electronic techs left. Most of them were transferred to Prime Base last week."

Commander Krogson blew up. "How in the name of the Bloody Blue Pleiades am I supposed to keep a war base going without technicians? You tell me, Schninkle, you always seem to know all the answers."

Schninkle coughed modestly. "Well, sir," he said, "as long as you have a situation where technicians are sent to the uranium mines for making mistakes, it's going to be an unpopular vocation. And, as long as the Lord Protector of the moment is afraid that Number Two, Number Three, and so on have ideas about grabbing his job—which they generally do—he's going to keep his fleet as strong as possible and their fleets so weak they aren't dangerous. The best way to do that is to grab techs. If most of the base's ships are sitting around waiting repair, the commander won't be able to do much about any ambitions he may happen to have. Add that to the obvious fact that our whole technology has been on a downward spiral for the last three hundred years and you have your answer."

Krogson nodded gloomy agreement. "Sometimes I feel as if we were all on a dead ship falling into a dying sun," he said. His voice suddenly altered. "But in the meantime we have our necks to save. Get going, Schninkle!" Schninkle bobbed and darted out of the office.

III

It was exactly ten o'clock in the morning when Sergeant Dixon of the Imperial Space Marines snapped to attention before his commanding officer.

"Sergeant Dixon reporting as ordered, sir!" His voice cracked a bit in spite of his best efforts to control it.

The colonel looked at him coldly. "Nice of you to drop in, Dixon," he said. "Shall we go ahead with our little chat?"

Kurt nodded nervousy.

"I have here," said the colonel, shuffling a sheaf of papers, "a report of an unauthorized expedition made by you into *Off Limits* territory."

"Which one do you mean, sir?" asked Kurt without thinking.

"Then there has been more than one?" asked the colonel quietly.

Kurt started to stammer.

Colonel Harris silenced him with a gesture of his hand. "I'm talking about the country to the north, the tableland back of the Twin Peaks."

"It's a beautiful place!" burst out Kurt enthusiastically. "It's… it's like Imperial Headquarters must be. Dozens of little streams full of fish, trees heavy with fruit, small game so slow and stupid that they can be knocked over with a club. Why, the battalion could live there without hardly lifting a finger!"

"I've no doubt that they could," said the colonel.

"Think of it, sir!" continued the sergeant. "No more plowing details, no more hunting details, no more nothing but taking it easy!"

"You might add to your list of 'no mores,' no more tech schools," said Colonel Harris. "I'm quite aware that the place is all you say it is, sergeant. As a result, I'm placing all information that pertains to it in a 'Top Secret' category. That applies to what is inside your head as well!"

"But, sir!" protested Kurt. "If you could only see the place—"

"I have," broke in the colonel, "thirty years ago."

Kurt looked at him in amazement. "Then why are we still on the plateau?"

"Because my commanding officer did just what I've just done, classified the information Top Secret. Then he gave me thirty days' extra detail on the plows. After he took my stripes away, that is." Colonel Harris rose slowly to his feet. "Dixon," he said softly, "it's not every man who can be a noncommissioned officer in the Space Marines. Sometimes we guess wrong. When we do, we do something about it!" There was the hissing crackle of distant summer lightning in his voice and storm clouds seemed to gather about his head. "Wipe those chevrons off!" he roared.

Kurt looked at him in mute protest.

"You heard me!" the colonel thundered.

"Yes-s-s, sir," stuttered Kurt, reluctantly drawing his forearm across his forehead and wiping off the three triangles of white grease paint that marked him a sergeant in the Imperial Space Marines. Quivering with shame, he took a tight grip on his temper and choked back the angry protests that were trying to force their way past his lips.

"Maybe," suggested the colonel, "you'd like to make a complaint to the I.G. He's due in a few days and he might reverse my decision. It has happened before, you know."

"No, sir," said Kurt woodenly.

"Why not?" demanded Harris.

"When I was sent out as a scout for the hunting parties, I was given direct orders not to range farther than twenty kilometers to the north. I went sixty." Suddenly his forced composure broke. "I couldn't help it, sir," he said. "There was something behind those peaks that kept pulling me and pulling me and"—he threw up his hands—"you know the rest."

There was a sudden change in the colonel's face as a warm human smile swept across it, and he broke into a peal of laughter. "It's a hell of a feeling, isn't it, son? You know you shouldn't, but at the same time there's something inside you that says you've got to know what's behind those peaks or die. When you get a few more years under your belt, you'll find that it isn't just mountains that make you feel like that. Here, boy, have a seat." He gestured toward a woven wicker chair that stood by his desk.

Kurt shifted uneasily from one foot to the other, stunned by the colonel's sudden change of attitude and embarrassed by his request. "Excuse me, sir," he said, "but we aren't out on work detail, and–"

The colonel laughed. "And enlisted men not on work detail don't sit in the presence of officers. Doesn't the way we do things ever strike you as odd, Dixon? On one hand you'd see nothing strange about being yoked to a plow with a major, and on the other, you'd never dream of sitting in his presence off duty."

Kurt looked puzzled. "Work details are different," he said. "We all have to work if we're going to eat. But in the garrison, officers are officers and enlisted men are enlisted men and that's the way it's always been."

Still smiling, the colonel reached into his desk drawer, fished out something, and tossed it to Kurt.

"Stick this in your scalp lock," he said.

Kurt looked at it, stunned. It was a golden feather crossed with a single black bar, the insignia of rank of a second lieutenant of the Imperial Space Marines. The room swirled before his eyes.

"Now," said the older officer, "sit down!"

Kurt slowly lowered himself into the chair and looked at the colonel through bemused eyes.

"Stop gawking!" said Colonel Harris. "You're an officer now! When a man gets too big for his sandals, we give him a new pair—after we let him sweat a while!"

He suddenly grew serious. "Now that you're one of the family, you have a right to know why I'm hushing up the matter of the tableland to the north. What I have to say won't make much sense at first. Later I'm hoping it will. Tell me," he said suddenly, "where did the battalion come from?"

"We've always been here, I guess," said Kurt. "When I was a recruit, Granddad used to tell me stories about us being brought from some-place else a long time ago by an iron bird, but it stands to reason that something that heavy can't fly!"

A faraway look came into the colonel's eyes. "Six generations," he mused, "and history becomes legend. Another six and the legends themselves become tales for children. Yes, Kurt," he said softly, "it stands to reason that something that heavy couldn't fly so we'll forget it for a while. We did come from someplace else though. Once there was a great empire, so great that all the stars you see at night were only part of it. And then, as things do when age rests too heavily on them, it began to crumble. Commanders fell to fighting among themselves and the emperor grew weak. The battalion was set down here to operate a forward maintenance station for his ships. We waited but no ships came. For five hundred years no ships have come," said the colonel somberly. "Perhaps they tried to relieve us and couldn't, perhaps the Empire fell with such a crash that we were lost in the wreckage. There are a thousand perhapses that a man can tick off in his mind when the nights are long and sleep comes hard! Lost… forgotten… who knows?"

Kurt stared at him with a blank expression on his face. Most of what the colonel had said made no sense at all. Wherever Imperial Headquarters was, it hadn't forgotten them. The I.G. still made his inspection every year or so.

The colonel continued as if talking to himself. "But our operational orders said that we would stand by to give all necessary maintenance to Imperial warcraft until properly relieved, and stand by we have."

The old officer's voice seemed to be coming from a place far distant in. time and space.

"I'm sorry, sir," said Kurt, "but I don't follow you. If all these things did happen, it was so long ago that they mean nothing to us now."

"But they do!" said Colonel Harris vigorously. "It's because of them that things like your rediscovery of the tableland to the north have to be suppressed for the good of the battalion! Here on the plateau the living is hard. Our work in the fields and the meat brought in by our hunting parties give us just enough to get by on. But here we have the garrison and the Tech Schools—and vague as it has become—a reason for remaining together as the battalion. Out there where the living is easy, we'd lose that. We almost did once. A wise commander stopped it before it went too far. There are still a few signs of that time left—left deliberately as reminders of what can happen if commanding officers forget why we're here!"

"What things?" asked Kurt curiously.

"Well, son," said the colonel, picking up his great war bonnet from the desk and gazing at it quizzically, "I don't think you're quite ready for that information yet. Now take off and strut your feather. I've got work to do!"

IV

At War Base Three nobody was happy. Ships that were supposed to be light-months away carrying on the carefully planned search for General Carr's hideout were fluttering down out of the sky like senile penguins, disabled by blown jets, jammed computers, and all the other natural ills that worn-out and poorly serviced equipment is heir to. Technical maintenance was quietly going mad. Commander Krogson was being noisy about it.

"Schninkle!" he screamed. "Isn't anything happening anyplace?"

"Nothing yet, sir," said the little man.

"Well, *make* something happen!" He hoisted his battered brogans onto the scarred top of the desk and chewed savagely on a frayed cigar. "How are the other sectors doing?"

"No better than we are," said Schninkle. "Commander Snork of Sector Six tried to pull a fast one but he didn't get away with it. He sent his STAP into a plantation planet out at the edge of the Belt and had them hypno the whole population. By the time they were through, there were about fifteen million greenies running around yelling 'Up with General Carr!' 'Down with the Lord Protector!' 'Long Live the People's Revolution!' and things like that. Snork even gave them a few medium-vortex blasters to make it look more realistic. Then he sent in his whole fleet, tipped off the press at Prime Base, and waited. Guess what the Bureau of Essential Information finally sent him?"

"I'll bite," said Commander Krogson.

"One lousy cub reporter. Snork couldn't back out then so he had to go ahead and blast the planet down to bedrock. This morning he got a three-line notice in *Space* and a citation as Third-Rate Protector of the People's Space Ways, Eighth Grade."

"That's better than the nothing we've got so far!" said the commander gloomily.

"Not when the press notice is buried on the next to last page right below the column on 'Our Feathered Comrades,'" said Schninkle, "and when the citation is posthumous. They even misspelled his name; it came out Snark!"

V

As Kurt turned to go, there was a sharp knock on Colonel Harris' door.

"Come in!" called the colonel.

Lieutenant Colonel Blick, the battalion executive officer, entered with an arrogant stride and threw his commander a slovenly salute. For a moment he didn't notice Kurt standing at attention beside the door.

"Listen, Harris!" he snarled. "What's the idea of pulling that clean-up detail out of my quarters?"

"There are no servants in this battalion, Blick," the older man said quietly. "When the men come in from work detail at night, they're tired. They've earned a rest and as long as I'm C.O., they're going to get it. If you have dirty work that has to be done, do it yourself. You're better able to do it than some poor devil who's been dragging a plow all day. I suggest you check pertinent regulations!"

"Regulations!" growled Blick. "What do you expect me to do, scrub my own floors?"

"I do," said the colonel dryly, "when my wife is too busy to get to it. I haven't noticed that either my dignity or my efficiency have suffered appreciably. I might add," he continued mildly, "that staff officers are supposed to set a good example for their juniors. I don't think either your tone or your manner are those that Lieutenant Dixon should be encouraged to emulate." He gestured toward Kurt and Blick spun on one heel.

"*Lieutenant* Dixon!" he roared in an incredulous voice. "By whose authority?"

"Mine," said the colonel mildly. "In case you've forgotten, I am still commanding officer of this battalion."

"I protest!" said Blick. "Commissions have always been awarded by decision of the entire staff."

"Which you now control," replied the colonel.

Kurt coughed nervously. "Excuse me, sir," he said, "but I think I'd better leave."

Colonel Harris shook his head. "You're one of our official family now, son, and you might as well get used to our squabbles. This particular one has been going on between Colonel Blick and me for years. He has no patience with some of our old customs." He turned to Blick. "Have you, Colonel?"

"You're right, I haven't!" growled Blick. "And that's why I'm going to change some of them as soon as I get the chance. The sooner we stop this Tech School nonsense and put the recruits to work in the fields where they belong, the better off we'll all be. Why should a plowman or a hunter have to know how to read wiring diagrams or set tubes? It's nonsense, superstitious nonsense. You!" he said, stabbing his finger into the chest of the startled lieutenant. "You! Dixon! You spent fourteen years in the Tech Schools just like I did when I was a recruit. What for?"

"To learn maintenance, of course," said Kurt.

"What's maintenance?" demanded Blick.

"Taking stuff apart and putting it back together and polishing jet bores with microplanes and putting plates in alignment and checking the meters when we're through to see the job was done right. Then there's class work in Direc calculus and subelectronics and–"

"That's enough!" interrupted Blick. "And now that you've learned all that, what can you do with it?"

Kurt looked at him in surprise.

"Do with it?" he echoed. "You don't *do* anything with it. You just learn it because regulations say you should."

"And this," said Blick, turning to Colonel Harris, "is one of your prize products. Fourteen of his best years poured down the drain and he doesn't even know what for!" He paused and then said in an arrogant voice, "I'm here for a showdown, Harris!"

"Yes?" said the colonel mildly.

"I demand that the Tech Schools be closed at once and the recruits released for work details. If you want to keep your command, you'll issue that order. The staff is behind me on this!"

Colonel Harris rose slowly to his feet. Kurt waited for the thunder to roll, but strangely enough, it didn't. It almost seemed to him that there was an expression of concealed amusement playing across the colonel's face.

"Someday, just for once," he said, "I wish somebody around here would do something that hasn't been done before."

"What do you mean by that?" demanded Blick.

"Nothing," said the colonel. "You know," he continued conversationally, "a long time ago I walked into my C.O.'s office and made the same demands and the same threats that you're making now. I didn't get very far, though—just as you aren't going to—because I overlooked the little matter of the Inspector General's annual visit. He's due in from Imperial Headquarters Saturday night, isn't he, Blick?"

"You know he is!" growled the other.

"Aren't worried, are you? It occurs to me that the I.G. might take a dim view of your new order."

"I don't think he'll mind," said Blick with a nasty grin. "Now will you issue the order to close the Tech Schools or won't you?"

"Of course not!" said the colonel brusquely.

"That's final?"

Colonel Harris just nodded.

"All right," barked Blick, "you asked for it!"

There was an ugly look on his face as he barked, "Kane! Simmons! Amett! The rest of you! Get in here!"

The door to Hams' office swung slowly open and revealed a group of officers standing sheepishly in the anteroom.

"Come in, gentlemen," said Colonel Harris.

They came slowly forward and grouped themselves just inside the door.

"I'm taking over!" roared Blick. "This garrison has needed a house-cleaning for a long time and I'm just the man to do it!"

"How about the rest of you?" asked the colonel.

"Beg pardon, sir," said one hesitantly, "but we think Colonel Blick's probably right. I'm afraid we're going to have to confine you for a few days. Just until after the I.G.'s visit," he added apologetically.

"And what do you think the I.G. will say to all this?"

"Colonel Blick says we don't have to worry about that," said the officer. "He's going to take care of everything."

A look of sudden anxiety played across Harris' face and for the first time he seemed on the verge of losing his composure.

"How?" he demanded, his voice betraying his concern.

"He didn't say, sir," the other replied. Harris relaxed visibly.

"All right," said Blick. "Let's get moving!" He walked behind the desk and plumped into the colonel's chair. Hoisting his feet on the desk, he gave his first command.

"Take him away!"

There was a sudden roar from the far corner of the room. "No you don't!" shouted Kurt. His battle-ax leaped into his hand as he jumped in front of Colonel Harris, his muscular body taut and his gray eyes flashing defiance.

Blick jumped to his feet. "Disarm that man!" he commanded. There was a certain amount of scuffling as the officers in the front of the group by the door tried to move to the rear and those behind them resolutely defended their more protected positions.

Blick's face grew so purple that he seemed on the verge of apoplexy. "Major Kane," he demanded, "place that man under restraint!"

Kane advanced toward Kurt with a noticeable lack of enthusiasm. Keeping a cautious eye on the glittering ax head, he said in what he obviously hoped to be a placating voice, "Come now, old man. Can't have this sort of thing, you know." He stretched out his hand hesitantly toward Kurt. "Why don't you give me your ax and we'll forget that the incident ever occurred."

Kurt's ax suddenly leaped toward the major's head. Kane stood petrified as death whizzed toward him. At the last split second Kurt gave a practiced twist to his wrist and the ax jumped up, cutting the air over the major's head with a vicious whistle. The top half of his silver staff plume drifted slowly to the floor.

"You want it," roared Kurt, his ax flicking back and forth like a snake's tongue, "you come get it. That goes for the rest of you, too!"

The little knot of officers retreated still farther. Colonel Harris was having the time of his life.

"Give it to 'em, son!" he whooped.

Blick looked contemptuously at the staff and slowly drew his own ax. Colonel Harris suddenly stopped laughing.

"Wait a minute, Blick!" he said. "This has gone far enough." He turned to Kurt.

"Give them your ax, son."

Kurt looked at him with an expression of hurt bewilderment in his eyes, hesitated for a moment, and then glumly surrendered his weapon to the relieved major.

"Now," snarled Blick, "take that insolent puppy out and feed him to the lizards!"

Kurt drew himself up in injured dignity. "That is no way to refer to a brother officer," he said reproachfully.

The vein in Blick's forehead started to pulse again. "Get him out of here before I tear him to shreds!" he hissed through clenched teeth. There was silence for a moment as he fought to regain control of himself. Finally he succeeded.

"Lock him up!" he said in an approximation of his normal voice. "Tell the provost sergeant I'll send down the charges as soon as I can think up enough."

Kurt was led resentfully from the room.

"The rest of you clear out," said Blick. "I want to talk with Colonel Harris about the I.G."

VI

There was a saying in the protectorate that when the Lord Protector was angry, stars and heads fell. Commander Krogson felt his wobble on his neck. His far-sweeping scouts were sending back nothing but reports of equipment failure, and the sector commander had coldly informed him that morning that his name rested securely at the bottom of the achievement list. It looked as if War Base Three would shortly have a change of command. "Look, Schninkle," he said desperately, "even if we can't give them anything, couldn't we make a promise that would look good enough to take some of the heat off us?"

Schninkle looked dubious.

"Maybe a new five-year plan?" suggested Krogson.

The little man shook his head. "That's a subject we'd better avoid entirely," he said. "They're still asking nasty questions about what happened to the last one. Mainly on the matter of our transport quota. I took the liberty of passing the buck on down to Logistics. Several of them have been… eh… removed as a consequence."

"Serves them right!" snorted Krogson. "They got me into that mess with their 'If a freighter and a half flies a light-year and a half in a month and a half, ten freighters can fly ten light-years in ten months!' I knew there was something fishy about it at the time, but I couldn't put my finger on it."

"It's always darkest before the storm," said Schninkle helpfully.

VII

"Take off your war bonnet and make yourself comfortable," said Colonel Harris hospitably.

Blick grunted assent. "This thing is sort of heavy," he said. "I think I'll change uniform regulations while I'm at it."

"There was something you wanted to tell me?" suggested the colonel.

"Yeah," said Blick. "I figure that you figure the I.G.'s going to bail you out of this. Right?"

"I wouldn't be surprised."

"I would," said Blick. "I was up snoopin' around the armory last week. There was something there that started me doing some heavy thinking. Do you know what it was?"

"I can guess," said the colonel.

"As I looked at it, it suddenly occurred to me what a happy coincidence it is that the Inspector General always arrives just when you happen to need him."

"It is odd, come to think of it."

"Something else occurred to me, too. I got to thinking that if I were C.O. and I wanted to keep the troops whipped into line, the easiest way to do it would be to have a visible symbol of Imperial Headquarters appear in person once in a while."

"That makes sense," admitted Harris, "especially since the chaplain has started preaching that Imperial Headquarters is where good marines go when they die—*if* they follow regulations while they're alive. But how would you manage it?"

"Just the way you did. I'd take one of the old battle suits, wait until it was good and dark, and then slip out the back way and climb up six or seven thousand feet. Then I'd switch on my landing lights and drift slowly down to the parade field to review the troops." Blick grinned triumphantly.

"It might work," admitted Colonel Harris, "but I was under the impression that those rigs were so heavy that a man couldn't even walk in one, let alone fly."

Blick grinned triumphantly. "Not if the suit was powered. If a man were to go up into the tower of the arsenal and pick the lock of the little door labeled 'Danger! Absolutely No Admittance,' he might find a whole stack of shiny little cubes that look suspiciously like the illustrations of power packs in the tech manuals."

"That he might," agreed the colonel.

Blick shifted back in his chair. "Aren't worried, are you?"

Colonel Harris shook his head. "I was for a moment when I thought you'd told the rest of the staff, but I'm not now."

"You should be! When the I.G. arrives this time, I'm going to be inside that suit. There's going to be a new order around here, and he's just what I need to put the stamp of approval on it. When the Inspector General talks, nobody questions!"

He looked at Harris expectantly, waiting for a look of consternation to sweep across his face. The colonel just laughed.

"Blick," he said, "you're in for a big surprise!"

"What do you mean?" said the other suspiciously.

"Simply that I know you better than you know yourself. You wouldn't be executive officer if I didn't. You know, Blick, I've got a hunch that the battalion is going to change the man more than the man is going to change the battalion. And now if you'll excuse me—" He started toward the door. Blick moved to intercept him.

"Don't trouble yourself," chuckled the colonel. "I can find my own way to the cell block." There was a broad grin on his face. "Besides, you've got work to do."

There was a look of bewilderment in Blick's face as the erect figure went out the door. "I don't get it," he said to himself. "I just don't get it!"

VIII

Flight Officer Ozaki was unhappy. Trouble had started two hours after he lifted his battered scout off War Base Three and showed no signs of letting up. He sat glumly at his controls and enumerated his woes. First there was the matter of the air conditioner, which had acquired an odd little hum and discharged into the cabin oxygen redolent with the rich, ripe odor of rotting fish. Second, something had happened to the complex insides of his food synthesizer and no matter what buttons he punched, all that emerged from the ejector were quivering slabs of undercooked protein base smeared with a raspberry-flavored goo.

Not last, but worst of all, the ship's fuel converter was rapidly becoming more erratic. Instead of a slow, steady feeding of the plutonite ribbon into the combustion chamber, there were moments when the mechanism would falter and then leap ahead. The resulting sudden injection of several square millimicrons of tape would send a sudden tremendous flare of energy spouting out through the rear jets. The pulse lasted for only a fraction of a second, but the sudden application of several Gs meant a momentary blackout and, unless he was strapped carefully into the pilot seat, several new bruises to add to the old.

What made Ozaki the unhappiest was that there was nothing he could do about it. Pilots who wanted to stay alive just didn't tinker with the mechanism of their ships.

Glumly he pulled out another red-bordered IMMEDIATE MAINTENANCE card from the rack and began to fill it in.

Description of item requiring maintenance: "Shower thermostat, M7, Small Standard."

Nature of malfunction: "Shower will deliver only boiling water."

Justification for immediate maintenance: Slowly in large, block letters Ozaki bitterly inked in "Haven't had a bath since I left base!" and tossed the card into the already overflowing gripe box with a feeling of helpless anger.

"Kitchen mechanics," he muttered. "Couldn't do a decent repair job if they wanted to—and most of the time they don't. I'd like to see one of them three days out on a scout sweep with a toilet that won't flush!"

IX

It was a roomy cell as cells go but Kurt wasn't happy there. His continual striding up and down was making Colonel Harris nervous.

"Relax, son," he said gently, "you'll just wear yourself out."

Kurt turned to face the colonel, who was stretched out comfortably on his cot. "Sir," he said in a conspiratorial whisper, "we've got to break out of here."

"What for?" asked Harris. "This is the first decent rest I've had in years."

"You aren't going to let Blick get away with this?" demanded Kurt in a shocked voice.

"Why not?" said the colonel. "He's the exec, isn't he? If something happened to me, he'd have to take over command anyway. He's just going through the impatient stage, that's all. A few days behind my desk will settle him down. In two weeks he'll be so sick of the job he'll be down on his knees begging me to take over again."

Kurt decided to try a new tack. "But, sir, he's going to shut down the Tech Schools!"

"A little vacation won't hurt the kids," said the colonel indulgently.

"After a week or so the wives will get so sick of having them underfoot all day that they'll turn the heat on him. Blick has six kids himself, and I've a hunch his wife won't be any happier than the rest. She's a very determined woman, Kurt, a very determined woman!"

Kurt had a feeling he was getting no place rapidly. "Please, sir," he said earnestly, "I've got a plan."

"Yes?"

"Just before the guard makes his evening check-in, stretch out on the bed and start moaning. I'll yell that you're dying and when he comes in to check, I'll jump him!"

"You'll do no such thing!" said the colonel sternly. "Sergeant Wetzel is an old friend of mine. Can't you get it through your thick head that I don't want to escape? When you've held command as long as I have, you'll welcome a chance for a little peace and quiet. I know Blick inside out, and I'm not worried about him. But, if you've got your heart set on escaping, I suppose there's no particular reason why you shouldn't. Do it the easy way though. Like this." He walked to the bars that fronted the cell and bellowed, "Sergeant Wetzel! Sergeant Wetzel!"

"Coming, sir!" called a voice from down the corridor. There was a shuffle of running feet and a gray scalp-locked and extremely portly sergeant puffed into view.

"What will it be, sir?" he asked.

"Colonel Blick or any of the staff around?" questioned the colonel.

"No, sir," said the sergeant. "They're all upstairs celebrating."

"Good!" said Harris. "Unlock the door, will you?"

"Anything you say, Colonel," said the old man agreeably and produced a large key from his pouch and fitted it into the lock. There was a slight creaking and the door swung open.

"Young Dixon here wants to escape," said the colonel.

"It's all right by me," replied the sergeant, "though it's going to be awkward when Colonel Blick asks what happened to him."

"The lieutenant has a plan," confided the colonel. "He's going to overpower you and escape."

"There's more to it than just that!" said Kurt. "I'm figuring on swapping uniforms with you. That way I can walk right out through the front gate without anybody being the wiser."

"That," said the sergeant, slowly looking down at his sixty-three-inch waist, "will take a heap of doing. You're welcome to try though."

"Let's get on with it then," said Kurt, winding up a roundhouse swing.

"If it's all the same with you, Lieutenant," said the old sergeant, eyeing Kurt's rocklike fist nervously, "I'd rather have the colonel do any overpowering that's got to be done."

Colonel Harris grinned and walked over to Wetzel.

"Ready?"

"Ready!"

Harris' fist traveled a bare five inches and tapped Wetzel lightly on the chin.

"Oof!" grunted the sergeant cooperatively and staggered back to a point where he could collapse on the softest of the two cots.

The exchange of clothes was quickly effected. Except for the pants—which persisted in dropping down to Kurt's ankles—and the war bonnet—which with equal persistence kept sliding down over his ears—he was ready to go. The pants problem was solved easily by stuffing a pillow inside them. This Kurt fondly believed made him look more like the rotund sergeant than ever. The garrison bonnet presented a more difficult problem, but he finally achieved a partial solution. By holding it up with his left hand and keeping the palm tightly pressed against his forehead, it should appear to the casual observer that he was walking engrossed in deep thought.

The first two hundred yards were easy. The corridor was deserted and he plodded confidently along, the great war bonnet wobbling sedately on his head in spite of his best efforts to keep it steady. When he finally reached the exit gate, he knocked on it firmly and called to the duty sergeant.

"Open up! It's Wetzel."

Unfortunately, just then he grew careless and let go of his headgear. As the door swung open, the great war bonnet swooped down over his ears and came to rest on his shoulders. The result was that where his head normally was there could be seen only a nest of weaving feathers. The duty sergeant's jaw suddenly dropped as he got a good look at the strange figure that stood in the darkened corridor. And then with remarkable presence of mind, he slammed the door shut in Kurt's face and clicked the bolt.

"Sergeant of the guard!" he bawled. "Sergeant of the guard! There's a *thing* in the corridor!"

"What kind of a thing?" inquired a sleepy voice from the guard room.

"A horrible kind of a thing with wiggling feathers where its head ought to be," replied the sergeant.

"Get its name, rank, and serial number," said the sleepy voice.

Kurt didn't wait to hear any more. Disentangling himself from the headdress with some difficulty, he hurled it aside and pelted back down the corridor.

Lieutenant Dixon wandered back into the cell with a crestfallen look on his face. Colonel Harris and the old sergeant were so deeply engrossed in a game of "rockets high" that they didn't even see him at first. Kurt coughed and the colonel looked up.

"Change your mind?"

"No, sir," said Kurt. "Something slipped."

"What?" asked the colonel.

"Sergeant Wetzel's war bonnet. I'd rather not talk about it." He sank down on his bunk and buried his head in his hands.

"Excuse me," said the sergeant apologetically, "but if the lieutenant's through with my pants, I'd like to have them back. There's a draft in here."

Kurt silently exchanged clothes and then moodily walked over to the grille that barred the window and stood looking out.

"Why not go upstairs to officers' country and out that way?" suggested the sergeant, who hated the idea of being overpowered for nothing. "If you can get to the front gate without one of the staff spotting you, you can walk right out. The sentry never notices faces, he just checks for insignia."

Kurt grabbed Sergeant Wetzel's plump hand and wrung it warmly. "I don't know how to thank you," he stammered.

"Then it's about time you learned," said the colonel. "The usual practice in civilized battalions is to say 'thank you.'"

"Thank you!" said Kurt.

"Quite all right," said the sergeant. "Take the first stairway to your left. When you get to the top, turn left again and the corridor will take you straight to the exit."

Kurt got safely to the top of the stairs and turned right. Three hundred feet later the corridor ended in a blank wall. A small passageway angled off to the left and he set off down it. It also came to a dead end in a small anteroom whose farther wall was occupied by a set of great bronze doors. He turned and started to retrace his steps. He had almost reached the main corridor when he heard angry voices sounding from it. He peeked cautiously around the corridor. His escape route was blocked by two officers engaged in acrimonious argument. Neither was too sober and the captain obviously wasn't giving the major the respect that a field officer usually commanded.

"I don't care what she said!" the captain shouted. "I saw her first."

The major grabbed him by the shoulder and pushed him back against the wall. "It doesn't matter who saw her first. You keep away from her or there's going to be trouble!"

The captain's face flushed with rage. With a snarl he tore off the major's breechcloth and struck him in the face with it.

The major's face grew hard and cold. He stepped back, clicked his calloused heels together, and bowed slightly.

"Axes or fists?"

"Axes," snapped the captain.

"May I suggest the armory anteroom?" said the major formally. "We won't be disturbed there."

"As you wish, sir," said the captain with equal formality. "Your breechcloth, sir." The major donned it with dignity and they started down the hall toward Kurt. He turned and fled back down the corridor.

In a second he was back in the anteroom. Unless he did something quickly, he was trapped. Two flaming torches were set in brackets on each side of the great bronze door. As flickering pools of shadow chased each other across the worn stone floor, Kurt searched desperately for some other way out. There was none. The only possible exit was through the bronze portals. The voices behind him grew louder. He ran forward, grabbed a projecting handle, and pulled. One door creaked open slightly and with a sigh of relief, Kurt slipped inside.

There were no torches here. The great hall stood in half-darkness, its only illumination the pale moonlight that streamed down through the arching skylight that formed the central ceiling. He stood for a moment in awe, impressed in spite of himself by the strange, unfamiliar shapes that loomed before him in the half-darkness. He was suddenly brought back to reality by the sound of voices in the anteroom.

"Hey! The armory door's open!"

"So what? That place is off limits to everybody but the C.O."

"Blick won't care. Let's fight in there. There should be more room."

Kurt quickly scanned the hall for a safe hiding place. At the far end stood what looked like a great bronze statue, its burnished surface gleaming dimly in the moonlight. As the door swung open behind him, he slipped cautiously through the shadows until he reached it. It looked like a coffin with feet, but to one side of it there was a dark pool of shadow. He slipped into it and pressed himself close against the cold metal. As he did so, his hipbone pressed against a slight protrusion and with a slight clicking sound, a hinged middle section of the metallic figure swung open, exposing a dark cavity. The thing was hollow!

Kurt had a sudden idea. "Even if they do come down here," he thought, "they'd never think of looking inside this thing!" With some difficulty he wiggled inside and pulled the hatch shut after him. There were legs to the thing—his own fit snugly into them—but no arms.

The two officers strode out of the shadows at the other end of the hall. They stopped in the center of the armory and faced each other like fighting cocks. Kurt gave a sigh of relief. It looked as if he were safe for the moment.

There was a sudden wicked glitter of moonlight on ax-heads as their weapons leaped into their hands. They stood frozen for a moment in a murderous tableau and then the captain's ax hummed toward his opponent's head in a vicious slash. There was a shower of sparks as the major parried and then with a quick wrist twist sent his own weapon looping down toward the captain's midriff. The other pulled his ax down to ward the blow, but he was only partially successful. The keen obsidian edge raked his ribs and blood dripped darkly in the moonlight.

As Kurt watched intently, he began to feel the first faint stirrings of claustrophobia. The Imperial designers had planned their battle armor for efficiency rather than comfort and Kurt felt as if he were locked away in a cramped dark closet. His malaise wasn't helped by a sudden realization that when the men left, they might very well lock the door behind them. His decision to change his hiding place was hastened when a bank of dark clouds swept across the face of the moon. The flood of light pouring down through the skylight suddenly dimmed until Kurt could barely make out the pirouetting forms of the two officers who were fighting in the center of the hall.

This was his chance. If he could slip down the darkened side of the hall before the moon lighted up the hall again, he might be able to slip out of the hall unobserved. He pushed against the closed hatch through which he entered. It refused to open. A feeling of trapped panic started to roll over him, but he fought it back. "There must be some way to open this from the inside," he thought.

As his fingers wandered over the dark interior of the suit looking for a release lever, they encountered a bank of keys set just below his midriff. He pressed one experimentally. A quiet hum filled the armor and suddenly a feeling of weightlessness came over him. He stiffened in fright. As he did so, one of his steel-shod feet pushed lightly backwards against the floor. That was enough. Slowly, like a child's balloon caught in a light draft, he drifted toward the center of the hall. He struggled violently, but since he was now several inches above the floor and rising slowly, it did him no good.

The fight was progressing splendidly. Both men were master axmen, and in spite of being slightly drunk, were putting on a brilliant exhibition. Each was bleeding from a dozen minor slashes, but neither had been seriously axed as yet. Their flashing strokes and counters were masterful, so masterful that Kurt slowly forgot his increasingly awkward situation as he became more and more absorbed in the fight before him. The blond captain was slightly the better axman, but the major compensated for it by occasionally whistling in cuts that to Kurt's experienced eye seemed perilously close to fouls. He grew steadily more partisan in his feelings until one particularly unscrupulous attempt broke down his restraint altogether.

"Pull down your guard!" he screamed to the captain. "He's trying to cut you below the belt!" His voice reverberated within the battle suit and boomed out with strange metallic overtones.

Both men whirled in the direction of the sound. They could see nothing for a moment and then the major caught sight of the strange, menacing figure looming above him in the murky darkness.

Dropping his ax, he dashed frantically toward the exit shrieking: "It's the Inspector General!"

The captain's reflexes were a second slower. Before he could take off, Kurt poked his head out of the open faceport and shouted down, "It's only me, Dixon! Get me out of here, will you?"

The captain stared up at him goggle-eyed. "What kind of a contraption is that?" he demanded. "And what are you doing in it?"

Kurt by now was floating a good ten feet off the floor. He had visions of spending the night on the ceiling and he wasn't happy about it. "Get me down now," he pleaded. "We can talk after I get out of this thing."

The captain gave a leap upward and tried to grab Kurt's ankles. His jump was short and his outstretched fingers gave the weightless armor a slight shove that sent it bobbing up another three feet.

He cocked his head back and called up to Kurt. "Can't reach you now. We'll have to try something else. How did you get into that thing in the first place?"

"The middle section is hinged," said Kurt. "When I pulled it shut, it clicked."

"Well, unclick it!"

"I tried that. That's why I'm up here now."

"Try again," said the man on the floor. "If you can-open the hatch, you can drop down and I'll catch you."

"Here I come!" said Kurt, his fingers selecting a stud at random. He pushed. There was a terrible blast of flame from the shoulder jets and he screamed skyward on a pillar of fire. A microsecond later, he reached the skylight. Something had to give. It did!

At fifteen thousand feet the air pressure dropped to the point where the automatics took over and the faceplate clicked shut. Kurt didn't notice that. He was out like a light. At thirty thousand feet the heaters cut in. Forty seconds later he was in free space. Things could have been worse though; he still had air for two hours.

X

Flight Officer Ozaki was taking a catnap when the alarm on the radiation detector went off. Dashing the sleep out of his eyes, he slipped rapidly into the control seat and cut off the gong. His fingers danced over the controls in a blur of movement. Swiftly the vision screen shifted until the little green dot that indicated a source of radiant energy was firmly centered. Next he switched on the pulse analyzer and watched carefully as it broke down the incoming signal into components and sent them surging across the scope in the form of sharp-toothed sine waves. There was an odd peak to them, a strength and sharpness that he hadn't seen before.

"Doesn't look familiar," he muttered to himself, "but I'd better check to make sure."

He punched the comparison button and while the analyzer methodically began to check the incoming trace against the known patterns stored up in its compact little memory bank, he turned back to the vision screen. He switched on high magnification and the system rushed toward him. It expanded from a single pinpoint of light into a distinct planetary system. At its center a giant dying sun expanded on the plate like a malignant red eye. As he watched, the green dot moved appreciably, a thin red line stretching out behind it to indicate its course from point of first detection. Ozaki's fingers moved over the controls and a broken line of white light came into being on the screen. With careful adjustments he moved it up toward the green track left by the crawling red dot. When he had an exact overlay, he carefully moved the line back along the course that the energy emitter had followed prior to detection.

Ozaki was tense. It looked as if he might have something. He gave a sudden whoop of excitement as the broken white line intersected the orange dot of a planetary mass. A vision of the promised thirty-day leave and six months' extra pay danced before his eyes as he waited for the pulse analyzer to clear.

"Home!" he thought ecstatically. "Home and unplugged plumbing!"

With a final whir of relays, the analyzer clucked like a contented chicken and dropped an identity card out of its emission slot. Ozaki grabbed it and scanned it eagerly. At the top was printed in red, "Identity. Unknown," and below in smaller letters, "Suggest check of trace pattern on base analyzer." He gave a sudden whistle as his eyes caught the energy utilization index. 927! That was fifty points higher than it had any right to be. The best tech in the Protectorate considered himself lucky if he could tune a propulsion unit so that it delivered a thrust of forty-five per cent of rated maximum. Whatever was out there was hot! Too hot for one man to handle alone. With quick decision he punched the transmission key of his space communicator and sent a call winging back to War Base Three.

XI

Commander Krogson stormed up and down his office in a frenzy of impatience.

"It shouldn't be more than another fifteen minutes, sir," said Schninkle.

Krogson snorted. "That's what you said an hour ago. What's the matter with those people down there? I want the identity of that ship and I want it now."

"It's not Identification's fault," explained the other. "The big analyzer is in pretty bad shape and it keeps jamming. They're afraid that if they take it apart, they won't be able to get it back together again."

The next two hours saw Krogson's blood pressure steadily rising toward the explosion point. Twice he ordered the whole identification section transferred to a labor battalion and twice he had to rescind the command when Schninkle pointed out that scrapings from the bottom of the barrel were better than nothing at all. His fingernails were chewed down to the quick when word finally came through.

"Identification, sir," said a hesitant voice on the intercom.

"Well?" demanded the commander.

"The analyzer says–" The voice hesitated again.

"The analyzer says what?" shouted Krogson in a fury of impatience.

"The analyzer says that the trace pattern is that of one of the old Imperial drive units."

"That's impossible!" sputtered the commander. "The last Imperial base was smashed five hundred years ago. What of their equipment was salvaged has long since been worn out and tossed on the scrap heap. The machine must be wrong!"

"Not this time," said the voice. "We checked the memory bank manually and there's no mistake. It's an Imperial all right. Nobody can produce a drive unit like that these days."

Commander Krogson leaned back in his chair, his eyes veiled in deep thought. "Schninkle," he said finally, thinking out loud, "I've got a hunch that maybe we've stumbled on something big. Maybe the Lord

Protector is right about there being a plot to knock him over, but maybe he's wrong about who's trying to do it. What if all these centuries since the Empire collapsed a group of Imperials have been hiding out waiting for their chance?"

Schninkle digested the idea for a moment. "It could be," he said slowly. "If there is such a group, they couldn't pick a better time than now to strike; the Protectorate is so wobbly that it wouldn't take much of a shove to topple it over."

The more he thought about it, the more sense the idea made to Krogson. Once he felt a fleeting temptation to hush up the whole thing. If there were Imperials and they did take over, maybe they would put an end to the frenzied rat race that was slowly ruining the galaxy—a race that sooner or later entangled every competent man in the great web of intrigue and power politics that stretched through the Protectorate and forced him in self-defense to keep clawing his way toward the top of the heap.

Regretfully he dismissed the idea. This was a matter of his own neck, here and now!

"It's a big IF, Schninkle," he said, "but if I've guessed right, we've bailed ourselves out. Get hold of that scout and find out his position."

Schninkle scooted out of the door. A few minutes later he dashed back in. "I've just contacted the scout!" he said excitedly. "He's closed in on the power source and it isn't a ship after all. It's a man in space armor! The drive unit is cut off, and it's heading out of the system at fifteen hundred per. The pilot is standing by for instructions."

"Tell him to intercept and capture!" Schninkle started out of the office. "Wait a second; what's the scout's position?"

Schninkle's face fell. "He doesn't quite know, sir."

"He *what?*" demanded the commander.

"He doesn't quite know," repeated the little man. "His astrocomputer went haywire six hours out of base."

"Just our luck!" swore Krogson. "Well, tell him to leave his transmitter on. We'll ride in on his beam. Better call the sector commander while you're at it and tell him what's happened."

"Beg pardon, Commander," said Schninkle, "but I wouldn't advise it."

"Why not?" asked Krogson.

"You're next in line to be sector commander, aren't you, sir?"

"I guess so," said the commander.

"If this pans out, you'll be in a position to knock him over and grab his job, won't you?" asked Schninkle slyly.

"Could be," admitted Krogson in a tired voice. "Not because I want to, though—but because I have to. I'm not as young as I once was, and the boys below are pushing pretty hard. It's either up or out—and out is always feet first."

"Put yourself in the sector commander's shoes for a minute," suggested the little man. "What would you do if a war-base commander came through with news of a possible Imperial base?" A look of grim comprehension came over Krogson's face. "Of course! I'd ground the commander's ships and send out my own fleet. I must be slipping; I should have thought of that at once!"

"On the other hand," said Schninkle, "you might call him and request permission to conduct routine maneuvers. He'll approve as a matter of course and you'll have an excuse for taking out the full fleet. Once in deep space, you can slap on radio silence and set course for the scout. If there is an Imperial base out there, nobody will know anything about it until it's blasted. I'll stay back here and keep my eyes on things for you."

Commander Krogson grinned. "Schninkle, it's a pleasure to have you in my command. How would you like me to make you Devoted Servant of the Lord Protector, Eighth Class? It carries an extra shoe-ration coupon!"

"If it's all the same with you," said Schninkle, "I'd just as soon have Saturday afternoons off."

XII

As Kurt struggled up out of the darkness, he could hear a gong sounding in the faint distance. *Bong*! bong! *BONG*! It grew nearer and louder. He shook his head painfully and groaned. There was light from some-place beating against his eyelids. Opening them was too much effort. He was in some sort of a bunk. He could feel that. But the gong. He lay there concentrating on it. Slowly he began to realize that the beat didn't come from outside. It was his head. It felt swollen and sore and each pulse of his heart sent a hammer thud through it.

One by one his senses began to return to normal. As his nose reassumed its normal acuteness, it began to quiver. There was a strange scent in the air, an unpleasant sickening scent as of—he chased the scent down his aching memory channels until he finally had it cornered—rotting fish. With that to anchor on, he slowly began to reconstruct reality. He had been floating high above the floor in the armory and the captain had been trying to get him down. Then he had pushed a button. There had been a microsecond of tremendous acceleration and then a horrendous crash. That must have been the skylight. After the crash was darkness, then the gongs, and now fish—dead and rotting fish.

"I must be alive," he decided. "Imperial Headquarters would never smell like this!"

He groaned and slowly opened one eye. Wherever he was, he hadn't been there before. He opened the other eye. He was in a room. A room with a curved ceiling and curving walls. Slowly, with infinite care, he hung his head over the side of the bunk. Below him in a form-fitting chair before a bank of instruments sat a small man with yellow skin and blue-black hair. Kurt coughed. The man looked up. Kurt asked the obvious question.

"Where am I?"

"I'm not permitted to give you any information," said the small man. His speech had an odd, slurred quality to Kurt's ear.

"Something stinks!" said Kurt.

"It sure does," said the small man gloomily. "It must be worse for you. I'm used to it."

Kurt surveyed the cabin with interest. There were a lot of gadgets tucked away here and there that looked familiar. They were like the things he had worked on in Tech School except that they were cruder and simpler. They looked as if they had been put together by an eight-year-old recruit who was doing the first trial assembly. He decided to make another stab at establishing some sort of communication with the little man.

"How come you have everything in one room? We always used to keep different things in different shops."

"No comment," said Ozaki.

Kurt had a feeling he was butting his head against a stone wall. He decided to make one more try.

"I give up," he said, wrinkling his nose, "where'd you hide it?"

"Hide what?" asked the little man.

"The fish," said Kurt.

"No comment."

"Why not?" asked Kurt.

"Because there isn't anything that can be done about it," said Ozaki. "It's the air conditioner. Something's haywire inside."

"What's an air conditioner?" asked Kurt.

"That square box over your head."

Kurt looked at it, closed his eyes, and thought for a moment. The thing did look familiar. Suddenly a picture of it popped into his mind. Page 318 in the "Manual of Auxiliary Mechanisms."

"It's fantastic!" he said.

"What is?" said the little man.

"This," Kurt pointed to the conditioner. "I didn't know they existed in real life. I thought they were just in books. You got a first-echelon kit?"

"Sure," said Ozaki. "It's in the recess by the head of the bunk. Why?"

Kurt pulled the kit out of its retaining clips and opened its cover, fishing around until he found a small screwdriver and a pair of needle-nose pliers.

"I think I'll fix it," he said conversationally.

"Oh, no you won't!" howled Ozaki. "Air with fish is better than no air at all." But before he could do anything, Kurt had pulled the cover off the air conditioner and was probing into the intricate mechanism with his screwdriver. A slight thumping noise came from inside. Kurt cocked his ear and thought. Suddenly his screwdriver speared down through the maze of whirring parts. He gave a slow quarter-turn and the internal thumping disappeared.

"See," he said triumphantly, "no more fish!"

Ozaki stopped shaking long enough to give the air a tentative sniff. He had got out of the habit of smelling in self-defense and it took him a minute or two to detect the difference. Suddenly a broad grin swept across his face.

"It's going away! I do believe it's going away!"

Kurt gave the screwdriver another quarter of a turn and suddenly the sharp, spicy scent of pines swept through the scout. Ozaki took a deep ecstatic breath and relaxed in his chair. His face lost its pallor.

"How did you do it?" he said finally.

"No comment," said Kurt pleasantly.

There was silence from below. Ozaki was in the throes of a brain-storm. He was more impressed by Kurt's casual repair of the air conditioner than he liked to admit.

"Tell me," he said cautiously, "can you fix other things beside air conditioners?"

"I guess so," said Kurt, "if it's just simple stuff like this." He gestured around the cabin. "Most of the stuff here needs fixing. They've got it together wrong."

"Maybe we could make a dicker," said Ozaki. "You fix things, I answer questions—some questions, that is," he added hastily.

"It's a deal," said Kurt, who was filled with a burning curiosity as to his whereabouts. Certain things were already clear in his mind. He knew that wherever he was, he'd never been there before. That meant evidently that there was a garrison on the other side of the mountains whose existence had never been suspected. What bothered him was how he had got there.

"Check," said Ozaki. "First, do you know anything about plumbing?"

"What's plumbing?" asked Kurt curiously. "Pipes," said Ozaki. "They're plugged. They've been plugged for more time than I like to think about."

"I can try," said Kurt.

"Good!" said the pilot and ushered him into the small cubicle that opened off the rear bulkhead. "You might tackle the shower while you're at it."

"What's a shower?"

"That curved dingbat up there," said Ozaki, pointing. "The thermostat's out of whack."

"Thermostats are kid stuff," said Kurt, shutting the door.

Ten minutes later Kurt came out. "It's all fixed."

"I don't believe it," said Ozaki, shouldering his way past Kurt. He reached down and pushed a small curved handle. There was the satisfying sound of rushing water. He next reached into the little shower compartment and turned the knob to the left. With a hiss, a needle-spray of cold water burst forth. The pilot looked at Kurt with awe in his eyes.

"If I hadn't seen it, I wouldn't have believed it! That's two answers you've earned."

Kurt peered back into the cubicle curiously. "Well, first," he said, "now that I've fixed them, what are they *for*?"

Ozaki explained briefly and a look of amazement came over Kurt's face. Machinery he knew, but the idea that it could be used for something was hard to grasp.

"If I hadn't seen it, I wouldn't have believed it!" he said slowly. This would be something to tell when he got home. Home! The pressing question of location popped back into his mind.

"How far are we from the garrison?" he asked.

Ozaki made a quick mental calculation.

"Roughly two light-seconds," he said.

"How far's that in kilometers?"

Ozaki thought again. "Around six hundred thousand. I'll run off the exact figures if you want them."

Kurt gulped. No place could be that far away. Not even Imperial Headquarters! He tried to measure out the distance in his mind in terms of days' marches, but he soon found himself lost. Thinking wouldn't do it. He had to see with his own eyes where he was.

"How do you get outside?" he asked.

Ozaki gestured toward the air lock that opened at the rear of the compartment. "Why?"

"I want to go out for a few minutes to sort of get my bearings."

Ozaki looked at him in disbelief. "What's your game, anyhow?" he demanded.

It was Kurt's turn to look bewildered. "I haven't any game. I'm just trying to find out where I am so I'll know which way to head to get back to the garrison."

"It'll be a long, cold walk." Ozaki laughed and hit the stud that slid back the ray screens on the vision ports. "Take a look."

Kurt looked out into nothingness, a blue-black void marked only by distant pinpoints of light. He suddenly felt terribly alone, lost in a blank immensity that had no boundaries. *Down* was gone and so was *up*. There was only this tiny lighted room with nothing underneath it. The port began to swim in front of his eyes as a sudden, strange vertigo swept over him. He felt that if he looked out into that terrible space for another moment, he would lose his sanity. He covered his eyes with his hands and staggered back to the center of the cabin.

Ozaki slid the ray screens back in place. "Kind of gets to you first time, doesn't it?"

Kurt had always carried a little automatic compass within his head. Wherever he had gone, no matter how far afield he had wandered, it had always pointed steadily toward home. Now for the first time in his life, the needle was spinning helplessly. It was an uneasy feeling. He had to get oriented.

"Which way is the garrison?" he pleaded.

Ozaki shrugged. "Over there someplace. I don't know whereabouts on the planet you come from. I didn't pick up your track until you were in free space."

"Over where?" asked Kurt.

"Think you can stand another look?"

Kurt braced himself and nodded. The pilot opened a side port to vision and pointed. There, seemingly motionless in the black emptiness of space, floated a great greenish-gray globe. It didn't make sense to Kurt. The satellite that hung somewhat to the left did. Its face was different, the details were sharper than he'd ever seen them before, but the features he knew as well as his own. Night after night on scouting detail for the hunting parties while waiting for sleep he had watched the silver sphere ride through the clouds above him.

He didn't want to believe but he had to!

His face was white and tense as he turned back to Ozaki. A thousand sharp and burning questions milled chaotically through his mind.

"Where am I?" he demanded. "How did I get out here? Who are you? Where did you come from?"

"You're in a spaceship," said Ozaki, "a two-man scout. And that's all you're going to get out of me until you get some more work done. You might as well start on this microscopic projector. The thing burned out just as the special investigator was about to reveal who had blown off the commissioner's head by wiring a bit of plutonite into his autoshave. I've been going nuts ever since trying to figure out who did it!"

Kurt took some tools out of the first-echelon kit and knelt down obediently beside the small projector.

Three hours later they sat down to dinner. Kurt had repaired the food machine and Ozaki was slowly masticating synthasteak that for the first time in days tasted like synthasteak. As he ecstatically lifted the last savory morsel to his mouth, the ship gave a sudden leap that plastered him and what remained of his supper against the rear bulkhead. There was darkness for a second and then the ceiling lights flickered on, then off, and then on again. Ozaki picked himself up and gingerly ran his fingers over the throbbing lump that was beginning to grow out of the top of his head. His temper wasn't improved when he looked up and saw Kurt still seated at the table calmly cutting himself another piece of pie.

"You should have braced yourself," said Kurt conversationally. "The converter's out of phase. You can hear her build up for a jump if you listen. When she does, you ought to brace yourself. Maybe you don't hear so good?" he asked helpfully.

"Don't talk with your mouth full, it isn't polite," snarled Ozaki.

Late that night the converter cut out altogether. Ozaki was sleeping the sleep of the innocent and didn't find out about it for several hours. When he did awake, it was to Kurt's gentle shaking.

"Hey!" Ozaki groaned and buried his face in the pillow.

"Hey!" This time the voice was louder. The pilot yawned and tried to open his eyes.

"Is it important if all the lights go out?" the voice queried. The import of the words suddenly struck home and Ozaki sat bolt upright in his bunk. He opened his eyes, blinked, and opened them again. The lights *were* out. There was a strange, unnatural silence about the ship.

"Good Lord!" he shouted and jumped for the controls. "The power's off."

He hit the starter switch but nothing happened. The converter was jammed solid. Ozaki began to sweat. He fumbled over the control board until he found the switch that cut the emergency batteries into the lighting circuit. Again nothing happened.

"If you're trying to run the lights on the batteries, they won't work," said Kurt in a conversational tone.

"Why not?" snapped Ozaki as he punched savagely and futilely at the starter button.

"They're dead," said Kurt. "I used them all up."

"You what?" yelled the pilot in anguish.

"I used them all up. You see, when the converter went out, I woke up. After a while the sun started to come up, and it began to get awfully hot so I hooked the batteries into the refrigeration coils. Kept the place nice and cool while they lasted."

Ozaki howled. When he swung the shutter of the forward port to let in some light, he howled again. This time in dead earnest. The giant red sun of the system was no longer perched off to the left at a comfortable distance. Instead, before Ozaki's horrified eyes was a great red mass that stretched from horizon to horizon.

"We're falling into the sun!" he screamed.

"It's getting sort of hot," said Kurt. "Hot" was an understatement. The thermometer needle pointed at a hundred and ten and was climbing steadily.

Ozaki jerked open the stores-compartment door and grabbed a couple of spare batteries. As quickly as his trembling fingers would work, he connected them to the emergency power line. A second later the cabin lights flickered on and Ozaki was warming up the space communicator. He punched the transmitter key and a call went arcing out through hyperspace. The vision screen flickered and the bored face of a communication tech, third class, appeared.

"Give me Commander Krogson at once!" demanded Ozaki.

"Sorry, old man," yawned the other, "but the commander's having breakfast. Call back in half an hour, will you?"

"This is an emergency! Put me through at once!"

"Can't help it," said the other, "nobody can disturb the Old Man while he's having breakfast!"

"Listen, you knucklehead," screamed Ozaki, "if you don't get me through to the commander as of right now, I'll have you in the uranium mines so fast that you won't know what hit you!"

"You and who else?" drawled the tech.

"Me and my cousin Takahashi!" snarled the pilot. "He's Reclassification Officer for the Base STAP."

The tech's face went white. "Yes, sir!" he stuttered. "Right away, sir! No offense meant, sir!" He disappeared from the screen. There was a moment of darkness and then the interior of Commander Krogson's cabin flashed on.

The commander was having breakfast. His teeth rested on the white tablecloth and his mouth was full of mush.

"Commander Krogson!" said Ozaki desperately.

The commander looked up with a startled expression. When he noticed his screen was on, he swallowed his mush convulsively and popped his teeth back into place.

"Who's there?" he demanded in a neutral voice in case it might be somebody important.

"Flight Officer Ozaki," said Flight Officer Ozaki.

A thundercloud rolled across the commander's face. "What do you mean by disturbing me at breakfast?" he demanded.

"Beg pardon, sir," said the pilot, "but my ship's falling into a red sun."

"Too bad," grunted Commander Krogson and turned back to his mush and milk.

"But, sir," persisted the other, "you've got to send somebody to pull me off. My converter's dead!"

"Why tell me about it?" said Krogson in annoyance. "Call Space Rescue, they're supposed to handle things like this."

"Listen, Commander," wailed the pilot, "by the time they've assigned me a priority and routed the paper through proper channels, I'll have gone up in smoke. The last time I got in a jam it took them two weeks to get to me; I've got only hours left!"

"Can't make exceptions," snapped Krogson testily. "If I let you skip the chain of command, everybody and his brother will think he has a right to."

"Commander," howled Ozaki, "we're frying in here!"

"All right. All right!" said the commander sourly. "I'll send somebody after you. What's your name?"

"Ozaki, sir. Flight Officer Ozaki."

The commander was in the process of scooping up another spoonful of mush when suddenly a thought struck him squarely between the eyes.

"Wait a second," he said hastily, "you aren't the scout who located the Imperial base, are you?"

"Yes, sir," said the pilot in a cracked voice.

"Why didn't you say so?" roared Krogson. Flipping on his intercom, he growled, "Give me the exec." There was a moment's silence.

"Yes, sir?"

"How long before we get to that scout?"

"About six hours, sir."

"Make it three!"

"Can't be done, sir."

"It will be done!" snapped Krogson and broke the connection.

The temperature needle in the little scout was now pointing to a hundred and fifteen.

"I don't think we can hold on that long," said Ozaki.

"Nonsense!" said the commander and the screen went blank.

Ozaki slumped into the pilot chair and buried his face in his hands. Suddenly he felt a blast of cold air on his neck. "There's no use in prolonging our misery," he said without looking up. "Those spare batteries won't last five minutes under this load."

"I knew that," said Kurt cheerfully, "so while you were doing all the talking, I went ahead and fixed the converter. You sure have mighty hot summers out here!" he continued, mopping his brow.

"You what?" yelled the pilot, jumping half out of his seat. "You couldn't even if you did have the know-how. It takes half a day to get the shielding off so you can get at the thing!"

"Didn't need to take the shielding off for a simple job like that," said Kurt. He pointed to a tiny inspection port about four inches in diameter. "I worked through there."

"That's impossible!" interjected the pilot. "You can't even see the injector through that, let alone get to it to work on!"

"Shucks," said Kurt, "a man doesn't have to see a little gadget like that to fix it. If your hands are trained right, you can feel what's wrong and set it to rights right away. She won't jump on you anymore either.

The syncromesh thrust baffle was a little out of phase so I fixed that, too, while I was at it."

Ozaki still didn't believe it, but he hit the controls on faith. The scout bucked under the sudden strong surge of power and then, its converter humming sweetly, arced away from the giant sun in a long, sweeping curve.

There was silence in the scout. The two men sat quietly, each immersed in an uneasy welter of troubled speculation.

"That was close!" said Ozaki finally. "Too close for comfort. Another hour or so and–!" He snapped his fingers.

Kurt looked puzzled. "Were we in trouble?"

"Trouble!" snorted Ozaki. "If you hadn't fixed the converter when you did, we'd be cinders by now!"

Kurt digested the news in silence. There was something about this super-being who actually made machines work that bothered him. There was a note of bewilderment in his voice when he asked: "If we were really in danger, why didn't you fix the converter instead of wasting time talking on that thing?" He gestured toward the space communicator.

It was Ozaki's turn to be bewildered. "Fix it?" he said with surprise in his voice. "There aren't a half a dozen techs on the whole base who know enough about atomics to work on a propulsion unit. When something like that goes out, you call Space Rescue and chew your nails until a wrecker can get to you."

Kurt crawled into his bunk and lay back, staring at the curved ceiling. He had thinking to do, a lot of thinking!

Three hours later the scout flashed up alongside the great flagship and darted into a landing port. Flight Officer Ozaki was stricken by a horrible thought as he gazed affectionately around his smoothly running ship.

"Say," he said to Kurt hesitantly, "would you mind not mentioning that you fixed this crate up for me? If you do, they'll take it away from me sure. Some captain will get a new gig and I'll be issued another clunk from Base Junkpile."

"Sure thing," said Kurt.

A moment later the flashing of a green light on the control panel signaled that the pressure in the lock had reached normal.

"Back in a minute," said Ozaki. "You wait here."

There was a muted hum as the exit hatch swung slowly open. Two guards entered and stood silently beside Kurt as Ozaki left to report to Commander Krogson.

XIII

The battle fleet of War Base Three of Sector Seven of the Galactic Protectorate hung motionless in space twenty thousand kilometers out from Kurt's home planet. A hundred tired detection techs sat tensely before their screens, sweeping the globe for some sign of energy radiation. Aside from the occasional light spatters caused by space static, their scopes remained dark. As their reports filtered into Commander Krogson, he became more and more exasperated.

"Are you positive this is the right planet?" he demanded of Ozaki.

"No question about it, sir."

"Seems funny there's nothing running down there at all," said Krogson. "Maybe they spotted us on the way in and cut off power. I've got a hunch that–" He broke off in mid-sentence as the red top-priority light on the communication panel began to flash. "Get that," he said. "Maybe they've spotted something at last."

The executive office flipped on the vision screen and the interior of the flagship's communication room was revealed.

"Sorry to bother you, sir," said the tech whose image appeared on the screen, "but a message just came through on the emergency band."

"What does it say?"

The tech looked unhappy. "It's coded, sir."

"Well, decode it!" barked the executive.

"We can't," said the technician diffidently. "Something's gone wrong with the decoder. The printer is pounding out random groups that don't make any sense at all."

The executive grunted his disgust. "Any idea where the call's coming from?"

"Yes, sir; it's coming in on a tight beam from the direction of Base. Must be from a ship emergency rig, though. Regular hyperspace transmission isn't directional. Either the ship's regular rig broke down or the operator is using the beam to keep anybody else from picking up his signal."

"Get to work on that decoder. Call back as soon as you get any results." The tech saluted and the screen went black.

"Whatever it is, it's probably trouble," said Krogson morosely. "Well, we'd better get on with this job. Take the fleet into atmosphere. It looks as if we are going to have to make a visual check."

"Maybe the prisoner can give us a lead," suggested the executive officer.

"Good idea. Have him brought in."

A moment later Kurt was ushered into the master control room. Krogson's eyes widened at the sight of scalp lock and paint.

"Where in the name of the Galactic Spirit," he demanded, "did you get that rig?"

"Don't you recognize an Imperial Space Marine when you see one?" Kurt answered coldly.

The guard that had escorted Kurt in made a little twirling motion at his temple with one finger. Krogson took another look and nodded agreement.

"Sit down, son," he said in a fatherly tone. "We're trying to get you home, but you're going to have to give us a little help before we can do it. You see, we're not quite sure just where your base is."

"I'll help all I can," said Kurt.

"Fine!" said the commander, rubbing his palms together. "Now just where down there do you come from?" He pointed out the vision port to the curving globe that stretched out below.

Kurt looked down helplessly. "Nothing makes sense, seeing it from up here," he said apologetically.

Krogson thought for a moment. "What's the country like around your base?" he asked.

"Mostly jungle," said Kurt. "The garrison is on a plateau though and there are mountains to the north."

Krogson turned quickly to his exec. "Did you get that description?"

"Yes, sir!"

"Get all scouts out for a close sweep. As soon as the base is spotted, move the fleet in and hover at forty thousand!"

Forty minutes later a scout came streaking back.

"Found it, sir!" said the exec. "Plateau with jungle all around and mountains to the north. There's a settlement at one end. The pilot saw movement down there, but they must have spotted us on our way in. There's still no evidence of energy radiation. They must have everything shut down."

"That's not good!" said Krogson. "They've probably got all their heavy stuff set up waiting for us to sweep over. We'll have to hit them hard and fast. Did they spot the scout?"

"Can't tell, sir."

"We'd better assume that they did. Notify all gunnery officers to switch their batteries over to central control. If we come in fast and high and hit them with simultaneous fleet concentration, we can vaporize the whole base before they can take a crack at us."

"I'll send the order out at once, sir," said the executive officer.

The fleet pulled into tight formation and headed toward the Imperial base. They were halfway there when the fleet gunnery officer entered the control room and said apologetically to Commander Krogson, "Excuse me, sir, but I'd like to suggest a trial run. Fleet concentration is a tricky thing, and if something went haywire—we'd be sitting ducks for the ground batteries."

"Good idea," said Krogson thoughtfully. "There's too much at stake to have anything go wrong. Select an equivalent target, and we'll make a pass."

The fleet was now passing over a towering mountain chain.

"How about that bald spot down there?" said the exec, pointing to a rocky expanse that jutted out from the side of one of the towering peaks.

"Good enough," said Krogson.

"All ships on central control!" reported the gunnery officer.

"On target!" repeated the tech on the tracking screen. "One. Two. Three. Four—"

Kurt stood by the front observation port watching the ground far below sweep by. He had been listening intently, but what had been said didn't make sense. There had been something about *batteries*—the term was alien to him—and something about the garrison. He decided to ask the commander what it was all about, but the intentness with which Krogson was watching the tracking screen deterred him. Instead, he gazed moodily down at the mountains below him.

"Five. Six. Seven. Ready. FIRE!"

A savage shudder ran through the great ship as her ground-pointed batteries blasted in unison. Seconds went by and then suddenly the rocky expanse on the shoulder of the mountain directly below twinkled as blinding flashes of actinic light danced across it. Then as Kurt watched, great masses of rock and earth moved slowly skyward from the center of the spurting nests of tangled flame. Still slowly, as if buoyed up by the thin mountain air, the debris began to fall back again until it was lost from sight in quick-rising mushrooms of jet-black smoke. Kurt turned and looked back toward Commander Krogson. *Batteries* must be the things that had torn the mountains below apart. And *garrison*—there was only one garrison!

"I ordered fleet fire," barked Krogson. "This ship was the only one that cut loose. What happened?"

"Just a second, sir," said the executive officer, "I'll try and find out." He was busy for a minute on the intercom system. "The other ships were ready, sir," he reported finally. "Their guns were all switched over to our control, but no impulse came through. Central fire control must be on the blink!" He gestured toward a complex bank of equipment that occupied one entire corner of the control room.

Commander Krogson said a few appropriate words. When he reached the point where he was beginning to repeat himself, he paused and stood in frozen silence for a good thirty seconds.

"Would you mind getting a fire-control tech in here to fix that obscenity bank?" he asked in a voice that put everyone's teeth on edge.

The other seemed to have something to say, but he was having trouble getting it out.

"Well?" said Krogson.

"Prime Base grabbed our last one two weeks ago. There isn't another left with the fleet."

"Doesn't look like much to me," said Kurt as he strolled over to examine the bank of equipment.

"Get away from there!" roared the commander. "We've got enough trouble without you making things worse."

Kurt ignored him and began to open inspection ports.

"Guard!" yelled Krogson. "Throw that man out of here!"

Ozaki interrupted timidly. "Beg pardon, Commander, but he can fix it if anybody can."

Krogson whirled on the flight officer. "How do you know?"

Ozaki caught himself just in time. If he talked too much, he was likely to lose the scout that Kurt had fixed for him.

"Because he... eh... talks like a tech," he concluded lamely.

Krogson looked at Kurt dubiously. "I guess there's no harm in giving it a trial," he said finally. "Give him a set of tools and turn him loose. Maybe for once a miracle will happen."

"First," said Kurt, "I'll need the wiring diagrams for this thing."

"Get them!" barked the commander and an orderly scuttled out of the control, headed aft.

"Next you'll have to give me a general idea of what it's supposed to do," continued Kurt.

Krogson turned to the gunnery officer. "You'd better handle this."

When the orderly returned with the circuit diagrams, they were spread out on the plotting table and the two men bent over them.

"Got it!" said Kurt at last and sauntered over to the control bank. Twenty minutes later he sauntered back again.

"She's all right now," he said pleasantly.

The gunner officer quickly scanned his testing board. Not a single red trouble light was on. He turned to Commander Krogson in amazement.

"I don't know how he did it, sir, but the circuits are all clear now."

Krogson stared at Kurt with a look of new respect in his eyes. "What were you down there, chief maintenance tech?"

Kurt laughed. "Me? I was never chief anything. I spent most of my time on hunting detail."

The commander digested that in silence for a moment. "Then how did you become so familiar with fire-control gear?"

"Studied it in school like everyone else does. There wasn't anything much wrong with that thing anyway except a couple of sticking relays."

"Excuse me, sir," interrupted the executive officer, "but should we make another trial run?"

"Are you sure the bank is in working order?"

"Positive, sir!"

"Then we'd better make straight for that base. If this boy here is a fair example of what they have down there, their defenses may be too tough for us to crack if we give them a chance to get set up!"

Kurt gave a slight start which he quickly controlled. Then he had guessed right! Slowly and casually he began to sidle toward the semicircular bank of controls that stood before the great tracking screen.

"Where do you think you're going!" barked Krogson.

Kurt froze. His pulses were pounding within him, but he kept his voice light and casual.

"No place," he said innocently.

"Get over against the bulkhead and keep out of the way!" snapped the commander. "We've got a job of work coming up."

Kurt injected a note of bewilderment into his voice.

"What kind of work?"

Krogson's voice softened and a look approaching pity came into his eyes. "It's just as well you don't know about it until it's over," he said gruffly.

"There she is!" sang out the navigator, pointing to a tiny brown projection that jutted up out of the green jungle in the far distance. "We're about three minutes out, sir. You can take over at any time now."

The fleet gunnery officer's fingers moved quickly over the keys that welded the fleet into a single instrument of destruction, keyed and ready to blast a barrage of ravening thunderbolts of molecular disruption down at the defenseless garrison at a single touch on the master fire-control button.

"Whenever you're ready, sir," he said deferentially to Krogson as he vacated the controls. A hush fell over the control room as the great tracking screen brightened and showed the compact bundle of white dots that marked the fleet crawling slowly toward the green triangle of the target area.

"Get the prisoner out of here," said Krogson. "There's no reason why he should have to watch what's about to happen."

The guard that stood beside Kurt grabbed his arm and shoved him toward the door.

There was a sudden explosion of fists as Kurt erupted into action. In a blur of continuous movement, he streaked toward the gunnery control panel. He was halfway across the control room before the pole-axed guard hit the floor. There was a second of stunned amazement, and then before anyone could move to stop him, he stood beside the controls, one hand poised tensely above the master stud that controlled the combined fire of the fleet.

"Hold it!" he shouted as the moment of paralysis broke and several of the officers started toward him menacingly. "One move and I'll blast the whole fleet into scrap!"

They stopped in shocked silence, looking to Commander Krogson for guidance.

"Almost on target, sir," called the tech on the tracking screen.

Krogson stalked menacingly toward Kurt. "Get away from those controls!" he snarled. "You aren't going to blow anything to anything. All that you can do is let off a premature blast. If you are trying to alert your base, it's no use. We can be on a return sweep before they have time to get ready for us."

Kurt shook his head calmly. "Wouldn't do you any good," he said. "Take a look at the gun ports on the other ships. I made a couple of minor changes while I was working on the control bank."

"Quit bluffing," said Krogson.

"I'm not bluffing," said Kurt quietly. "Take a look. It won't cost you anything."

"On target!" called the tracking tech.

"Order the fleet to circle for another sweep," snapped Krogson over his shoulder as he stalked toward the forward observation port. There was something in Kurt's tone that had impressed him more than he liked to admit. He squinted out toward the nearest ship. Suddenly his face blanched!

"The gunports! They're closed!"

Kurt gave a whistle of relief. "I had my fingers crossed," he said pleasantly. "You didn't give me enough time with the wiring diagrams for me to be sure that cutting out that circuit would do the trick. Now... guess what the results would be if I should happen to push down on this stud."

Krogson had a momentary vision of several hundred shells ramming their sensitive noses against the thick chrome steel of the closed gun ports.

"Don't bother trying to talk," said Kurt, noticing the violent contractions of the commander's Adam's apple. "You'd better save your breath for my colonel."

"Who?" demanded Krogson.

"My colonel," repeated Kurt. "We'd better head back and pick him up. Can you make these ships hang in one place or do they have to keep moving fast to stay up?"

The commander clamped his jaws together sullenly and said nothing.

Kurt made a tentative move toward the firing stud.

"Easy!" yelled the gunnery officer in alarm. "That thing has hair-trigger action!"

"Well?" said Kurt to Krogson.

"We can hover," grunted the other.

"Then take up a position a little to one side of the plateau." Kurt brushed the surface of the firing stud with a casual finger. "If you make me push this, I don't want a lot of scrap iron falling down on the battalion. Somebody might get hurt."

As the fleet came to rest above the plateau, the call light on the communication panel began to flash again.

"Answer it," ordered Kurt, "but watch what you say."

Krogson walked over and snapped on the screen.

"Communications, sir."

"Well?"

"It's that message we called you about earlier. We've finally got the decoder working—sort of, that is." His voice faltered and then stopped.

"What does it say?" demanded Krogson impatiently.

"We still don't know," admitted the tech miserably. "It's being decoded all right, but it's coming out in a North Vegan dialect that nobody down here can understand. I guess there's still something wrong with the selector. All that we can figure out is that the message has something to do with General Carr and the Lord Protector."

"Want me to go down and fix it?" interrupted Kurt in an innocent voice.

Krogson whirled toward him, his hamlike hands clenching and unclenching in impotent rage.

"Anything wrong, sir asked the technician on the screen.

Kurt raised a significant eyebrow to the commander.

"Of course not," growled Krogson. "Go find somebody to translate that message and don't bother me until it's done."

A new face appeared on the screen.

"Excuse me for interrupting, sir, but translation won't be necessary. We just got a flash from Detection that they've spotted the ship that sent it. It's a small scout heading in on emergency drive. She should be here in a matter of minutes."

Krogson flipped off the screen impatiently. "Whatever it is, it's sure to be more trouble," he said to nobody in particular. Suddenly he became aware that the fleet was no longer in motion. "Well," he said sourly to Kurt, "we're here. What now?"

"Send a ship down to the garrison and bring Colonel Harris back up here so that you and he can work this thing out between you. Tell him that Dixon is up here and has everything under control."

Krogson turned to the executive officer. "All right," he said, "do what he says." The other saluted and started toward the door.

"Just a second," said Kurt. "If you have any idea of telling the boys outside to cut the transmission leads from fire control, I wouldn't advise it. It's a rather lengthy process, and the minute a trouble light blinks on that board, up we go! Now on your way!"

XIV

Lieutenant Colonel Blick, acting commander of the 427th Light Maintenance Battalion of the Imperial Space Marines, stood at his office window and scowled down upon the whole civilized world, all twenty-six square kilometers of it. It had been a hard day. Three separate delegations of mothers had descended upon him demanding that he reopen the Tech Schools for the sake of their sanity. The recruits had been roaming the company streets in bands composed of equal numbers of small boys and large dogs, creating havoc wherever they went. He tried to cheer himself up by thinking of his forthcoming triumph when he, in the guise of the Inspector General, would float magnificently down from the skies and once and for all put the seal of final authority upon the new order. The only trouble was that he was beginning to have a sneaking suspicion that maybe that new order wasn't all that he had planned it to be. As he thought of his own six banshees screaming through quarters, his suspicion deepened almost to certainty.

He wandered back to his desk and slumped behind it gloomily. He couldn't backwater now, his pride was at stake. He glanced at the water clock on his desk and then rose reluctantly and started toward the door. It was time to get into battle armor and get ready for the inspection.

As he reached the door, there was a sudden slap of running sandals down the hall. A second later, Major Kane burst into the office, his face white and terrified.

"Colonel," he gasped, "the I.G.'s here!"

"Nonsense," said Blick. "I'm the I.G. now!"

"Oh yeah?" whimpered Kane. "Go look out the window. He's here, and he's brought the whole Imperial fleet with him!"

Blick dashed to the window and looked up. High above, so high that he could see them only as silver specks, hung hundreds of ships.

"Headquarters *does* exist!" he gasped.

He stood stunned. What to do... what to do... what to do? The question swirled around in his brain until he was dizzy. He looked to Kane for advice, but the other was as bewildered as he was.

"Don't stand there, man," he stormed. "Do something!"

"Yes, sir," said Kane. "What?"

Blick thought for a long, silent moment. The answer was obvious, but there was a short, fierce inner struggle before he could bring himself to accept it.

"Get Colonel Harris up here at once. He'll know what we should do."

A stubborn look came across Kane's face. "We're running things now," he said angrily.

Blick's face hardened and he let out a roar that shook the walls. "Listen, you pup, when you get an order, you follow it. Now get!"

Forty seconds later Colonel Harris stormed into the office. "What kind of a mess have you got us into this time?" he demanded.

"Look up there, sir," said Blick, leading him to the window.

Colonel Harris snapped back into command as if he'd never left it.

"Major Kane!" he shouted.

Kane popped into the office like a frightened rabbit.

"Evacuate the garrison at once! I want everyone off the plateau and into the jungle immediately. Get litters for the sick and the veterans who can't walk and take them to the hunting camps. Start the rest moving north as soon as you can."

"Really, sir," protested Kane, looking to Blick for a cue.

"You heard the colonel," barked Blick. "On your way!" Kane bolted.

Colonel Harris turned to Blick and said in a frosty voice: "I appreciate your help, Colonel, but I feel perfectly competent to enforce my own orders."

"Sorry, sir," said the other meekly. "It won't happen again."

Harris smiled. "O.K., Jimmie," he said, "let's forget it. We've got work to do!"

XV

It seemed to Kurt as if time was standing still. His nerves were screwed up to the breaking point and although he maintained an air of outward composure for the benefit of those in the control room of the flagship, it took all his willpower to keep the hand that was resting over the firing stud from quivering. One slip and they'd be on him. Actually it was only a matter of minutes between the time the scout was dispatched to the garrison below and the time it returned, but to him it seemed as if hours had passed before the familiar form of his commanding officer strode briskly into the control room.

Colonel Harris came to a halt just inside the door and swept the room with a keen, penetrating gaze.

"What's up, son?" he asked Kurt.

"I'm not quite sure. All that I know is that they're here to blast the garrison. As long as I've got control of this," he indicated the firing stud, "I'm top dog, but you'd better work something out in a hurry."

The look of strain on Kurt's face was enough for the colonel.

"Who's in command here?" he demanded.

Krogson stepped forward and bowed stiffly. "Commander Conrad Krogson of War Base Three of the Galactic Protectorate."

"Colonel Marcus Harris, 427th Light Maintenance Battalion of the Imperial Space Marines," replied the other briskly. "Now that the formalities are out of the way, let's get to work. Is there some place here where we can talk?"

Krogson gestured toward a small cubicle that opened off the control room. The two men entered and shut the door behind them.

A half-hour went by without agreement. "There may be an answer somewhere," Colonel Harris said finally, "but I can't find it. We can't surrender to you, and we can't afford to have you surrender to us. We haven't the food, facilities, or anything else to keep fifty thousand men under guard. If we turn you loose, there's nothing to keep you from coming back to blast us—except your word, that is, and since it would obviously be given under duress, I'm afraid that we couldn't attach much weight to it. It's a nice problem. I wish we had more time to spend on it, but unless you can come up with something workable during the next five minutes, I'm going to give Kurt orders to blow the fleet."

Krogson's mind was operating at a furious pace. One by one he snatched at possible solutions, and one by one he gave them up as he realized that they would never stand up under the scrutiny of the razor-sharp mind that sat opposite him.

"*Look,*" he burst out finally, "your empire is dead and our protectorate is about to fall apart. Give us a chance to come down and join you and we'll chuck the past. We need each other and you know it!"

"I know we do," said the colonel soberly, "and I rather think you are being honest with me. But we just can't take the chance. There are too many of you for us to digest and if you should change your mind—" He threw up his hands in a helpless gesture.

"But I wouldn't," protested Krogson. "You've told me what your life is like down there and you know what kind of a rat race I've been caught up in. I'd welcome the chance to get out of it. All of us would!"

"You might to begin with," said Harris, "but then you might start thinking what your Lord Protector would give to get his hands on several hundred trained technicians. No, Commander," he said, "we just couldn't chance it." He stretched his hand out to Krogson and the other after a second's hesitation took it.

Commander Krogson had reached the end of the road and he knew it. The odd thing about it was that now he found himself there, he didn't particularly mind. He sat and watched his own reactions with a sense of vague bewilderment. The strong drive for self-preservation that had kept him struggling ahead for so long was petering out and there was nothing to take its place. He was immersed in a strange feeling of emptiness and though a faint something within him said that he should go out fighting, it seemed pointless and without reason.

Suddenly the moment of quiet was broken. From the control room came a muffled sound of angry voices and scuffling feet. With one quick stride, Colonel Harris reached the door and swung it open. He was almost bowled over by a small, disheveled figure who darted past him into the cubicle. Close behind came several of the ship's officers. As the figure came to a stop before Commander Krogson, one of them grabbed him and started to drag him back into the control room.

"Sorry, sir," the officer said to Krogson, "but he came busting in demanding to see you at once. He wouldn't tell us why and when we tried to stop him, he broke away."

"Release him!" ordered the commander. He looked sternly at the little figure. "Well, Schninkle," he said sternly, "what is it this time?"

"Did you get my message?"

Krogson snorted. "So it was you in that scout! I might have known it. We got it all right, but Communication still hasn't got it figured out. What are you doing out here? You're supposed to be back at base keeping knives out of my back!"

"It's private, sir," said Schninkle.

"The rest of you clear out!" ordered Krogson. A second later, with the exception of Colonel Harris, the cubicle stood empty. Schninkle looked questioningly at the oddly uniformed officer.

"Couldn't put him out if I wanted to," said Krogson, "now go ahead."

Schninkle closed the door carefully and then turned to the commander and said in a hushed voice, "There's been a blowup at Prime Base. General Carr was hiding out there after all. He hit at noon yesterday. He had two-thirds of the Elite Guard secretly on his side and the Lord Protector didn't have a chance. He tried to run but they chopped him down before he got out of the atmosphere."

Krogson digested the news in silence for a moment. "So the Lord Protector is dead." He laughed bitterly. "Well, long live the Lord Protector!" He turned slowly to Colonel Harris. "I guess this lets us both off. Now that the heat's off me, you're safe. Call off your boy out there, and we'll make ourselves scarce. I've got to get back to the new Lord Protector to pay my respects. If some of my boys get to Carr first, I'm apt to be out of a job."

Harris shook his head. "It isn't as simple as that. Your new leader needs technicians as much as your old one did. I'm afraid we are still back where we started."

As Krogson broke into an impatient denial, Schninkle interrupted him. "You can't go back, Commander. None of us can. Carr has the whole staff down on his 'out' list. He's making a clean sweep of all possible competition. We'd all be under arrest now if he knew where we were!"

Krogson gave a slow whistle. "Doesn't leave me much choice, does it?" he said to Colonel Harris. "If you don't turn me loose, I get blown up; if you do, I get shot down."

Schninkle looked puzzled. "What's up, sir?" he asked.

Krogson gave a bitter laugh. "In case you didn't notice on your way in, there is a young man sitting at the fire controls out there who can blow up the whole fleet at the touch of a button. Down below is an ideal base with hundreds of techs, but the colonel here won't take us in, and he's afraid to let us go."

"I wouldn't," admitted Harris, "but the last few minutes have rather changed the picture. My empire has been dead for five hundred years and your protectorate doesn't seem to want you around anymore. It looks like we're both out of a job. Maybe we both ought to find a new one. What do you think?"

"I don't know what to think," said Krogson. "I can't go back and I can't stay here, and there isn't anyplace else. The fleet can't keep going without a base."

A broad grin came over the face of Colonel Harris. "You know," he said, "I've got a hunch that maybe we can do business after all. Come on!" He threw open the cubicle door and strode briskly into the control room, Krogson and Schninkle following close at his heels. He walked over to Kurt, who was still poised stiffly at the fire-control board.

"You can relax now, lad. Everything is under control."

Kurt gave a sigh of relief and, pulling himself to his feet, stretched luxuriantly. As the other officers saw the firing stud deserted, they tensed and looked to Commander Krogson questioningly. He frowned for a second and then slowly shook his head.

"Well?" he said to Colonel Harris.

"It's obvious," said the other, "you've a fleet, a darn good fleet, but it's falling apart for lack of decent maintenance. I've got a base down there with five thousand lads who can think with their fingers. This knucklehead of mine is a good example." He walked over to Kurt and slapped him affectionately on the shoulder. "There's nothing on this ship that he couldn't tear down and put back together blindfolded if he was given a little time to think about it. I think he'll enjoy having some real work to do for a change."

"I may seem dense," said Krogson with a bewildered expression on his face, "but wasn't that the idea that I was trying to sell you?"

"The idea is the same," said Harris, "but the context isn't. You're in a position now where you have to cooperate. That makes a difference. A big difference!"

"It sounds good," said Krogson, "but now you're overlooking something. Carr will be looking for me. We can't stand off the whole galaxy!"

"You're overlooking something too, sir," Schninkle interrupted. "He hasn't the slightest idea where we are. It will be months before he has things well enough under control to start an organized search for us. When he does, his chances of ever spotting the fleet are mighty slim if we take reasonable precautions. Remember that it was only by a fluke that we ever happened to spot this place to begin with."

As he talked, a calculating look came into his eyes. "A year of training and refitting here and there wouldn't be a fleet in the galaxy that could stand against us." He casually edged over until he occupied a position between Kurt and the fire-control board. "If things went right, there's no reason why you couldn't become Lord Protector, Commander."

A flash of the old fire stirred within Krogson and then quickly flickered out. "No, Schninkle," he said heavily. "That's all past now. I've had enough. It's time to try something new."

"In that case," said Colonel Harris, "let's begin! Out there a whole galaxy is breaking up. Soon the time will come when a strong hand is going to be needed to piece it back together and put it in running order again. You know," he continued reflectively, "the name of the old empire still has a certain magic to it. It might not be a bad idea to use it until we are ready to move on to something better."

He walked silently to the vision port and looked down on the lush greenness spreading far below. "But whatever we call ourselves," he continued slowly, half talking to himself, "we have something to work for now." A quizzical smile played over his lips and his wise old eyes seemed to be scanning the years ahead. "You know, Kurt, there's nothing like a visit from the Inspector General once in a while to keep things in line. The galaxy is a big place, but when the time comes, we'll make our rounds!"

XVI

On the parade ground behind the low buildings of the garrison, the 427th Light Maintenance Battalion of the Imperial Space Marines stood in rigid formation, the feathers in their war bonnets moving slightly in the breeze that blew in from the west and their war paint glowing redly in the slanting rays of the setting sun.

A quiver ran through the hard-surface soil of the plateau as the great mass of the fleet flagship settled down ponderously to rest. There was a moment of expectant silence as a great port clanged open and a gangplank extended to the ground. From somewhere within the ship a fanfare of trumpets sounded. Slowly and with solemn dignity, surrounded by his staff, Conrade Krogson, Inspector General of the Imperial Space Marines, advanced to review the troops.

THIS EARTH OF HOURS

by James Blish

Editor's Introduction

James Blish was a highly influential science fiction writer until his death in 1974. As "W. Atheling," he became one of the field's best-known critics.

His work tended to be philosophical in nature. Even his "straight" adventure stories, beginning with "Surface Tension" (which became the novel *The Seedling Stars*), had a deeper theme: What is human? His *A Case of Conscience*, including as it does an ethical problem as old as the Roman Catholic Church, is rightly regarded as a science fiction classic. His best-known novels are the stories of *The Okies*, or *Cities in Flight*.

Blish's military career was brief and undistinguished. According to Damon Knight, Blish, a medical technician at Fort Dix, New Jersey, was "always in trouble over unshined shoes, or pajamas showing under his trousers at reveille." In 1945 he refused a direct order to do KP. According to Knight, "Since it was wartime, he could have been court-martialed, but his father pulled strings in Washington and got him discharged."

Blish's later work shows a far different view of the military: It does not always win his approval, but he pays the military all due respect.

Kipling called the non-commissioned officers the backbone of the army. In this story Marine Master Sergeant Oberholzer shows why.

Enrico Fermi once asked of alien civilizations, "Where are they?" He reasoned that there had to be a large number of intelligent life forms in the universe, and some had to be a great deal older and more advanced than we; why, then, have they never visited us? James Blish offers one possible answer.

––––––––––––––––

I

The advance squadron was coming into line as Master Sergeant Oberholzer came onto the bridge of the *Novoe Washingtongrad*, saluted, and stood stiffly to the left of Lieutenant Campion, the exec, to wait for orders. The bridge was crowded and crackling with tension, but after twenty years in the Marines, it was all old stuff to Oberholzer. The *Hobo* (as most of the enlisted men called her, out of earshot of the brass) was at the point of the formation, as befitted a virtually indestructible battleship already surfeited with these petty conquests. The rest of the cone was sweeping on ahead in the swift enveloping maneuver which had reduced so many previous planets before they had been able to understand what was happening to them.

This time the planet at the focus of all those shifting conic sections of raw naval power was a place called Calle. It was showing now on a screen that Oberholzer could see, turning as placidly as any planet turned when you were too far away from it to see what guns it might be pointing at you. Lieutenant Campion was watching it too, though he had to look out of the very corners of his eyes to see it at all.

If the exec were caught watching the screen instead of the meter board assigned to him, Captain Hammer would probably reduce him to an ensign. Nevertheless, Campion never took his eyes off the image of Calle. This one was going to be rough.

Captain Hammer was watching, too. After a moment he said, "Sound!" in a voice like sandpaper.

"By the pulse six, sir," Lieutenant Spring's voice murmured from the direction of the 'scope. His junior, a very raw youngster named Rover, passed him a chit from the plotting table. "For that read: By the briefs five eight nine, sir," the invisible navigator corrected.

Oberholzer listened without moving while Captain Hammer muttered under his breath to Flo-Mar 12-Upjohn, the only civilian allowed on the bridge—and small wonder, since he was the Consort of State of the Matriarchy itself. Hammer had long ago become accustomed enough to his own bridge to be able to control who overheard him, but 12-Upjohn's answering whisper must have been audible to every man there.

"The briefing said nothing about a second inhabited planet," the Consort said a little peevishly. "But then there's very little we *do* know about this system—that's part of our trouble. What makes you think it's a colony?"

"A colony from Calle, not one of ours," Hammer said in more or less normal tones; evidently he had decided against trying to keep only half of the discussion private. "The electromagnetic 'noise' from both planets has the same spectrum—the energy level, the output, is higher on Calle, that's all. That means similar machines being used in similar ways. And let me point out, Your Excellency, that the outer planet is in opposition to Calle now, which will put it precisely in our rear if we complete this maneuver."

"*When* we complete this maneuver," 12-Upjohn said firmly. "Is there any evidence of communication between the two planets?"

Hammer frowned. "No," he admitted.

"Then we'll regard the colonization hypothesis as unproved—and stand ready to strike back hard if events prove us wrong. I think we have sufficient force here to reduce *three* planets like Calle if we're driven to that pitch."

Hammer grunted and resigned the argument. Of course it was quite possible that 12-Upjohn was right; he did not lack for experience—in fact, he wore the Silver Earring as the most-traveled Consort of State ever to ride the Standing Wave. Nevertheless Oberholzer repressed a sniff with difficulty. Like all military, he was a colonial; he had never seen the Earth, and never expected to; and both as a colonial and as a Marine who had been fighting the Matriarchy's battles all his adult life, he was more than a little contemptuous of Earthmen, with their tandem names and all that they implied. Of course it was not the Consort of State's fault that he had been born on Earth and so had been named only Marvin 12 out of the misfortune of being a male; nor that he had married into Florence Upjohn's cabinet, that being the only way one could become a cabinet member and Marvin 12 having been taught from birth to believe such a post the highest honor a man might covet. All the same, neither 12-Upjohn nor his entourage of drones filled Oberholzer with confidence.

Nobody, however, had asked M. Sgt. Richard Oberholzer what he thought, and nobody was likely to. As the chief of all the non-Navy enlisted personnel on board the *Hobo*, he was expected to be on the bridge when matters were ripening toward criticality; but his duty there was to listen, not to proffer advice. He could not in fact remember any occasion when an officer had asked his opinion, though he had received—and executed—his fair share of near-suicidal orders from bridges long demolished.

"By the pulse five point five," Lieutenant Spring's voice sang.

"Sergeant Oberholzer," Hammer said.

"Aye, sir."

"We are proceeding as per orders. You may now brief your men and put them into full battle gear."

Oberholzer saluted and went below. There was little enough he could tell the squad—as 12-Upjohn had said, Calle's system was nearly unknown—but even that little would improve the total ignorance in which they had been kept till now. Luckily, they were not much given to asking questions of a strategic sort; like impressed spacehands everywhere, the huge mass of the Matriarchy's interstellar holdings meant nothing to them but endlessly riding the Standing Wave, with battle and death lurking at the end of every jump. Luckily also, they were inclined to trust Oberholzer, if only for the low cunning he had shown in keeping most of them alive, especially in the face of unusually Crimean orders from the bridge.

This time Oberholzer would need every ounce of trust and erg of obedience they would give him. Though he never expected anything but the worst, he had a queer cold feeling that this time he was going to get it. There were hardly any data to go on yet, but there had been something about Calle that looked persuasively like the end of the line.

Very few of the forty men in the wardroom even looked up as Oberholzer entered. They were checking their gear in the dismal light of the fluorescents with the single-mindedness of men to whom a properly wound gun-tube coil, a properly set face-shield gasket, a properly fueled and focused vaulting jet, have come to mean more than parents, children, retirement pensions, the rule of law, or the logic of empire. The only man to show any flicker of interest was Sergeant Cassirir—as was normal, since he was Oberholzer's understudy—and he did no more than look up from over the straps of his antigas suit and say, "Well?"

"Well," Oberholzer said, "now hear this."

There was a sort of composite jingle and clank as the men lowered their gear to the deck or put it aside on their bunks.

"We're investing a planet Called Calle in the Canes Venatici cluster," Oberholzer said, sitting down on an olive-drab canvas pack stuffed with lysurgic acid grenades. "A cruiser Called the *Assam Dragon*—you were with her on her shakedown, weren't you, Himber?—touched down here ten years ago with a flock of tenders and got swallowed up. They got two or three quick yells for help out and that was that—nothing anybody could make much sense of, no weapons named or description of the enemy. So here we are, loaded for the kill."

"Wasn't any Calley in command of the *Assam Dragon* when I was aboard," Himber said doubtfully.

"Nah. Place was named for the astronomer who spotted her, from the rim of the cluster, a hundred years ago," Oberholzer said. "Nobody names planets for ship captains. Anybody got any sensible questions?"

"Just what kind of trouble are we looking for?" Cassirir said.

"That's just it—we don't know. This is closer to the center of the Galaxy than we've ever gotten before. It may be a population center too; could be that Calle is just one piece of a federation, at least inside its own cluster. That's why we've got the boys from Momma on board; this one could be damn important."

Somebody sniffed. "If this cluster is full of people, how come we never picked up signals from it?"

"How do you know we never did?" Oberholzer retorted. "For all I know, maybe that's why the *Assam Dragon* came here in the first place. Anyhow that's not our problem. All we're–"

The lights went out. Simultaneously the whole mass of the *Novoe Washingtongrad* shuddered savagely, as though a boulder almost as big as she was had been dropped on her.

Seconds later the gravity went out too.

II

Flo-Mar 12-Upjohn knew no more of the real nature of the disaster than did the wardroom squad, nor did anybody on the bridge, for that matter. The blow had been indetectable until it struck, and then most of the fleet was simply annihilated; only the *Hobo* was big enough to survive the blow, and she survived only partially—in fact, in five pieces. Nor did the Consort of State ever know by what miracle the section he was in hit Calle still partially under power; he was not privy to the self-salvaging engineering principles of battleships. All he knew—once he struggled back to consciousness—was that he was still alive, and that there was a broad shaft of sunlight coming through a top-to-bottom split in one wall of what had been his office aboard ship.

He held his ringing head for a while, then got up in search of water. Nothing came out of the dispenser, so he unstrapped his dispatch case from the underside of his desk and produced a pint palladium flask of vodka. He had screwed up his face to sample this—at the moment he would have preferred water—when a groan reminded him that there might be more than one room in his suddenly shrunken universe, as well as other survivors.

He was right on both counts. Though the ship section he was in consisted mostly of engines of whose function he had no notion, there were also three other staterooms. Two of these were deserted, but the third turned out to contain a battered member of his own staff, by name Robin One.

The young man was not yet conscious and 12-Upjohn regarded him with a faint touch of despair. Robin One was perhaps the last man in space that the Consort of State would have chosen to be shipwrecked with.

That he was utterly expendable almost went without saying; he was, after all, a drone. When the perfection of sperm electrophoresis had enabled parents for the first time to predetermine the sex of their children, the predictable result had been an enormous glut of males—which was directly accountable for the present regime on Earth. By the time the people and the law-makers, thoroughly frightened by the crazy years of fashion upheavals, "beefcake," polyandry, male prostitution, and all the rest, had come to their senses, the Matriarchy was in to stay; a weak electric current had overturned civilized society as drastically as the steel knife had demoralized the Eskimos.

Though the tide of excess males had since receded somewhat, it had left behind a wrack, of which Robin One was a bubble. He was a drone, and hence superfluous by definition—fit only to be sent colonizing, on diplomatic missions or otherwise thrown away.

Superfluity alone, of course, could hardly account for his presence on 12-Upjohn's staff. Officially, Robin One was an interpreter; actually—since nobody could know the language the Consort of State might be Called upon to understand on this mission—he was a poet, a class of unattached males with special privileges in the Matriarchy, particularly if what they wrote was of the middling-difficult or Hillyer Society sort. Robin One was an eminently typical member of this class, distractible, sulky, jealous, easily wounded, homosexual, lazy except when writing, and probably (to give him the benefit of the doubt, for 12-Upjohn had no ear whatever for poetry) the second-worst poet of his generation.

It had to be admitted that assigning 12-Upjohn a poet as an interpreter on this mission had not been a wholly bad idea, and that if
Hildegard Muller of the Interstellar Understanding Commission had
not thought of it, no mere male would have been likely to—least of all
Bar-Rob 4-Agberg, Director of Assimilation. The nightmare of finding
the whole of the center of the Galaxy organized into one vast federation,
much older than Earth's, had been troubling the State Department
for a long time, at first from purely theoretical considerations—all
those heart-stars were much older than those in the spiral arms, and
besides, where star density in space is so much higher, interstellar
travel does not look like quite so insuperable an obstacle as it long
had to Earthmen—and later from certain practical signs, of which the
obliteration of the *Assam Dragon* and her defenders had been only
the most provocative. Getting along with these people on the first
contact would be vital, and yet the language barrier might well provoke
a tragedy wanted by neither side, as the obliteration of Nagasaki in
World War II had been provoked by the mistranslation of a single
word. Under such circumstances, a man with a feeling for strange
words in odd relationships might well prove to be useful, or even
vital.

Nevertheless, it was with a certain grim enjoyment that 12-Upjohn
poured into Robin One a good two-ounce jolt of vodka. Robin
coughed convulsively and sat up, blinking.

"Your Excellency—how—what's happened? I thought we were dead.
But we've got lights again, and gravity."

He was observant, that had to be granted. "The lights are ours but
the gravity is Calle's," 12-Upjohn explained tersely. "We're in a part of
the ship that cracked up."

"Well, it's good that we've got power."

"We can't afford to be philosophical about it. Whatever shape it's in,
this derelict is a thoroughly conspicuous object and we'd better get out
of it in a hurry."

"Why?" Robin said. "We were supposed to make contact with these
people. Why not just sit here until they notice and come to see us?"

"Suppose they just blast us to smaller bits instead? They didn't stop to parley with the fleet, you'll notice."

"This is a different situation," Robin said stubbornly. "I wouldn't have stopped to parley with that fleet myself if I'd had the means of knocking it out first. It didn't look a bit like a diplomatic mission. But why should they be afraid of a piece of a wreck?"

The Consort of State stroked the back of his neck reflectively. The boy had a point. It was risky; on the other hand, how long would they survive foraging in completely unknown territory? And yet obviously they couldn't stay cooped up in here forever—especially if it was true that there was already no water.

He was spared having to make up his mind by a halloo from the direction of the office. After a startled stare at each other, the two hit the deck running.

Sergeant Oberholzer's face was peering grimly through the split in the bulkhead.

"Oh ho!" he said. "So you *did* make it." He said something unintelligible to some invisible person outside and then squirmed through the breach into the room, with considerable difficulty since he was in full battle gear. "None of the officers did, so I guess that puts you in command."

"In command of what?" 12-Upjohn said dryly.

"Not very much," the Marine admitted. "I've got five men surviving, one of them with a broken hip, and a section of the ship with two drive units in it. It would lift, more or less, if we could jury-rig some controls, but I don't know where we'd go in it without supplies or a navigator—or an overdrive, for that matter." He looked about speculatively. "There was a Standing Wave transceiver in this section, I think, but it'd be a miracle if it still functioned."

"Would you know how to test it?" Robin asked.

"No. Anyhow we've got more immediate business than that. We've picked up a native. What's more, he speaks English—must have picked it up from the *Assam Dragon*. We started to ask him questions, but it turns out he's some sort of top official, so we brought him over here on the off chance that one of you was alive."

"What a break!" Robin One said explosively.

"A whole series of them," 12-Upjohn agreed, none too happily. He had long ago learned to be at his most suspicious when the breaks seemed to be coming his way. "Well, better bring him in."

"Can't," Oberholzer said. "Apologies, Your Excellency, but he wouldn't fit. You'll have to come to him."

III

It was impossible to imagine what sort of stock the Callean had evolved from. He seemed to be a thorough-going mixture of several different phyla. Most of him was a brown, segmented tube about the diameter of a barrel and perhaps twenty-five feet long, rather like a cross between a python and a worm. The front segments were carried upright, raising the head a good ten feet off the ground.

Properly speaking, 12-Upjohn thought, the Callean really had no head, but only a front end, marked by two enormous faceted eyes and three upsetting simple eyes which were usually closed. Beneath these there was a collar of six short, squidlike tentacles, carried wrapped around the creature in a ropy ring. He was as impossible-looking as he was fearsome, and 12-Upjohn felt at a multiple disadvantage from the beginning.

"How did you learn your language?" he said, purely as a starter.

"I learned it from you," the Callean said promptly. The voice was unexpectedly high, a quality which was accentuated by the creature's singsong intonation; 12-Upjohn could not see where it was coming from. "From your ship which I took apart, the dragon-of-war."

"Why did you do that?"

"It was evident that you meant me ill," the Callean sang. "At that time I did not know that you were sick, but that became evident at the dissections."

"Dissection! You dissected the crew of the *Dragon*?"

"All but one."

There was a growl from Oberholzer. The Consort of State shot him a warning glance.

"You may have made a mistake," 12-Upjohn said. "A natural mistake, perhaps. But it was our purpose to offer you trade and peaceful relationships. Our weapons were only precautionary."

"I do not think so," the Callean said, "and I never make mistakes. That you make mistakes is natural, but it is not natural to me."

12-Upjohn felt his jaw dropping. That the creature meant what he said could not be doubted: his command of the language was too complete to permit any more sensible interpretation. 12-Upjohn found himself at a loss; not only was the statement the most staggering he had ever heard from any sentient being, but while it was being made he had discovered how the Callean spoke: the sounds issued at low volume from a multitude of spiracles or breath-holes all along the body, each hole producing only one pure tone, the words and intonations being formed in mid-air by intermodulation— a miracle of co-ordination among a multitude of organs obviously unsuitable for sound-forming at all. This thing was formidable— that would have been evident even without the lesson of the chunk of the *Novoe Washingtongrad* canted crazily in the sands behind them.

Sands? He looked about with a start. Until that moment the Callean had so hypnotized his attention that he had forgotten to look at the landscape, but his unconscious had registered it. Sand, and nothing but sand. If there were better parts of Calle than this desert, they were not visible from here, all the way to the horizon.

"What do you propose to do with us?" he said at last. There was really nothing else to say; cut off in every possible sense from his home world, he no longer had any base from which to negotiate.

"Nothing," the Callean said. "You are free to come and go as you please."

"You're no longer afraid of us?"

"No. When you came to kill me, I prevented you, but you can no longer do that."

"There you've made a mistake, all right," Oberholzer said, lifting his rifle toward the multicolored, glittering jewels of the Callean's eyes. "You know what this is—they must have had them on the *Dragon*."

"Don't be an idiot, Sergeant," 12-Upjohn said sharply. "We're in no position to make any threats." Nor, he added silently, should the Marine have called attention to his gun before the Callean had taken any overt notice of it.

"I know what it is," the creature said. "You cannot kill me with that. You tried it often before and found you could not. You would remember this if you were not sick."

"I never saw anything that I couldn't kill with a Sussmann flamer," Oberholzer said between his teeth. "Let me try it on the bastard, Your Excellency."

"Wait a minute," Robin One said, to 12-Upjohn's astonishment. "I want to ask some questions—if you don't mind, Your Excellency?"

"I don't mind," 12-Upjohn said after an instant. Anything to get the Marine's crazy impulse toward slaughter sidetracked. "Go ahead."

"Did you dissect the crew of the *Assam Dragon* personally?" Robin asked the Callean.

"Of course."

"Are you the ruler of this planet?"

"Yes."

"Are you the only person in this system?"

"No."

Robin paused and frowned. Then he said: "Are you the only person of your species in your system?"

"No. There is another on Xixobrax—the fourth planet."

Robin paused once more, but not, it seemed to 12-Upjohn, as though he were in any doubt; it was only as though he were gathering his courage for the key question of all. 12-Upjohn tried to imagine what it might be, and failed.

"How many of you are there?" Robin One said.

"I cannot answer that. As of the instant you asked me that question, there were eighty-three hundred thousand billion, one hundred and eighty-nine million, four hundred and sixty-five thousand, one hundred and eighty; but now the number has changed, and it goes on changing."

"Impossible," 12-Upjohn said, stunned. "Not even two planets could support such a number—and you'd never allow a desert like this to go on existing if you had even a fraction of that population to support. I begin to think, sir, that you are a type normal to my business: the ordinary, unimaginative liar."

"He's not lying," Robin said, his voice quivering. "It all fits together. Just let me finish, sir, please. I'll explain, but I've got to go through to the end first."

"Well," 12-Upjohn said, helplessly, "all right, go ahead." But he was instantly sorry, for what Robin One said was:

"Thank you. I have no more questions."

The Callean turned in a great liquid wheel and poured away across the sand dunes at an incredible speed. 12-Upjohn shouted after him, without any clear idea of what it was that he was shouting—but no matter, for the Callean took no notice. Within seconds, it seemed, he was only a threadworm in the middle distance, and then he was gone. They were all alone in the chill desert air.

Oberholzer lowered his rifle bewilderedly. "He's fast," he said to nobody in particular. "Cripes, but he's fast. I couldn't even keep him in the sights."

"That proves it," Robin said tightly. He was trembling, but whether with fright or elation, 12-Upjohn could not tell; possibly both.

"It had better prove something," the Consort of State said, trying hard not to sound portentous. There was something about this bright remote desert that made empty any possible pretense to dignity. "As far as I can see, you've just lost us what may have been our only chance to treat with these creatures… just as surely as the sergeant would have done it with his gun. Explain, please."

"I didn't really catch on until I realized that he was using the second person singular when he spoke to us," Robin said. If he had heard any threat implied in 12-Upjohn's charge, it was not visible; he seemed totally preoccupied. "There's no way to tell them apart in modern English. We thought he was referring to us as 'you' plural, but he wasn't, any more than his I was a plural. He thinks we're all a part of the same personality—including the men from the *Dragon*, too—*just as he is himself.* That's why he left when I said I had no more questions. He can't comprehend that each of us has an independent ego. For him such a thing doesn't exist."

"Like ants?" 12-Upjohn said slowly. "I don't see how an advanced technology… but no, I do see. And if it's so, it means that any Callean we run across could be their chief of state but that no one of them actually is. The only other real individual is next door, on the fourth planet—another hive ego."

"Maybe not," Robin said. "Don't forget that he thinks we're part of one, too."

12-Upjohn dismissed that possibility at once. "He's sure to know his own system, after all… What alarms me is the population figure he cited. It's got to be *at least* clusterwide—and from the exactness with which he was willing to cite it, for a given instant, he had to have immediate access to it. An instant, effortless census."

"Yes," Robin said. "Meaning mind-to-mind contact, from one to all, throughout the whole complex. That's what started me thinking about the funny way he used pronouns."

"If that's the case, Robin, we are *spurlos versenkt.* And my pronoun includes Earth."

"They may have some limitations," Robin said, but it was clear that he was only whistling in the dark. "But at least it explains why they butchered the *Dragon's* crew so readily—and why they're willing to let us wander around their planet as if we didn't even exist. We don't, for them. They can't have any respect for a single life. No wonder they didn't give a damn for the sergeant's gun!"

His initial flush had given way to a marble paleness; there were beads of sweat on his brow in the dry, hot air, and he was trembling harder than ever. He looked as though he might faint in the next instant, though only the slightest of stutters disturbed his rush of words. But for once the Consort of State could not accuse him of agitation over trifles.

Oberholzer looked from one to the other, his expression betraying perhaps only disgust, or perhaps blank incomprehension—it was impossible to tell. Then, with a sudden sharp *snick* which made them both start, he shot closed the safety catch on the Sussmann.

"Well," he said in a smooth, cold, empty voice, "now we know what we'll eat."

IV

Their basic and dangerous division of plans and purposes began with that.

Sergeant Oberholzer was not a fool, as the hash marks on his sleeve and the battle stars on his ribbons attested plainly; he understood the implications of what the Callean had said—at least after the Momma's boy had interpreted them; and he was shrewd enough not to undervalue the contribution the poor terrified fairy had made to their possible survival on this world. For the moment, however, it suited the Marine to play the role of the dumb sergeant to the hilt. If a full understanding of what the Calleans were like might reduce him to a like state of trembling impotence, he could do without it.

Not that he really believed that any such thing could happen to him; but it was not hard to see that Momma's boys were halfway there already—and if the party as a whole hoped to get anything done, they had to be jolted out of it as fast as possible.

At first he thought he had made it. "Certainly not!" the Consort of State said indignantly. "You're a man, Sergeant, not a Callean. Nothing the Calleans do is any excuse for your behaving otherwise than as a man."

"I'd rather eat an enemy than a friend," Oberholzer said cryptically. "Have you got any supplies inside there?"

"I—I don't know. But that has nothing to do with it."

"Depends on what you mean by 'it.' But maybe we can argue about that later. What are your orders, Your Excellency?"

"I haven't an order in my head," 12-Upjohn said with sudden, disarming frankness. "We'd better try to make some sensible plans first and stop bickering. Robin, stop snuffling, too. The question is, what can we do besides trying to survive, and cherishing an idiot hope for a rescue mission?"

"For one thing, we can try to spring the man from the *Dragon's* crew that these worms have still got alive," Oberholzer said. "If that's what he meant when he said they dissected all but one."

"That doesn't seem very feasible to me," 12-Upjohn said. "We have no idea where they're holding him–"

"Ask them. This one answered every question you asked him."

–and even supposing that he's nearby, we couldn't free him from a horde of Calleans, no matter how many dead bodies they let you pile up. At best, sooner or later you'd run out of ammunition."

"It's worth trying," Oberholzer said. "We could use the manpower."

"What for?" Robin One demanded. "He'd be just one more mouth to feed. At the moment, at least, they're feeding him."

"For raising ship," Oberholzer retorted, "*If* there's any damn chance of welding our two heaps of junk together and getting off this mudball. We ought to look into it, anyhow."

Robin One was looking more alarmed by the minute. If the prospect of getting into a fight with the Calleans had scared him, Oberholzer thought, the notion of hard physical labor evidently was producing something close to panic.

"Where could we go?" he said. "Supposing that we could fly such a shambles at all?"

"I don't know," Oberholzer said. "We don't know what's possible yet. But anything's better than sitting around here and starving. First off, I want that man from the *Dragon*."

"I'm opposed to it," 12-Upjohn said firmly. "The Calleans are leaving us to our own devices now. If we cause any real trouble, they may well decide that we'd be safer locked up, or dead. I don't mind planning to lift ship if we can—but no military expeditions."

"Sir," Oberholzer said, "military action on this planet is what I was sent here for. I reserve the right to use my own judgment. You can complain if we ever get back—but I'm not going to let a man rot in a worm burrow while I've got a gun on my back. You can come along or not, but we're going."

He signaled to Cassirir, who seemed to be grinning slightly. 12-Upjohn stared at him for a moment and then shook his head. "We'll stay," he said. "Since we have no water, Sergeant, I hope you'll do us the kindness of telling us where your part of the ship lies."

"That way, about two kilometers," Oberholzer said. "Help yourself. If you want to settle in there, you'll save us the trouble of toting Private Hannes with us on a stretcher."

"Of course," the Consort of State said. "We'll take care of him. But, Sergeant…"

"Yes, Your Excellency?"

"If this stunt of yours still leaves us all alive afterwards and we do get back to any base of ours, I will *certainly* see to it that a complaint is lodged. I'm not disowning you now because it's obvious that we'll all have to work together to survive, and a certain amount of amity will be essential. But don't be deceived by that."

"I understand, sir," Oberholzer said levelly. "Cassirir, let's go. We'll backtrack to where we nabbed the worm and then follow his trail to wherever he came from. Fall in."

The men shouldered their Sussmanns. 12-Upjohn and Robin One watched them go. At the last dune before the two would go out of sight altogether, Oberholzer turned and waved, but neither waved back. Shrugging, Oberholzer resumed plodding. "Sarge?" "Yeah?"

"How *do* you figure to spring this joker with only four guns?"

"Five guns if we spring him—I've got a side arm," Oberholzer reminded him. "We'll play it by ear, that's all. I want to see just how serious these worms are about leaving us alone and letting us shoot them if we feel like it. I've got a hunch that they aren't very bright, one at a time, and don't react fast to strictly local situations. If this whole planet is like one huge body, and the worms are its brain cells, then we're germs—and maybe it'd take more than four germs to make the body do anything against us that counted, at least fast enough to do any good."

Cassirir was frowning absurdly; he did not seem to be taking the theory in without pain. Well, Cassirir had never been much of a man for tactics.

"Here's where we found the guy," one of the men said, pointing at the sand.

"That's not much of a trail," Cassirir said. "If there's any wind, it'll be wiped out like a shot."

"Take a sight on it, that's all we need. You saw him run off—straight as a ruled line, no twists or turns around the dunes or anything. Like an army ant. If the trail sands over, we'll follow the sight. It's a cinch it leads someplace."

"All right," Cassirir said, getting out his compass. After a while the four of them resumed trudging.

There were only a few drops of hot, flat-tasting water left in the canteens, and their eyes were gritty and red from dryness and sand, when they topped the ridge that overlooked the nest. The word sprang instantly into Oberholzer's mind, though perhaps he had been expecting some such thing ever since Robin One had compared the Calleans to ants.

It was a collection of rough white spires, each perhaps fifty feet high, rising from a common doughlike mass which almost filled a small valley. There was no greenery around it and no visible source of water, but there were three roads, two of them leading into oval black entrances which Oberholzer could see from here. Occasionally—not often—a

Callean would scuttle out and vanish, or come speeding over the horizon and dart into the darkness. Some of the spires bore masts carrying
what seemed to be antennae or more recondite electronic devices, but
there were no windows to be seen; and the only sound in the valley,
except for the dry, dusty wind, was a subdued composite hum.

"Man!" Cassirir said, whispering without being aware of it.

"It must be as black as the ace of spades in there. Anybody got a
torch?"

Nobody had. "We won't need one anyhow," Oberholzer said confidently. "They've got eyes, and they can see in desert sunlight. That
means they can't move around in total darkness. Let's go—I'm thirsty."

They stumbled down into the valley and approached the nearest
black hole cautiously. Sure enough, it was not as black as it had
appeared from the hill; there was a glow inside which had been hidden
from them against the contrast of the glaringly lit sands. Nevertheless,
Oberholzer found himself hanging back.

While he hesitated, a Callean came rocketing out of the entrance
and pulled to a smooth, sudden stop.

"You are not to get in the way," he said in exactly the same piping
singsong voice the other had used.

"Tell me where to go and I'll stay out of your way," Oberholzer said.
"Where is the man from the warship that you didn't dissect?"

"In Gnitonis, halfway around the world from here." Oberholzer felt
his shoulders sag, but the Callean was not through. "You should have
told me that you wanted him," he said. "I will have him brought to
you. Is there anything else that you need?"

"Water," Oberholzer said hopefully.

"That will be brought. There is no water you can use here. Stay out
of the cities; you will be in the way."

"How else can we eat?"

"Food will be brought. You should make your needs known; you
are of low intelligence and helpless. I forbid nothing, I know you are
harmless, and your life is short in any case; but I do not want you to
get in the way."

The repetition was beginning to tell on Oberholzer, and the frustration created by his having tried to use a battering ram against a freely swinging door was compounded by his mental picture of what the two Momma's boys would say when the squad got back.

"Thank you," he said, and bringing the Sussmann into line, he trained it on the Callean's squidlike head and squeezed the trigger.

It was at once established that the Calleans were as mortal to Sussmann flamers as is all other flesh and blood; this one made a very satisfactory corpse. Unsatisfied, the flamer bolt went on to burn a long slash in the wall of the nest, not far above the entrance. Oberholzer grounded the rifle and waited to see what would happen next; his men hefted their weapons tensely.

For a few minutes there was no motion but the random twitching of the headless Callean's legs. Evidently he was still not entirely dead, though he was a good four feet shorter than he had been before and plainly was feeling the lack. Then there was a stir inside the dark entrance.

A ten-legged animal about the size of a large rabbit emerged tentatively into the sunlight, followed by two more and then by a whole series of them, perhaps as many as twenty. Though Oberholzer had been unabashed by the Calleans themselves, there was something about these things that made him feel sick. They were coal black and shiny, and they did not seem to have any eyes; their heavily armored heads bore nothing but a set of rudimentary palps and a pair of enormous pincers, like those of a June beetle.

Sightless or no, they were excellent surgeons. They cut the remains of the Callean swiftly into sections, precisely one metamere to a section, and bore the carrion back inside the nest. Filled with loathing, Oberholzer stepped forward quickly and kicked one of the last in the procession. It toppled over like an unstable kitchen stool but regained its footing as though nothing had happened. The kick had not hurt it visibly, though Oberholzer's toes felt as though he had kicked a Victorian iron dog. The creature, still holding its steak delicately in its living tongs, mushed implacably after the others back into the dubiety of the nest. Then all that was left in the broiling sunlight was a few pools of blackening blood seeping swiftly into the sand.

"Let's get out of here," Cassirir said raggedly.

"Stand fast," Oberholzer growled. "If they're mad at us, I want to know about it right now."

But the next Callean to pass them, some twenty eternal minutes later, hardly even slowed down. "Keep out of the way," he said and streaked away over the dunes. Snarling, Oberholzer caromed a bolt after him, but missed him clean.

"All right," he said. "Let's go back. No hitting the canteens till we're five kilometers past the mid-point cairn. March!"

The men were all on the verge of prostration by the time that point was passed, but Oberholzer never once had to enforce the order. Nobody, it appeared, was eager to come to an end on Calle as a series of butcher's cuts in the tongs of a squad of huge black beetles.

V

"I know what they think," the man from the *Assam Dragon* said. "I've heard them say it often enough."

He was a personable youngster, perhaps thirty, with blond wavy hair which had been turned almost white by the strong Callean sunlight: His captors had walked him for three hours every day on the desert. He had once been the *Assam Dragon's* radioman, a post which in interstellar flight is a branch of astronomy, not of communications; nevertheless Oberholzer and the Marines called him Sparks in deference to a tradition which, 12-Upjohn suspected, the Marines did not even know existed.

"Then why wouldn't there be a chance of our establishing better relations with the 'person' on the fourth planet?" 12-Upjohn said. "After all, there's never been an Earth landing there."

"Because the 'person' on Xixobrax is a colony of Calle and knows everything that goes on here. It took the two planets in cooperation to destroy the fleet. There's almost full telepathic communion between the two—in fact, all through the Central Empire. The only rapport that seems to weaken over short distances—interplanetary distances— is the sense of identity. That's why each planet has an I of its own, its own ego. But it's not the kind of ego we know anything about. Xixobrax wouldn't give us any better deal than Calle has, any more than I'd give Calle a better deal than you would, Your Excellency. They have common purposes and allegiances. All the Central Empire seems to be like that."

12-Upjohn thought about it; but he did not like what he thought. It was a knotty problem, even in theory.

Telepathy among men had never amounted to anything. After the pioneer exploration of the microcosm with the Arpe Effect—the second of two unsuccessful attempts at an interstellar drive, long before the discovery of the Standing Wave—it had become easy to see why this would be so. Psi forces in general were characteristic only of the subspace in which the primary particles of the atom had their being; their occasional manifestations in the macrocosm were statistical accidents, as weak and indirigible as spontaneous radioactive decay.

Up to now this had suited 12-Upjohn. It had always seemed to him' that the whole notion of telepathy was a dodge—an attempt to bypass the plain duty of each man to learn to know his brother and, if possible, to learn to love him; the telepathy fanatics were out to short-circuit the task, to make easy the most difficult assignment a human being might undertake. He was well aware, too, of the bias against telepathy which was inherent in his profession of diplomat; yet he had always been certain of his case, hazy though it was around the edges. One of his proofs was that telepathy's main defenders invariably were incorrigibly lazy writers, from Upton Sinclair and Theodore Dreiser all the way down to...

All the same, it seemed inarguable that the whole center of the Galaxy, an enormously diverse collection of peoples and cultures, was being held together in a common and strife-free union by telepathy alone, or perhaps by telepathy and its even more dubious adjuncts: a whole galaxy held together by a force so unreliable that two human beings sitting across from each other at a card table had never been able to put it to an even vaguely practicable use.

Somewhere there was a huge hole in the argument.

While he had sat helplessly thinking in these circles, even Robin One was busy, toting power packs to the welding crew which was working outside to braze together on the desert the implausible, misshapen lump of metal which the Marine sergeant was fanatically determined would become a ship again. Now the job was done, though no shipwright would admire it, and the question of where to go with it was being debated in full council. Sparks, for his part, was prepared to bet that the Calleans would not hinder their departure.

"Why would they have given us all this oxygen and stuff if they were going to prevent us from using it?" he said reasonably. "They know what it's for—even if they have no brains, collectively they're plenty smart enough."

"No brains?" 12-Upjohn said. "Or are you just exaggerating?"

"No brains," the man from the *Assam Dragon* insisted. "Just lots of ganglia. I gather that's the way all of the races of the Central Empire are organized, regardless of other physical differences. That's what they mean when they say we're all sick—hadn't you realized that?"

"No," 12-Upjohn said in slowly dawning horror. "You had better spell it out."

"Why, they say that's why we get cancer. They say that the brain is the ultimate source of all tumors and is itself a tumor. They call it 'hostile symbiosis.' "

"Malignant?"

"In the long run. Races that develop them kill themselves off. Something to do with solar radiation; animals on planets of Population II stars develop them, Population I planets don't."

Robin One hummed an archaic twelve-tone series under his breath. There were no words to go with it, but the Consort of State recognized it; it was part of a chorale from a twentieth-century American opera, and the words went: *Weep, weep beyond time for this Earth of hours.*

"It fits," he said heavily. "So to receive and use a weak field like telepathy, you need a weak brain. Human beings will never make it."

"Earthworms of the galaxy, unite," Robin One said.

"They already have," Sergeant Oberholzer pointed out. "So where does all this leave us?"

"It means," 12-Upjohn said slowly, "that this Central Empire, where the stars are almost all Population I, is spreading out toward the spiral arms where the Earth lies. Any cluster civilizations they meet are natural allies—clusters are purely Population I—and probably have already been mentally assimilated. Any possible natural allies *we* meet, going around Population II stars, we may well pick a fight with instead."

"That's not what I meant," Sergeant Oberholzer said.

"I know what you meant; but this changes things. As I understand it, we have a chance of making a straight hop to the nearest Earth base if we go on starvation rations–"

"–and if I don't make more than a point zero five percent error in plotting the course," Sparks put in.

"Yes. On the other hand, we can make *sure* of getting there by going in short leaps via planets known to be inhabited, but never colonized and possibly hostile. The only other possibility is Xixobrax, which I think we've ruled out. Correct?"

"Right as rain," Sergeant Oberholzer said. "Now I see what you're driving at, Your Excellency. The only thing is—you didn't mention that the stepping-stone method will take us the rest of our lives."

"So I didn't," 12-Upjohn said bleakly. "But I hadn't forgotten it. The other side of *that* coin is that it will be even longer than that before the Matriarchy and the Central Empire collide."

"After which," Sergeant Oberholzer said with a certain relish, "I doubt that it'll be a Matriarchy, whichever wins. Are you calling for a vote, sir?"

"Well—yes, I seem to be."

"Then let's grasshopper," Sergeant Oberholzer said unhesitatingly. "The boys and I can't fight a point zero five percent error in navigation— but for hostile planets, we've got the flamers."

Robin One shuddered. "I don't mind the fighting part," he said unexpectedly. "But I *do* simply loathe the thought of being an old, old man when I get home. All the same, we do have to get the word back."

"You're agreeing with the sergeant?"

"Yes, that's what I said."

"I agree," Sparks said. "Either way we may not make it, but the odds are in favor of doing it the hard way."

"Very good," 12-Upjohn said. He was uncertain of his exact emotion at this moment; perhaps gloomy satisfaction was as close a description as any. "I make it unanimous. Let's get ready."

The sergeant saluted and prepared to leave the cabin; but suddenly he turned back.

"I didn't think very much of either of you, a while back," he said brutally. "But I'll tell you this: There must be something about brains that involves guts too. I'll back 'em any time against any critter that lets itself be shot like a fish in a barrel—whatever the odds."

The Consort of State was still mulling that speech over as the madman's caricature of an intersteller ship groaned and lifted its lumps and angles from Calle. Who knows, he kept telling himself, who knows, it might even be true.

But he noticed that Robin One was still humming the chorale from *Psyche and Eros*; and ahead the galactic night was as black as death.

007: "It is Enough, Ivan. Go Home!"

by Reginald Bretnor

Editor's Introduction

Reginald Bretnor and my father have at least this in common: They were both in the Horse Cavalry. I have heard identical tales from each about how they nearly castrated themselves attempting to sheathe the Patton sabre during mounted parade.

Reg Bretnor lives in Oregon now, but he used to live in the Bay Area of California. I first met him at Poul Anderson's house; I believe that was also the day I really got to know Randall Garrett. Reg is a fascinating character: inveterate (and expert!) poker player; sword collector; gun expert; historian; military theorist and excellent raconteur.

He and Randall Garrett had much in common: attitudes, and a fascination with puns, although Randall was much quicker to make them in ordinary conversation. Still in all, Bretnor for years published "Through Space and Time with Ferdinand Feghoot," certainly the most famous series of science fiction puns in our history. (Randall parodied them with "The Adventures of Benedict Breadfruit." I suppose that was inevitable.)

When not being a punster, Reginald Bretnor is a very serious writer. His Decisive Warfare is generally considered a real contribution to military theory, while the present essay indicates that he understands all too well the menace facing Western civilization.

It has become fashionable of late to act as if there were a symmetry between Western civilization and the Soviet bloc; to speak of "side A and side B" as if their national motives were the same. This is always done in speeches at the United Nations.

We all know better, of course. The Soviets slaughtered more of their own citizens than the Nazis ever managed, and their invasion of Afghanistan has little in common with the futile U.S. efforts to keep at least a part of Vietnam, if not free, then at least unenslaved. Intellectuals may be proud of their achievements in inducing the U.S. to withdraw from Vietnam; but they do not often say so when speaking to groups of Southeast Asian refugees.

Yet we continue to sell grain and butter to the Soviet Union, and the Europeans continue to build their pipelines. Worse, this is not done for cash, but for credit, so that Poland, West Germany, Czechoslovakia and the Soviet Union itself pile up ever-mounting debts to the West—and Western bankers agitate for further extensions of credit lest a Communist loan default upset the international monetary market.

This may not be entirely rational. As Henry Kissinger has recently pointed out ("The International Context For U.S. Security," in America's Security in the 1980's, International Institute for Strategic Studies Adelphi Paper 174), "The Soviet Union has great military strength and enormous political and sociological weaknesses. It is a system of government that has no legitimate means of succession… The economy is obviously not working, and all Communist countries, without exception, face the problem of what to do with the Communist Party in a developed state. The Party is not needed for government and it is not needed for economy. Under the socialist system you have the kind of absurdity that appeared in the Soviet press: the system operated on the basis of a tractor factory that was never built, and they fired a Minister because he reported the existence of a refinery that did not exist."

The paradox is that the West continues to supply the Soviet Union with the means for bailing itself out of economic hardships; it thus has surplus goods which it can devote to its continued buildup of military strength.

Reginald Bretnor continues that analysis.

————————————

In the fictional world of détente and of the suspense novel, Secret Agent 007—James Bond—entertained us with the excitements of his clandestine warfare against fictional Russians.

In the real world we live in, on September 2, 1983, real Russians shot down Korean Air Lines Flight 007—a cold-blooded, deliberate act of savagery—murdering two hundred sixty-nine men, women and children.

The aircraft was a passenger plane, unarmed, undefended, and there can be no doubt that the Russians knew exactly what they were doing. The monitored conversations of their fighter pilot show that. So do the reports of Japanese monitors. What we do not know—what none, or very few, of our leaders understand—is why they did it. I do not mean their immediate motive, whatever it may have been, but rather that mysterious twist in the Russian psyche—in the minds of those dire old men in the Kremlin who rule Russia—that seems to make such barbarities inevitable. They are the men who make decisions, decisions with possible worldwide implications, like the decision to kill Flight 007. In Russia such decisions are not made by impulsive junior officers, or even by impulsive generals.

We, in the world where Flight 007 was butchered, will profit if our revulsion and our anger bring us to the realization that the Russians most of us think we have been dealing with are as fictional as those in Secret Agent 007's world, or those in the imagination of such fuzzy-minded liberals as the late Eleanor Roosevelt.

The real Russians Solzhenitsyn writes about are much more true to life, even though they exist only in the minds of his readers.

We live in the same real world as the Russian Communists, and if we are determined to survive, it is up to us to understand them. In order to do this, we must consider their history, for Russian Communism is a nineteenth-century growth, dogmatic Marxist materialism grafted onto the ancient tree of Russian tyranny.

The Mongol Heritage and the October Revolution

For almost two hundred and fifty years those lands that were eventually consolidated into the Russian Empire were under Mongol rule, and though Ivan the Great completed their defeat and their expulsion in 1480, they had left their mark on the people they had conquered. When the first English travelers came to Muscovy in the mid-sixteenth century during the reign of Ivan the Grim, they found a nation deeply suspicious of foreigners and of everything foreign, a nation where no man was free, where the authority of the Czar and his officers was absolute and arbitrary. Talented foreigners were being recruited—artisans, architects and (notably) artillerists—but once in, they were never allowed to leave. Those who did leave, escaped. The Orthodox Church had immense power, but this power was scarcely ever used to sustain human rights and human dignity. Not until the middle of the seventeenth century, during the reign of Peter the Great's father, did Western influence become appreciable. Then came Peter the Great, himself a Russian tyrant in the classic mold, who, in spite of this, did more than any man to open Russia to the West. By the time of Catherine the Great a century later, Russia's aristocracy and intellectuals had become largely Westernized; French was the language of culture and fashion; wealthy Russians were beginning to travel abroad. Unfortunately, this Westernization was largely cosmetic, and the Communist revolution of October 1918 shattered it. The aristocracy, the upper middle class and vast numbers of intellectuals were destroyed or scattered as refugees throughout the world, and before too long, bloody-minded Lenin died and was followed by the even bloodier-minded Stalin.

Again there were wholesale purges and imprisonments, enforced migrations of entire peoples and heartlessly engineered famines.

The old men now in the Kremlin were shaped by all these forces; they are men who have survived and climbed to power by deceit, by treachery, by never letting principle prevail over policy.

Simply consider the countries that were free and independent between the two World Wars and are now under the Russian heel: Latvia,

Lithuania, Esthonia, Poland, Hungary, to say nothing of East Germany, North Korea, Outer Mongolia. Consider the spread of Communist subversion and Communist arms into every country where the Free West is vulnerable.

Reading the adventures of Secret Agent 007, one often felt that he and his Russian counterparts were playing games.

The old men in the Kremlin are not.

Unhappily, we are. We are playing *their* game: *Motivation and Deterrence.*

Let us consider what motivates these men. First—and I have never seen this adequately emphasized—they are men who live for power, and they justify its exercise at home and its exercise and exploitation abroad by repeating endlessly the empty promises of Marxism.

Second, they differ from almost all past tyrants in one thing: They are dedicated materialists; it is Marxist dogma that men have no souls, that at death, like a quenched candle flame, they simply cease to be. This has a very dangerous corollary. If you believe it, sooner or later you will think: *When I die, so far as I'm concerned, the universe will end. No matter what I do during my life, nothingness can exact no payment from me; there can be no retribution.*

We have failed to understand this, probably because so many materialistic thinkers in the West still believe in a humanistic philosophy the Communists have shucked off. One historical anecdote will serve to get the point across. In the Muscovy of Ivan the Grim, only one small group of people enjoyed freedom of speech. These were the "holy idiots," like the one in the opera *Boris Godunov.* Ivan was mad. He was a sadist and a sexual psychopath. On one occasion, becoming enraged at the city of Great Novgorod, he marched against it in mid-winter with an army of his police and spent a few weeks looting, torturing, killing. When he left, only sixteen of the city's men were still alive.

He then moved on to the city of Pskov, where he began the same sort of thing. However, there he was confronted by a "holy idiot," one Mikula Svyet, who demonstrated his holiness by, among other things, going naked summer and winter. Mikula pointed at the Czar and said, "It is enough, Ivan. Go home!"

And Ivan went. Aside from his derangement, he was intensely, fanatically, religious. Fearing the wrath of God, he was deterred.

Would Stalin have been? Would Andropov be?

Whose Game Are We Playing?

Even before the October Revolution, we of the West began to play the Marxists' game. First, the German general staff smuggled Lenin and Trotsky into Russia in a sealed boxcar to overthrow the liberal Kerensky government, which had deposed the Czar but had promised to continue fighting with the Allies. Then, in the twenties, American generosity, exercised through the Hoover Commission, saved millions from starvation. From then on, the Russian Communists continued to lift themselves by our bootstraps. The West lent them money, extended credit to them, sold them factories they themselves could not have built, technology they themselves could not have developed. We seemed determined to make Lenin's cynical prophesy come true: "When we hang the capitalists, they will sell us the rope to do it with." (Nor is it fair, by the way, to blame all this on left-leaning liberals. Some of our largest corporations have been, and still are, just as guilty.)

Let us not forget, too, that when Hitler was threatening the West, he and Stalin concluded their notorious pact, partitioning tormented Poland and giving the Nazis a secure Eastern frontier. And when France had fallen, while Britain alone resisted Hitler, Russia remained "neutral"—just as she remained "neutral" all through our own war with Japan until Hiroshima had been destroyed and Japan's surrender was a virtual certainty. And all the while, we had been pouring into Russia weapons, materiel, provisions, without which she would have been defeated.

Immediately after the war, we did nothing to halt the march of Russian Communist imperialism. Our first firm stand against it was

Truman's in Korea, which ended up as something less than victory; and then the bumbling of the Bay of Pigs; and then Vietnam, about which the less said now the better. And all this while, it was pretty much business as usual where "non-military" trade with the U.S.S.R. was concerned.

Business As Usual?

What business do we have to do with the Soviet Union? Much of it we do for our own profit. Some we undoubtedly do for our survival— strategic metals and minerals that otherwise might be in short supply. But by far the greater part of our trade with the Communists is strategically to our detriment. The reason for this is simple: *There is no such thing as non-military aid to the U.S.S.R.*

Every contract any Western firm accepts to build, say, an automobile factory, a truck factory, a dam, frees Russian technical personnel to build the tanks, the missiles, the aircraft and ships of war with which the Russian Communists implement their aggressive policy. Every sale of sophisticated electronic equipment, of laboratory equipment or of industrial know-how enables more Russian scientific personnel to devote their time to research for war. Every sale of wheat to this power that cannot even feed its own population adequately saves millions of Russian man-hours for work dedicated to our eventual destruction.

The coldly calculated brutality with which Korean Air Lines Flight 007 was destroyed may have been employed to test us, to determine just how far we'd let ourselves be pushed. Or its purpose may have been deliberately to outrage the civilized world and so divert attention from some other nasty business being planned elsewhere. At this writing, we do not know.

But we do know that the action was not exceptional, that it speaks eloquently of the total immorality of Soviet policy and that it warns us loudly and clearly of what we may expect in the future.

Business as usual? Perhaps so. Perhaps we will continue to sell the old men in the Kremlin the fruit of our scientific and technological superiority, to wink at their industrial espionage in this country, to ship them crops they cannot grow themselves. Or, even if we do not, very probably other industrial powers will.

The world forgets too easily when there is money to be made.

But the shadow of Ivan the Grim still looms over Russia, and perhaps the time has come for someone to say, with adequate authority:

"It is enough, Ivan. Go home!"

What the Soviet Pilots Said

Here is the transcript, distributed by the White House last night, of excerpts from the radio transmissions of two Soviet pilots who participated in the downing of the Korean Air Lines Flight 007 last week. This is a translation; the conversation was in Russian. All times are Greenwich Mean Time.

1818:34—SU-15 fighter to 1826:20—*SU-15 fighter to "Deputat," Soviet ground station call sign*: "The A.N.O. (air navigation lights) are burning. The strobe light is flashing."

1818:56—*MiG-23 fighter to Deputat*: "Roger. I'm at 7500, course 230."

1819:02—*SU fighter to Deputat*: "I am closing on the target."

1826:20—*SU fighter to Deputat*: "I have executed the launch."

1826:22—*SU fighter to Deputat*: "The target is destroyed."

1826:27—*SU fighter to Deputat*: "I am breaking off attack."

Associated Press: Washington

THE 'EATHEN

by Rudyard Kipling

Editor's Introduction

This book is dedicated to the non-commissioned officers of the armed forces of the United States. Allowing for Kipling's times, when there were no women non-coms, there have been few more powerful expressions of appreciation for this rare breed than this poem.

Sarge Workman tells me there's nothing more dangerous than a second lieutenant with a map.

To those Regulars who put up with *this* particular second lieutenant (complete with map) this book is dedicated.

The 'eathen in 'is blindness bows down to wood and stone;
'E don't obey no orders unless they is his own;
'E keeps 'is side-arms awful: 'e leaves 'em all about,
An' then comes up the Regiment an' pokes the 'eathen out.

> *All along o' dirtiness, all along o' mess.*
> *All along o' doin' things rather-more-or-less.*
> *All along of abby-nay* [1] *, kul* [2] *, an' hazar-ho* [3] *,*
> *Mind you keep your rifle and yourself jus' so!*

---

[1] Not now
[2] Tomorrow
[3] Wait a bit

The young recruit is 'aughty—'e draf's from Gawd knows where;
They bid 'im show 'is stockin's and lay 'is mattress square;
'E calls it bloomin' nonsense—'e doesn't know, no more—
An' then comes 'is Company and kicks 'im round the floor!

The young recruit is 'ammered—'e takes it very hard;
'E 'angs 'is 'ead an' mutters—'e sulks about the yard;
'E talks o' "cruel tyrants" which 'e'll swing for by-an-by,
An' the others 'ears and mocks 'im, and the boy goes orf to cry.

The young recruit is silly—'e thinks o' suicide.
'E's lost 'is gutter-devil; 'e 'asn't got 'is pride;
But day by day they kicks 'im, which 'elps 'im on a bit,
Till 'e finds 'isself one mornin' with a full an' proper kit.

> *Gettin' clear o' dirtiness, gettin' done with mess,*
> *Gettin shut o' doin' things rather more-or-less;*
> *Not so fond of abby-nay, kul, nor hazar-ho,*
> *Learns to keep 'is rifle an' 'isself jus' so!*

The young recruit is 'appy—'e throws a chest to suit;
You see 'im grow mustaches; you 'ear 'im slap 'is boot.
'E learns to drop the "bloodies" from every word 'e slings,
An' 'e shows an 'ealthy brisket when 'e strips for bars an' rings.

The cruel-tyrant-sergeants they watch 'im 'arf a year;
They watch 'im with 'is comrades, they watch 'im with 'is beer;
They watch 'im with the women at the regimental dance,
And the cruel-tyrant-sergeants send 'is name along for "Lance".

An' now 'e's 'arf o' nothin', an' all a private yet,
'Is room they up an' rags 'im to see what they will get.
They rags 'im low an' cunnin', each dirty trick they can.
But 'e learns to sweat 'is temper and 'e learns to sweat 'is man.

An', last, a Colour-Sergeant, as such to be obeyed,
'E schools 'is men at cricket, 'e tells 'em on parade;
They sees 'im quick and 'andy, uncommon set an' smart,
An' so 'e talks to orficers which 'ave the Core at 'eart.

'E learns to do 'is watchin' without it showin' plain;
'E learns to save a dummy, and shove 'im straight again;
'E learns to check a ranker that's buyin' leave to shirk;
'An 'e learns to make men like 'im so they'll learn to like their work.

An' when it comes to marchin' 'e'll see their socks are right,
An' when it comes to action 'e shows 'em how to sight.
'E knows their ways of thinkin' and just what's in their mind;
'E knows when they are takin' on an' when they've fell be'ind.

'E knows each talkin' corp'ral that leads a squad astray;
'E feels 'is innards 'eavin, 'is bowels givin' way;
'E sees the blue-white faces all tryin' 'ard to grin,
'An 'e stands an' waits an' suffers till it's time to cap 'em in.

An' now the hugly bullets come peckin' through the dust,
An' no one wants to face 'em, but every beggar must;
So, like a man in irons, which isn't glad to go,
They moves 'em off by companies uncommon stiff an' slow.

Of all 'is five years' schoolin' they don't remember much
Excep' the not retreatin', the step and keepin' touch.
It looks like teachin' wasted when they duck and spread an' 'op
But if 'e 'adn't learned 'em they be all about the shop.

An' now it's " 'Oo goes backward?" an' now it's " 'Oo comes on?"
And now it's "Get the doolies," and now the Captain's gone;
An' now it's bloody murder, but all the while they 'ear
'Is voice, the same as barrick-drill, a-shepherdin' the rear.

'E's just as sick as they are, 'is 'eart is like to split,
But 'e works 'em, works 'em, works 'em till he feels 'em take the bit;
The rest is 'oldin' steady till the watchful bugles play,
An' 'e lifts 'em, lifts 'em, lifts 'em through the charge that wins the day!

The 'eathen in 'is blindness bows down to wood and stone;
'E don't obey no orders unless they is his own;
The 'eathen in 'is blindness must end where 'e began,
But the backbone of the Army is the Non-commissioned Man!

> *Keep away from dirtiness—keep away from mess,*
> *Don't get into doin' things rather-more-or-less!*
> *Let's ha' done with abby-nay, kul, and hazar-ho;*
> *Mind you keep your rifle an' yourself jus' so!*

THE TOOLS OF WAR

by Roland J. Green and Clyde R. Jones

Editor's Introduction

I first met Roland Green at the World Science Fiction Convention held in Washington in 1974. The conversation soon turned to military history and future conflict, and I recognized him as a kindred spirit at once.

Since that time, we have collaborated on *JANISSARIES II: Clan and Crown*, and have plotted at least one more joint work.

I've never met Clyde Jones, who, like Roland, lives in the Chicago area.

Green and Jones discuss a wide range of new weapons, but they cannot consider everything in a work of this length. One area they neglect is space weaponry; but space weapons may yet prove to be decisive.

The chemical-powered laser "battle station" located high in orbit could dominate warfare for some time to come. The Laser Battle Station (LBS) has multi-shot capability; it can burn down an entire fleet of ICBMs, then take on the enemy's air fleet for an encore.

Indeed, if the laser frequency is chosen correctly, it can have a decisive effect on land and sea warfare. Blue-green lasers can destroy targets on the ground. Such lasers would operate only in clear weather; but the ability to deny the enemy ground movement in clear weather would be well-nigh decisive.

Another potential weapon is Project Thor: orbiting crowbars with guidance systems. A cloud of them could be made to reenter over the enemy's attacking armored army. The "crowbars" would seek out tanks, striking them with velocities of miles per second; the result would be the certain destruction of the tank.

Such weapons could also be used against ships.

Those interested in space weapons would do well to begin with General Daniel O. Graham's *High Frontier* (New York: Tor Books, 1983) as well as the essays in the first two volumes of this series. Also useful is the *Report of the Second Meeting of the Citizens' Advisory Council on National Space Policy* (L-5 Society, 1060 E. Elm St., Tucson, Arizona 85719, $10.00, 1983).

Another decisive weapon not here discussed is the "neutron bomb," also called an Enhanced Radiation Weapon. N-bombs put out most of their energy as neutrons and x-rays rather than as blast and heat. Thus they "kill people without destroying property." To be precise: A one-kiloton neutron weapon exploded some 2,000 feet above a city would render exposed personnel—such as enemy troops—helpless while doing little more physical damage than breaking windows.

Because there is no blast, shelter from N-bombs consists of having several feet of dirt between you and the bomb. Civilians and troops in deep foxholes would survive; troops aboard armored vehicles would not. At the very least, N-bombs would make blitzkrieg tactics very difficult to employ. They thus appear to aid the defense more than the offense.

N-bombs have given rise to a number of myths, including the notion that enemy soldiers, having received a lethal dose of radiation, would now fight all the harder since they would have nothing left to live for. This is sometimes known as the "zombies-make-great-tankers" theory. It is held by such diverse persons as Kosta Tsipis, an arms-control specialist at MIT; Herbert Scoville, Jr., a key arms-control and disarmament specialist in the Pentagon during the Carter administration; and science fiction writer Fred Pohl.

The theory doesn't explain how the enemy soldiers know they're zombies: Given the wide range of human tolerance to radiation, it's not likely they'd know. Moreover, the theory ignores the enemy troops directly under the weapon, who would be killed instantly; units with 50 percent and higher casualties rarely have high military effectiveness.

For a full discussion of N-bombs, see Sam Cohen, *The Truth About the Neutron Bomb* (New York, William Morrow, 1983). Cohen, the inventor of neutron weapons, discusses their effects and the political opposition he has encountered for the past ten years. He demonstrates that the Soviet Union almost certainly has neutron weapons.

The Tools of War is not precisely an original title. James R. Newman (who with Edward Kasner wrote *Mathematics and the Imagination*, probably the most popular book about mathematics ever published) wrote a four-hundred-page book with that title; it was published in early 1942 and is long out of print, although it ought to be available in libraries. I found mine in a Hollywood used bookstore. I recommend it to anyone interested in the history of weaponry (Garden City, New York, Doubleday, Doran & Company, Inc., 1942).

Newman's book gave an accurate description of the weapons to be used in the coming war. Of course it emphasized the battleship to the detriment of the aircraft carrier—but it did at least admit there was some controversy. After all, no military theorist and few Navy officers (other than upstarts like Halsey) really understood that the carrier would be the decisive arm of naval warfare in World War II.

Newman's book was notable in another way: Much of its text and at least one of its diagrams were lifted in their entirety and inserted, without credit, into the designer's notes for a well-known war game based on the fall of France. I suppose there is some justification since Newman's work had one of the best expositions on the Maginot Line, yet was written after the Germans bypassed it.

A final area neglected by nearly everyone is communications. Brigadier S. L. A. Marshall in his Pork Chop Hill speculates that wars of the future may be fought by small patrols able to call in immense firepower from far away. Lieutenant Asfaw of the Ethiopian Imperial

Guards showed how that might be done during one of the battles of the Korean War.

In 1963, using Asfaw's battle as an example, Corlin O. Beum and I designed a weapons system then code-named "Thoth" missiles. They would be launched from cargo aircraft far from the combat zone and guided in to an offset from the observer patrol. We also developed an autocorrelation communication system to aid in Thoth guidance. The weapons system was intended for Vietnam; alas, it was never built because no one believed that that war would last long enough to require such special weapons.

The Thoth missile system could be built today. The missiles and their guidance systems are standard off-the-shelf hardware. The communications systems are a bit trickier.

Indeed, Command, Control, Communications and Intelligence— the famous "C-cubed-I" factor—are the key to modern battle. Most C3I systems require space-based components; thus defense of one's space assets is a key to the future of war.

Meanwhile, Green and Jones provide a good introduction to speculation about the future of arms.

––––––––––––

The best reason for any study of the weapons of future land, sea and air warfare is also the simplest.

These are the weapons most likely to be used.

No one has dropped an atomic or hydrogen bomb in combat since 1945. No one has ever launched an ICBM at an enemy target or intercepted an incoming enemy warhead.

On the other hand, airplanes and helicopters have been flying in combat somewhere in the world each year since 1945. Every continent has seen tanks in action, if only against rioters or revolutionaries. Warships—from super-carriers down to motor-patrol boats—have sent planes, rockets, shells and torpedoes at enemy targets. Even relatively new developments such as tactical missiles, hovercraft, guided "smart" bombs and lasers have gone from the laboratories to the factories and from the factories to the firing line. Everywhere the infantryman has gone on practicing the basic skills of his craft.

This kind of warfare will continue because we're not likely to abolish war completely and the only other alternative is still worse. A world that used H-bombs where tanks could do the job wouldn't last long or be very interesting, except possibly to extra-terrestrial archeologists who came along after the ruins were no longer dangerously radioactive.

This article focuses on the next twenty years of warfare on Earth. Beyond that point, we're talking about something closer to soothsaying than prediction, and probably about a book rather than an article.

The Possibilities

1. Intermediate Weapons

The neutron bomb has already created an area of what might be called "intermediate weapons," neither strictly conventional (high-explosive) nor nuclear. We may expect to see at least two more kinds of these weapons before the year 2000, plus developments in chemical and biological warfare.

Cold-fusion Bombs: Thermonuclear weapons with the fusion initiated by a ring of magnets, charges of extremely powerful conventional explosives, or one-shot lasers. Such bombs might be smaller, cheaper, lighter and cleaner than any present tactical fission or fusion weapon. A cold-fusion bomb with a one-kiloton yield could conceivably be fired from a medium mortar or carried in an anti-tank missile.

Directed-radiation Weapons: Actual bombs emitting directional bursts of hard radiation on detonation; magnetic pulse weapons (particularly effective against computers); beamed radiation weapons producing focused, coherent microwaves, radio waves, sound, streams of charged particles, etc.

For the first two we'll probably need radically improved chemical explosives or cold-fusion triggers; for the third, a breakthrough in reliable, portable, high-capacity energy storage or generation. The last two can be used against equipment rather than people, and against people all may be adjustable to harass, disable or kill.

Chemical and Biological Warfare: Gases and germs each offer their share of potential horrors.

In sheer killing power, lethal chemical agents such as nerve gases hardly need "improvement." They need to be cheaper, safer to transport and store and more controllable as to the areas they'll affect and the time they'll remain potent.

Non-lethal agents, basically descendants of current riot-control gases, are a more fertile field for innovation. We can expect hallucinogens, tranquilizers, blistering gases many times more powerful than mustard gas, and so on quite literally *ad nauseam*.

As chemical agents become more reliable, they'll appear in a wider variety of projectiles, mine fields and booby traps. We may even see chemical agents that are themselves booby traps. Consider the possibilities of leaving behind when you retreat fuel dumps treated with a chemical agent which, under the heat of combustion, breaks down to release cyanide gas.

The potential of biological warfare is expanding alarmingly, thanks to recent developments in DNA research. Within the next generation we may see DNA expertise and laboratories within reach of some large corporations and many governments, responsible or otherwise.

In spite of this, we still may not see strategic biological warfare unless the world's political situation deteriorates so far that there's no longer a question of whether there will be war, but only of how many survivors there will be. Sowing cholera in the enemy's water supply or anthrax among his livestock may look like the same kind of total threat as dropping H-bombs, to be met by the same sort of total response.

Like fall-out, biological warfare is also no respecter of borders. Immunizing your own population in advance sacrifices surprise without guaranteeing that a strain of bacteria mutated once won't mutate again. Even those countries not deterred by their enemies may wind up deterred by the threat of a universal plague or intervention by outside parties. In the end, strategic biological warfare seems likely to wind up incorporated into the same rough and ready system of deterrence that so far has prevented the use of nuclear weapons.

It should be kept in mind, however, that the DNA-tailoring techniques can be used with *any* sort of organism. Contaminating the water supply of your opponent's capital city with a virulent strain of the twenty-four-hour flu or Montezuma's Revenge is not the sort of threat that really justifies his launching ICBMs. At the same time, it will do the efficiency of his government and military command structure no good at all.

2. Materials

The general trend since 1900 has been toward improved strength-to-weight ratios, and usually lighter weight. During the rest of the century we can expect improvements in stampings, castings, and powder metallurgy. We will see improved plastics, semi-organic materials, carbon-fiber reinforced materials (fiberglass as tough as steel), possibly woven metals or whole new categories of non-ferrous and non-metallic substances.

Some materials may prove too expensive to use in large items such as complete aircraft or in small, chronically expendable ones such as boots. Others may not be cost-effective under all circumstances. A one-pound bulletproof helmet with radio, gas mask, goggles, sound amplifiers, laser detector, neck armor, packet of Excedrin and tube of Brylcreem may not be acceptable if it costs ten times as much as an equally effective three-pounder.

In general, we can expect to see small warships, air and ground vehicles, all kinds of weapons and their projectiles, and the fighting man's personal equipment becoming lighter, stronger, or both. More vehicles and weapons will become air-portable, and the gap in firepower between ground-mobile and air-mobile troops will shrink. This will make air-mobile operations much less dangerous for the attacker and more so for the defender.

The much-burdened infantryman will be particularly happy. After millennia of trial, error and profanity, his individual load may actually begin to shrink, or at least stop increasing. This will reduce many types of non-combat casualties and also one of the barriers to the use of women in ground combat roles. Ground troops should also be able to wear extensive body armor, effective against blast, fragments and some types of small arms.

3. Hyper-explosives

By the year 2000 we could have chemical explosives five to ten times more powerful than today's. The practical limit is what can survive rough handling, both on the way to the battlefield and on the way to the target.

Propellant explosives are likely to be developed further. As long as the gun won't explode or the rocket tumble in flight, the more power from a given weight of propellant, the better. Explosives in warheads may be developed more conservatively. Most tactical weapons sooner or later have to be used in close proximity to your own troops. Some, like hand grenades, are designed for nothing else. A certain margin for error is always useful; otherwise you may wipe out one of your own platoons if a single shell drops fifty yards short.

We can be reasonably certain about some of the effects of hyper-explosives. Potentially ship-killing weapons will become still more compact, cheaper and more numerous. All types and sizes of solid-fuel missiles will become more effective. Some form of body armor may become not merely possible but essential for ground troops, and even warship crews. A wide range of currently unprotected vehicles, such as trucks and helicopters, may also have to develop some form of armor to survive.

Beyond this, exactly what happens depends on whether we use hyper-explosives to increase the performance or to decrease their size. Each course offers so many advantages that we are likely to see both.

Increasing weapons performance gives us higher velocities, longer ranges and more powerful warheads. It also permits improving two specific categories of weapons.

One is the rocket-assisted projectile, fired from a conventional artillery piece but given extra range by a small rocket. Current RAPs sacrifice accuracy and warhead size for range. With hyper-explosives, this sacrifice would be reduced.

The other category of improved weapons is the "smart projectile," the bomb or shell with a target-seeking capability. The target-seeking equipment is expensive and can reduce the load of explosives carried. With hyper-explosives we can increase the performance of smart projectiles enough to justify their much wider use in spite of cost. Hyper-explosives could permit a rocket-boosted eight-inch shell with three maneuverable warheads or a thousand-pound bomb carrying not only multiple warheads and target-seekers but decoys, anti-radar jammers and booby traps.

Shrinking the weapon offers equally interesting prospects. To begin with, the job of the saboteur, terrorist/freedom fighter/guerrilla or commando is going to become easier and the job of his opponents more difficult. The same principle will operate all the way up the scale of weaponry. Three near-certainties are:

- Improved infantry heavy weapons and better armament of all types of ground troops and vehicles armed with infantry weapons.
- Defensive air-to-air missiles and light guns carried aboard helicopters and transport aircraft.
- Heavy artillery pieces and mortars mounted on trucks instead of tracked vehicles. This will increase road speed and reduce cost, weight, fuel consumption, noise and maintenance.

4. Lasers

Reality's answer to the death ray has a promising future, although it also has certain weaknesses. Lasers require careful maintenance, use a great deal of energy and can be blocked by foul weather, spray, and natural or artificial smoke. They are always more likely to be useful on land than at sea and more useful above the weather than on the ground. Within these limits they are going to be increasingly effective, and even lethal, in combat.

For target illumination and range-finding, lasers have been in use since the 1960s. A comparatively low-powered portable laser can generate enough reflection to make a target visible to a human gunner or a missile's target-seeking mechanism. Such lasers are rapidly becoming smaller, cheaper, more reliable and more widely distributed; they will go on doing so.

The multiplication of lasers will inevitably generate counter-measures. Passive methods include high-intensity flares to confuse light-sensitive guidance systems and smoke generators to block the beam. More active methods might include rockets homing on the heat pulse of the laser generator or shells filled with highly reflective powder.

Laser weapons will undoubtedly start off mounted on vehicles and may stay there. Even a jeep can carry a fair-sized generator or a rack of storage batteries. As energy-storage methods improve, so will laser weapons. They will probably fire in short pulses, giving the hot gases generated from the target time to disperse. Even if such lasers can't penetrate heavy armor, they may destroy all sorts of lightly-protected targets and the external fittings and sensors of heavy vehicles.

A workable, cheap laser rifle or pistol is farther away but probably not impossible. Chemical cartridges made of hyper-explosives or high-capacity, quick-discharge batteries could solve the basic problem of storing energy. Such a weapon would fire in short pulses from a clip of the cartridges or batteries.

Lasers may also be the basis of future anti-aircraft and antimissile systems, even at the tactical level. Missiles and aircraft have fuel and electronic systems that are inherently vulnerable to heat. Their main defense has always been speed, less useful against a weapon that strikes at the speed of light.

For air-to-air combat, lasers are a high-performance weapon that could give comparatively low-performance aircraft considerable fighting power. Air-to-air lasers could be giant versions of the clip-fed ground soldiers' laser, probably mounted externally in self-contained pods slung on wing stations to reduce structural heating.

For close-range defense of ground targets, lasers can simply be added to the guns and missiles already mounted on warships or deployed with air-defense units. With adequate detection systems and high-speed computers, close-range air-defense lasers might even become effective against smart bombs and shells.

To protect larger areas, the air-defense laser may itself have to take to the air, in aircraft with long endurance and substantial pay loads. Such planes could carry long-range lasers, a power supply and a computerized detection and tracking system. They would also carry a few short-range weapons for self-defense but would normally operate over their own rear areas or fleets, well clear of the enemy's air-defense system. Flying above the weather and terrain obstacles, such airborne lasers could engage a wide variety of aircraft and missile targets at very respectable ranges.

5. Small Arms

Even without a laser rifle, the soldier of the year 2000 could be a distinctly formidable opponent. The use of basically off-the-shelf hardware has already produced a fully automatic 5.56 mm rifle with a laser sight. It is being used by police SWAT teams and will no doubt be appearing in the hands of their opponents before long. The Teflon-coated bullet has also received a good deal of unfortunately quite justifiable publicity for its ability to penetrate bulletproof vests and vehicles. (Antitank pistols, anyone?) There are other small-arms possibilities for the near future, each with its advantages, disadvantages and requirements.

The Caseless Cartridge: A conventional bullet with the propellant forming a hardened lump of explosive rather than contained in a metallic cartridge. This will reduce the size, weight and cost of the round. It will also allow increasing the ammunition load without decreasing the caliber of the round or using heavier and more penetrating bullets. It will require the solution of overheating problems and also some redesign of the firing mechanism.

The Rocket Bullet: The descendant of the Gyrojet round. Current rocket-propelled small-arms rounds seem to lack penetrating power at short ranges and accuracy at longer ones. A combination of hyper-explosives, heavier bullets and a rifle-length barrel should produce a more effective system. The great advantage is reduced recoil, but problems appear to remain with smoke, flash and noise.

The Electric Gun: A rifle discharging its rounds by creating mutually repelling electrical charges or activating a series of ring magnets set at intervals along the barrel—a miniature induction catapult. Such a system is probably the farthest away but would also have the least recoil, noise, flash and wear on the mechanism and the barrel. It is also likely to remain limited to solid-projectile small arms. Subjecting explosive warheads or electronic circuits to such powerful magnetic or electrical fields might not be a good idea.

The Exploding Bullet: A label for a variety of types: simple miniature shells filled with hyper-explosive; flechette rounds; discarding-sabot rounds with disintegrating plastic shells and depicted-uranium cores. The first two would be highly effective against personnel; the third would also be armor-piercing.

Making full use of these improved small arms needs a corresponding improvement in sights, using lasers and mini-computers. At a conservative estimate, the well-trained infantryman of the year 2000 could be able to hit anything he can see out to a range of about one thousand yards and penetrate most body armor and some vehicles at shorter ranges.

The basic shoulder weapon may even become capable of firing not only bullets but grenades, rockets and flares. The World War II rifle grenade was heavy, inaccurate, short-ranged and needed a high-powered cartridge, which damaged the rifle in prolonged use. Before 2000 a far more lethal grenade or high-intensity flare could be made light enough to go several hundred yards with a normally powered cartridge. A small rocket could be fired out to a safe distance, where its own motor would ignite to send it on the way. So infantry heavy weapons may disappear entirely from many types of units in favor of a soldier carrying one rifle, four different kinds of ammunition—and, it may be hoped, a bayonet.

6. Electronic Warfare

Here the sky is already nearly the limit and the rate of progress faster than in any other area.

As far as surveillance, detection and ranging techniques are concerned, we may not see any spectacular breakthroughs. Existing equipment in these areas already uses the entire electromagnetic spectrum as well as heat, sound, smells and chemicals. As with lasers, what we need is cheaper, more reliable equipment, more widely distributed and needing less skill for its operation and maintenance. Making even these improvements will be more than enough to keep alive the already frenzied race between one side's electronic systems and the other side's electronic counter-measures.

You use radar and the enemy begins to jam it. You fire homing rockets at his jammers and he invents a radar-negative paint. You switch to passive infrared sensors and he replies with random thermite charges to overload your sensors with heat pulses. You switch again, this time to laser rangers, which he blocks with efflorescent gases and rockets homing in on your illuminators. You abandon sophistication and use old-fashioned aluminum-foil chaff with propaganda printed on the back in three languages, none of them used by your opponent. He trains carrier pigeons to lay radio-sensitive eggs and you invent a robot chef to scramble them.

Now you decide to strike closer to home. You bug his headquarters with microphones. He returns the favor. You dig out his microphones and plant another batch of your own, including a few microminiaturized ones he misses. He plants radio transmitters in your coffee urn that clash with the microwave devices you've woven into his curtains and furniture. He bounces a laser off your window shades and reads the reflections while you are doing the same with sonic pulses. Meanwhile, your people have been finding cockroaches with serial numbers in Russian, Hindi and Hebrew. You replace them with microrobots with TV pickups and acetylene torches, disguised as mice, and he unleashes his robot cat that lives on your roof… And so on.

At the heart of electronic warfare lies the computer. Over the next twenty-five years the revolution in computer capacity and size, now underway, will affect every area of military activity.

Computers are vulnerable to faulty components, poor maintenance, inadequate data and incorrect programming. The bigger the computer, the more complex its intended functions, or the larger its data-gathering network, the more vulnerable it will be. The same principle also applies in reverse. The larger the number of activities controlled by one computer, the more vulnerable the whole system is to collapse through disruption of the central computer.

So we can expect to see the most developments among the smaller, more specialized computers. The present smart shells and bombs will multiply, with the larger ones becoming extremely sophisticated. All types and sizes of missile will become more accurate. By the year 2000 almost any weapon on the battlefield may suddenly appear with a miniature "brain." This includes such previously science-fictional devices as the thirty-second bomb from Heinlein's *Starship Troopers*, as well as a gruesome variety of booby traps and mines.

The use of electronic aids in all forms of combat vehicles will increase. Even today the SR-71 reconnaissance plane carries out most of a mission automatically, and the engines of many modern warships are controlled from the bridge. Pilots and engineers provide redundancy and discretionary judgment. We may see the automated tank with a computerized weapons system and a two-man crew; we will certainly see more electronic monitoring of vital systems for malfunctions.

We may also see what will be in all but name robot soldiers. The computerized security systems already protecting banks and luxury highrises could substitute for human sentries in many places. Farther afield, we can expect robot command posts, linked to a variety of sensors, programmed to tell friend from foe and controlling mine fields, shortrange missiles and demolition charges. Finally, there are literally hundreds of clerical and housekeeping chores that can be computerized—issuing pay, accounting for supplies, troubleshooting faulty equipment, monitoring hospital patients, etc.

These uses of computers have certain points in common. Their equipment and programming can be designed for a limited range of tasks and made comparatively immune to subsequent programming errors or changes in the environment. They also economize in manpower. This is essential in the industrial countries, where the individual enlisted man has already become the most difficult item for the armed forces to acquire and maintain. With the declining birth rate in these countries, the manpower shortage is going to become worse, and the intelligent use of computers is one of the most promising ways of meeting it.

The picture becomes more complicated when we move on to larger systems centralized around one or more computers. Such systems are indispensable for any sort of effective area defenses against aircraft and missiles, on land or at sea. They are the most effective method for coordinating tactical air strikes, amphibious landings or artillery bombardments. Finally, they are desirable backups for *all* command and control activities, where the ability to handle larger quantities of data faster than your enemy can often be a real advantage.

At the same time, we need to avoid making such systems more indispensable than they need to be. This is not going to be the easiest of jobs since military organizations are biased toward centralization and hierarchy. Computerized systems are invaluable for reinforcing this bias, far above and beyond what makes sense in a combat situation. If your system's main function becomes letting the general look over the shoulder of every platoon leader without leaving his headquarters, you should hope that enemy action will save you the trouble of fragging, if not the general, at least the general's computers.

Apart from reorienting commanders, we face problems in providing for movement and protection of the computers and their sensors. In the Yom Kippur War of 1973, the Egyptian air defense system lost its effectiveness as soon as their army advanced beyond the range of the radar stations on the west bank of the Suez Canal. The system disintegrated completely when the Israelis crossed the canal and attacked the radar stations on the ground.

So we should start planning to have more of the key elements of battlefield electronics systems mounted in aircraft, hovercraft, fast patrol boats and armored vehicles. We should also develop modular or packaged electronic systems that can be shifted from place to place and from vehicle to vehicle. Finally, with the increased capacity of smaller computers, we may want to develop systems with multiple computers, each capable of acting as the central component of the system.

Ideally, any system deployed on or near the firing line ought to be compact enough so that the company clerk can grab the vital elements and run just before the enemy overruns the CP. The farther back, the less trouble you need to take; by the time the computers at your main supply dump come under fire, so much else will have gone wrong that the inability to count socks and prophylactics will be among the least of the commanding general's worries.

Mobility, dispersal and decentralization also require reliable communications, able to carry large amounts of information and comparatively immune to either jamming or interception by the enemy. These will not always be available, although recent developments in lasers and glass-fiber optics look promising. Large computer systems face a future of continuously shifting balance points between risks and benefits, different for each type of warfare and probably for each opponent. The Egyptian air defense system might have been adequate against an opponent less aggressive and mobile than the Israelis. The only certainty we face is the need to design as much flexibility into the system and as much capacity into each element as technology and budgets permit.

7. Vehicles: Land, Sea and Air

Land: Battlefield vehicles will be lighter, faster, better armed, better protected and carry heavier payloads. Wheeled vehicles will have more cross-country mobility. Tracked vehicles should have higher road speeds and greater reliability, thanks to improved components. We may see greater use of gas turbines, or even electrical propulsion.

Air: High-performance aircraft such as the F-15 are already approaching the limits of existing power plants and materials, not to mention human physiology. Here we are likely to see primarily improvements in detail—more armor, payload and range, more sophisticated electronics (such as "fly-by-wire" systems), more use of variable-geometry wings and other unconventional designs for the lifting surfaces, and easier maintenance.

At lower speeds and altitudes, more and more aircraft will have short or vertical take-off and landing capabilities. The vertical take-off jet, the helicopter, and possibly the revived flying boat may replace some conventional aircraft for maritime uses. Modular armament systems will give all kinds of aircraft the capacity for self-defense. Finally, we will see increasingly sophisticated drone aircraft used for battlefield surveillance, reconnaissance, maritime patrol, airborne early warning, ECM and decoys; airborne missile launching is also possible.

Increased infantry firepower and the availability of better vertical landing systems may reduce the role of the helicopter on the battlefield. It will certainly have to become better protected and easier to maintain.

Current helicopters require much skilled maintenance at vulnerable fixed bases for each hour of flying time.

Sea: In the wake of the Falklands War, the future of navies no longer seems a simple linear process of the decline of the large warship. Small warships can be built cheaper, and with modern weapons and sensors, they can pack an enormous punch, including tactical aircraft. On the other hand, a larger ship can enjoy greater endurance, better sea-keeping qualities, a larger ammunition load and more ability to survive battle damage without the use of exotic and expensive materials for armor.

To make the warships of the near future more effective, we will probably see the extensive revival of armor protection and medium-caliber guns (six to eight inches), with rocket-boosted or smart shells.

Nuclear propulsion is too expensive for all except the largest ships, but there will be more gas turbines and diesels at sea. To simplify maintenance and reduce costs, more and more ships will be built with standardized modular weapons, fire-control systems and power plants. Large high-speed merchant ships are likely to be converted for many tasks, including ASW with VTOL aircraft and helicopters operating off portable flight decks.

The missile-armed fast patrol boat will become a major factor in naval strategy. As long as weapons and power plants for these craft are available on the open market, they can be built, manned and used by comparatively underdeveloped countries. In narrow seas, a force of FPBs can face a whole task force on dangerously even terms.

Nuclear submarines have virtually unlimited submerged endurance but are expensive, noisy and too large for use in shallow waters.

Improved electrical-power storage or the revival of the Walther hydrogen-peroxide system may give the conventional submarine a new lease on life in even the major navies.

Four types of vehicle need separate discussion:

Hovercraft today are noisy, hard to maneuver and poorly protected. As power plants, light-weight weapons and armor improve, hovercraft will become more effective. Large ones may serve as fast patrol boats; hovercraft are much less vulnerable to air attack than surface ships and nearly immune to submarines. Smaller hovercraft may replace most conventional landing craft for amphibious operations. On land they may help give high-speed ground mobility to command posts, radar stations, lasers and missile launchers.

The ducted fan, a shrouded propeller rotating horizontally to generate vertical lift, is simpler and more reliable than the helicopter. Experimental models during the 1950s had high fuel consumption, small payloads and stability problems. With better power plants and materials, as well as multiple fans giving stability, ducted-fan vehicles may replace the large and vulnerable heavy-lift helicopters.

The rocket belt has been experimental and largely unsuccessful for many years. With improved liquid or solid propellants, lighter materials and control by mini-computers, it may become a workable replacement for the parachute. Not only the individual soldier but any vehicle or weapon that is air-transportable may become air-droppable as well, ready to go into action the moment it lands.

The powered exoskeleton has appeared a number of times in science fiction as "powered armor" for the infantry. This ultimate development of the concept is probably more than twenty years away and may never be really practical or effective. Against the weapons of the future, a powered suit may simply increase the infantryman's value as a target without decreasing his vulnerability or increasing his fighting power. Less sophisticated exoskeletons undoubtedly will be developed and used for all sorts of engineering, construction and housekeeping jobs.

Conclusion: The New Range of Choices

The decision-makers in future wars will face a whole new range of choices in deciding how to accomplish any given objective.

1. Level of Violence

As weapons improve along the lines we've just examined, any military unit will be able to function at many different levels, high and low.

With only its regular weapons and ammunition, an infantry brigade will be able to suppress a riot in one neighborhood of a city or raze the city to the ground. A patrol boat will be able to stop a yacht smuggling marijuana or sink a super-tanker two hundred times her tonnage at a range of thirty miles. With the level of violence no longer tied particularly closely to the nature and size of the armed forces on the spot, the already complex job of the decision-makers in choosing which level to use will become still worse.

2. High-performance Platforms vs. High-performance Weapons

The high-performance platform such as the F-15, or super-carrier, has attracted most of the attention and distorted our perception of the range of possibilities. We can now build high-performance vehicles, sophisticated, specialized and extremely expensive. We can also build vehicles with a lower performance, carrying extremely powerful weapons. The missile-armed patrol boat, the subsonic attack aircraft with smart bombs, the jeep carrying a tank-killing missile are all existing examples of performance built into the weapons rather than into the weapons platform.

Now the United States is putting into service the Harpoon missile, designed to be fired from submerged submarines, surface ships of any reasonable size, aircraft and land vehicles. There is talk of using converted airliners or merchant ships to launch the cruise missile, a major strategic weapons system. Before long we may see jeeps able to carry anything from four MPs with pistols to missiles with kiloton fusion warheads, converted airliners mounting anti-missile lasers or long-range anti-aircraft missiles, merchant ships defending themselves with packaged missiles, guns, radar sets and even helicopters or VTOL aircraft.

The high-performance weapon isn't always the optimum solution but it is likely to be the preferable one in an increasing number of cases for economic reasons. It already costs more to build performance into the platform than into the weapon, and the gap is likely to increase. Also, any countermeasures effective against the weapon are likely to be even more effective against the weapons platform. Even if the enemy forces you to expend eight missiles instead of two, it's still cheaper than losing two planes and three crewmen.

3. The Mass Army vs. the Elite Force

Much conventional thought about war implies a dichotomy between large masses of moderately trained men with simple weapons and handfuls of super-troopers with immense firepower. This dichotomy began to erode with the development of automatic weapons and has been shrinking ever since. A World War I infantry company outgunned one of Napoleon's battalions; a modern platoon could beat either one; and a modern missile frigate could sink any of the battleships that fought at Jutland without getting her paint scratched.

Until recently the process has been slowed by the limitations of explosives and materials, as well as poor design. Increased firepower has tended to require more skill, training and education on the part of the soldiers. Now we are moving into an era of durable materials, hyper-explosives and solid-state electronics. All sorts of prepackaged, maintenance-free and nearly foolproof weapons become possible, putting great power into the hands of only marginally trained and educated soldiers.

As long as there are few restrictions on the spread of such weapons and the technology to manufacture them, the gap between the educated and the uneducated fighting man will continue to narrow. In a world where most of the educated soldiers come from rich countries and most of the uneducated ones come from poor countries, this narrowing gap could be more dangerous than the atomic bomb or nerve gas.

These are the tools of the next generation's warfare. What remains are the two old questions:

How fast will the decision-makers learn to use these tools?

Who will pay for their education?

ACT OF MERCY

by D.C. Poyer

Editor's Introduction

The mystique of the French Foreign Legion has fascinated many writers. Though called "French," there has seldom been a French majority among the Legionnaires. Germans, Belgians, Danes, Swedes, Britons—the list is endless. With every European war, the ranks of the Legion were filled as the defeated soldiers sought the only trade they knew.

This poses a formidable problem. Why would men of all nationalities—a veritable legion of strangers—fight so fiercely and so well? For fight they have. Few dared face them, for even in their defeats they sold their lives dearly.

Stationed for decades at Sidi Bel Abbes, the Legion was withdrawn to Corsica when the French left North Africa. There was then, and is now, considerable question as to what should happen to *La Legion Étrangere*.

Otto von Habsburg, whom some consider the legitimate sovereign of Europe, has thought long and hard on the future of the Legion. In 1975 he wrote:

"Since its background is European, should not the Foreign Legion come to Europe? Instead of being 'foreign,' could it not offically become that which in fact it is, in other words, European? Could it not find its niche in a new community defense organization, the European equivalent of what the Marine Corps is for the United States of America?"

The thought is intriguing; indeed, I had some such idea in mind when I wrote of the worlds of the CoDominium, whose Marines incorporated the Legion. Men who regard the Legion as their Fatherland should have little trouble giving allegiance to Europe, or to a larger entity.

Such a truly multi-national force could be useful in other ways. The accomplishments of the Legion go beyond battle. To this day, in Morocco the inscription on the famous Foum el Zabel tunnel reads:

The mountain stood in our way.
We were ordered to proceed nevertheless.
The Legion carried out the order.

The Legion carries battle banners from Lebanon and Syria, Madagascar, France and Spain, the Crimea, Hanoi and Hue and Saigon; from the glory of Camerone in Mexico to Kolwezi in Katanga. However, when one thinks of the Legion, what usually comes to mind is the desert, when Franks and Iberians and Saxons returned to North Africa in repayment for the time when only the strong sinews of Charles the Hammer halted the blood tide of Islaam and for half a millennium Arabs held Spain.

D. C. Poyer writes of the time when the Legion held the desert and feared only two things: capture by the Arabs, and *le cafard*.

———————————

It is cold in the Sahara at night, cold enough to freeze the water in a sleeping man's canteen. Cold enough, if a Legionnaire is unprepared, to kill him.

And tonight feels like the coldest night of the year: bundled up as I am for guard duty, I'm shivering as if with malaria. My rifle is cramping my right arm, so I shift it to my left. For the thousandth time tonight I sigh and wish for a cigar, for one of the long black ones they sell back home in France.

I console myself with the thought that my watch will be over in a few more minutes, and turn and look over the wall at the Sahara. The moon is full, and its light glistens on the dunes, making them hills of silver dust. It is a beautiful night.

Me, Jean-Paul Bergaine, I am not much of a soldier. As the girls say of me in the brothels of Mers-el-Kebir, I am a lover, not a fighter. So why did I join the *Legion Étrangère*? Ah, now, there's a question I ask myself a hundred times a day. Why did I lose myself in this empty place, this place that is not my own, this hell that perhaps can belong to no one but the desert Arabs? A hundred times a day I ask myself this. I spit over the wall and am in the middle of a vast yawn when the alarm bugle sounds behind me.

I spin, stuffing cartridges up the magazine of the Lebel, and at first I see nothing, because my eyes are sweeping the ramparts for Arabs. But then I realize that, in the flickering blue-white light, I can see the walls clearly and even the mountains far beyond them, and I look up at the ball of flame overhead.

I have not had much schooling, but I know what it is, the ball of white fire and red sparks that moves so slowly in the sky. It is a *bolide*, a meteor. But how slowly it moves! It must be very high. Every man in the post is awake now, craning his neck upward, but we hear nothing. The bluish light is harsh on the upturned faces, and shadows are sharp on the dark sand.

The *bolide* takes many minutes to disappear. It seems to be traveling south, into the desert. A good place for it, too; only the desert Arabs go far into the South Sahara. It will hurt no one. But it has put on quite a show for us; unless we should have women or a skirmish, it will furnish us conversation for days to come. My relief arrives, and I go back into the barracks. Spinelli and Petit and I speak wonderingly of it for a few minutes before we pull the blankets over our heads again.

The mud-walled office of the post commandant was very sparsely furnished; a battered wooden table, carried to the post over two hundred kilometers of camel-trail, and two rickety cane chairs were the sum of its appointments. The two men in tropical uniform rose politely as a short, perspiring man in a dirty white suit brushed aside the curtain at the door and entered the room.

"Ah, M. Paul-Boncour! It is indeed an honor to be able to assist the National Observatory!" said the older officer, ushering his junior forward with a gesture. "This is my assistant, Lieutenant de Dissonville. If you approve, I should like to send him with you on your expedition. Lieutenant, would you step outside and ask the orderly to bring in some wine? Thank you. Professor, a seat?"

"Thank you." Paul-Boncour sat down heavily. "I am happy to see that you appreciate the importance of my mission; I've been riding that damned camel for four days to get here. According to the calculations of the flight of the *bolide* I made at Koufra, it should have landed in the desert about fifty kilometers southeast of here. By the way, did you happen to time the passage of the object across the heavens?"

"Ah... no; we were, to be frank, startled by the apparition, and had no idea such a procedure was called for... but, monsieur, you say that you expect to find the *bolide* southeast of here?"

"Yes. Estimates made by myself, and also by Rawlings of the Royal Observatory, who happened to be vacationing in Koufra, agree that the low speed and southeasterly heading of the object would bring it down in an area just beyond your post. But—why do you look at me so strangely?"

The Army officer shifted his eyes to the scarred tabletop for a moment, brow furrowed in concentration, before he answered. "A *bolide* is a ballistic object, is it not? Falling through the air much like an artillery shell?"

"In general, yes. It falls in a straight line across the earth's face, and downward in a parabolic arc."

"But this *bolide*, Professor... when it passed over us, it was going due south, Monsieur! How could that be?"

The fat, sweating civilian and the officer in his wilted khakis regarded each other over the rickety table.

"Impossible," said the professor flatly.

It is a blazing hot day today, much hotter than yesterday. After five years in Africa, I am an old hand, a seasoned, sun-blackened *vieillard*, but the days like today are too hot for any European. The Arabs can stand the heat, though. When the column has fallen out for five minutes' rest, and the men cannot regain their feet for the fatigue and thirst, we see them sitting far off on the horizon, watching our agony from atop their camels. And enjoying it. They are not like us, the desert Arabs. They are bred to the savagery of the desert, and sometimes I wonder if we French will ever succeed in wresting it from them. But that is a silly thought; we are a cultured race, while they are uncivilized savages who enjoy nothing more than torturing a stranger to death. I have seen some of my comrades' bodies after the Arabs were done with them, and I would die before falling into their hands. Only our modern rifles keep them at a respectful distance from us as we march.

We started this morning from the post and marched south all morning. The fat civilian, who is riding a mule at the head of the column, has a compass, and we must go in a straight line. *Diable!* A mule— just so he can rest his fat ass! Even the lieutenant, that spoiled Parisian mama's boy, is marching. Mule or not, a fat man like that won't last the day out. When he faints, he'll fall off, and we can stop for a rest and perhaps a drink of water then. *Vive le soleil!*

We slog on through the heat of the day, and that night make camp on a small plain of gravel surrounded by sand drifts. We are slowly moving into the sandy part of the South Sahara, away from all the settled portions of the country. There are not even Legion posts ahead of us. After the sentries are posted we sit in small groups and shoot the bull for a while. Spinelli tells an old story about lost treasures in the South Sahara; Palewski laughs, telling him that there the only gold is on the buttons of dead Legionnaires. They are good comrades. We eat our hard bread and blood-sausages cold, and turn in.

The nineteen men marched onward the next day, and the next, through a lifeless, hostile and monotonous terrain of gravel and drifted sand.

In the lead walked the young lieutenant, pushing himself mercilessly to stay ahead of the common soldiers. His short hair was soaking wet under the neck-cloth of the cap, and the stinging sweat trickled into his eyes. Near mid-afternoon he began to feel nauseated, feeling the onset of heat exhaustion, but he kept his flushed face set forward, toward the emptiness ahead, and walked on.

Behind him, trailing him by ten or twelve paces, rode the savant. He slumped in a torpor on his mule, which plodded slowly along, lolling its tongue and panting loudly. From time to time the professor roused himself for a moment, glanced at a compass, and stared slowly around at the horizon before relapsing into semiconsciousness. A filthy red bandanna peeped from the neck of his shirt.

The sergeant, Kruger, marched at the right of his column, gliding across the sand with a snakelike, fluid step, wasting not a millimeter of motion. In the breathless silence that surrounded them, his occasional low commands rang out like the crack of a revolver.

The men marched in silence, their heads low like a herd of animals, their turned-up collars, caps and packs concealing their faces from the sun. They, too, glided across the sand, moving as if on parade in a compact body that moved among the low dunes like a many-legged blue caterpillar.

At eight in the evening the lieutenant held his arm above his head to halt the column, and heard behind him Kruger's soft voice commanding, "Legionnaires… *arretez-vous*." He turned to the scientist, who was slumped like a lump of melting lard on his saddle, eyes closed.

"With your permission, *M. le Professeur*, we will make camp here for the night," he said.

The mule had stopped when the lieutenant had halted, and stood with its knees locked and eyes closed. It looked as if it had died upright.

"*Monsieur*," said de Dissonville again.

They pulled the scientist from his perch, rubbed his face with a handful of water, and made camp.

They marched south for five days.

"The men can eat it, anyway," said de Dissonville. "It will be a change from marching rations."

The professor gave the carcass of the dead mule a final kick and turned away. "It was healthy enough yesterday," he growled. He looked different; his face was becoming browned, and he had lost much of his corpulence. The wrinkles around his face made him look a great deal older. The lieutenant, too, had lost some of his awkward youthfulness and was beginning to walk with the fluid, swaying motion that made marching in the desert bearable.

"I can't understand it," he said. "Professor, you were sure that the thing could not have landed more than seventy kilometers from the fort. We have gone three times that, perhaps more. Perhaps we've already passed it; it could have been on the other side of a dune. With all respect, *M. le Professeur*, I think we should turn back toward the post. We have enough water and food left, with the mule dead, to get back without trouble."

Paul-Boncour pondered, then shook his head. "You don't understand at all. My computations indicate a very large body. A mass like that striking the earth would cause an explosion many times more powerful than that of a powder magazine. It would leave an immense crater."

"Like that of an explosive shell?"

"Yes, but perhaps a kilometer across. Doubtless you conceived of the meteor quietly resting on the sand where it landed. But I suppose they don't teach you much science at Saint-Cyr, do they?"

De Dissonville began to reply, but Kruger signaled suddenly for silence. Over the baked sand stretching for miles ahead of them they heard two more pops of musketry, and then a rattle of fire all at once. Then silence again, covering the small group of men like a blanket.

"*Allons! Allons!* Sergeant Kruger, get these men in column!" shouted the lieutenant. "Quickly! Check your rifles as we march. Let's go!"

I am huddled under a small overhang of the thing, where one of the spheres joins another. My arm hurts, but the bleeding seems to have stopped. I can't tell if Spinelli, a few meters in front of me, is still alive, but if he is not dead yet, he soon will be. He has a musket ball in his guts and the sand under him is dark in the rapidly fading light. If the Arabs leave us alone for a few more minutes, I will crawl over to him and give him a drink if he wants it, or maybe tell him a joke. He has not made a sound since he was hit, though.

It happened fast. After we heard the shots, we fell in quickly and marched in their direction. The lieutenant had us check our rifles and the sergeant told us to take a long drink from our canteens, to fix our bayonets, and to loosen our cartridges in their belts.

We marched for about a kilometer, the deep sand deadening the noise of our boots, the lieutenant and the professor ahead. The fat one was talking to the lieutenant, and took his arm once, but was shaken off. The lieutenant handed him one of his pistols. The civilian said something else and then the lieutenant put out an arm and Lard-Face went on his back in the sand. We marched by him and he got up and ran after us. I was near the rear of the column and he ran up beside me, wheezing, and asked me if I knew where I was being led. I said, Yes, *Monsieur*, those were the muskets of the Arabs we heard. He said, It is not part of our mission to chase natives. That was not a question, so I said nothing. He said, Do you not care that there might be a hundred savages there? That that *enfant* could be leading all of us to death? I said, *Monsieur*, I am not an officer; you waste your time speaking to me. Sergeant Kruger had come back to the end of the column by then and he said to him, *Monsieur le Professeur*, the lieutenant sends his compliments and begs you to guard our rear while he conducts a reconnaissance in force. The professor stopped and I looked quickly around at him after a few steps and saw him standing kneedeep in the sand examining the service revolver the lieutenant had given him.

We marched over the edge of a small dune and there it was, about a hundred meters ahead of us, and beyond it were about fifty Arabs, some cross-legged on their camels and some standing in a small circle on the sand. They spotted us and the lieutenant saw right away that the only cover would be the big silver thing and so he shouted charge

and as they ran for their camels and their rifles, we ran for the shelter
of the big thing. It looked like five great big shiny cannonballs welded
together in a row, but what was important was that we were in the
open and if we could get it behind us and throw up some sand as a
breastwork, we couldn't ask for a better place to fight from.

But the sand was deep and we couldn't run fast enough and the Arabs
got the lieutenant and Kruger and twelve others, and I got a ball in the
arm, before we got to the thing and dug ourselves in. After the three
of us were under cover, we watched them drag away the men who were
still alive and begin cutting them up.

They must have been using very small, very sharp knives. We could
hear the screams for hours.

So now I am on this side of the thing and Petit and Palewski are on
the other side, so I guess they can't take us by surprise anyway. I don't
know what we can do if they attack in the dark. I guess I will have to
shoot Spinelli first and then myself so they can't cut us up.

The fat man had waited all night behind a dune, peeping over it
from time to time at the reflections of starlight and, later in the night,
moonlight on the multiple spheres of the object in the depression below.
When it began to grow brighter in the east, and he still saw no signs of
the Arabs, he finally rose and walked down the gentle slope.

"Soldier," he said to the man huddled under the curving side of the
object. "Soldier, wake up." The man finally did wake up, and blinked
his eyes slowly before focusing them on Paul-Boncour.

"Lard-Face," said the man, seemingly speaking to himself. "Then it
is morning, and we are still alive." Then his eyes widened, and with
a sudden lunge he flattened the savant on the sand. "Don't make a
sound," he whispered. "I don't know why they didn't kill us while we
slept, but if they see you walking around, they'll be on top of us. And
we are only four."

"Let me up, you fool," said Paul-Boncour loudly. "Do you think I
would have come down here if those savages were still around? Get up.
Act like a Frenchman! Where are the others?"

The Legionnaire stood up slowly and scanned the desert, warily at first, and then with a flicker of hope in his expression; finally he smiled broadly. He helped the sprawled scientist to his feet and called to the others. "Petit! Palewski! *Reveillez-vous*! The Arabs have left!" There was no answer. Still smiling, he shouldered his rifle, said to Paul-Boncour, "I'll go wake them," and disappeared around the end of the object.

The professor, left alone for a moment, investigated the corpse that lay huddled a few yards in front of Bergaine's little sandmound emplacement. He prodded it with his boot; frozen. A bad wound too, judging from the dried blood on the sand around the body.

Silly ass, he thought; it was his own fault for following wherever he was led. Still, it was too bad. A total waste of money to train and arm the man, to have him die here like this; and Paul-Boncour was, after all, a taxpayer.

The wounded Legionnaire reappeared from the other side of the object. He looked sick. Paul-Boncour swung on him. "Well, where are the others?" he asked. "You did say there were two others, *n'est-ce pas?*"

"They're dead," said Bergaine. His face was pale. "The Arabs…"

"Well," interrupted the civilian, shielding his eyes against the rising sun, "Too bad. But we've found our *bolide*, at any rate. Let's investigate it."

So every man in the platoon is dead, except me. I guess the professor's in command now; at least he has a compass, and a map. Even he can get us back to the post, now that we have the food and water the others won't be needing any more.

I am scraping a shallow grave in the sand for Spinelli, using my rifle butt, when the professor comes over to me and pulls me away. Follow me, he says. I say that I have to bury Spinelli and the others. Oh, they'll keep for a couple more minutes, says he, come here, I want you to be able to corroborate some things for me when we get back to civilization.

I don't understand what he means by "corroborate," but I follow him. First he shows me some lines, like the outline of a door, on the side of the silver thing; I say yes, I see them. He shows me some things like cannon muzzles at one end. I say yes sir, I see them, can I go bury Spinelli now? He says that there is one more thing that I have to see. I follow him, but I'm getting a little angry; after I get done with Spinelli, I am going to have to bury what is left of Petit and Palewski, and I am not looking forward to that.

This last thing he has to show me is a trail, like a trough or a shallow groove in the sand, with marks at intervals along the sides. There are stains in the sand, as if something had leaked into the ground here and there along the trail. I ask him what it is.

Look where it leads from, he says, and points back toward the thing. Sure enough, I can see that it leads right to the door-like markings, and I see also that at one place on the trail the sand is all scuffled and stamped over, as if a group of men had been dancing or fighting on that spot, and there is a great deal of the funny-looking stain around there.

They were waiting for it when it came out, I say. The professor is surprised, and says that for a common soldier, I am very quick. I say nothing; that is not a question. I ask him again if he will let me go and finish the burying now so that we can start back to the post before the Arabs decide to return with some friends and show off their work.

He looks surprised, and says, Start back? Of course we do not start back. Not now. Don't you understand what all this means? A creature of another celestial sphere has visited our planet for the first time. Perhaps he comes in peace, and then again, perhaps as a scout for a warlike race. It is our duty, to Science, to Humanity, to find this *étrangère* and to fathom his intentions toward mankind! He is shouting and waving his arms at me as he finishes his little speech.

I am beginning to think that the professor has gone just a little bit crazy from the sun and the deaths. After all, he is a cultured man and not used to such things. I look at him directly and say gently, *Monsieur*, we can carry enough water to get back alive only if we start walking now, while we are still strong. We must not linger here or the Arabs will return and find us. We must go back now. I speak very slowly, so that he knows I am in absolute earnest. Otherwise, I say, I will take the compass and the map and start back alone, and you can go after your creature, which is probably dead from the cold and the attentions of the savages anyway.

The professor pulls the lieutenant's revolver from his pocket and points it at me. We are going after the creature together, my brave Legionnaire, he says, with a little smile. Gather up the food and the canteens. And leave your rifle here, with the dead ones.

It was plain to Paul-Boncour that the creature, whatever it looked like, was badly hurt. The trough in the sand was deeper on one side than on the other, and on the deeper side most of the stains appeared. As the two plodded on, the stains became more frequent, forming a discolored line on the sand.

"The creature that left this trail," said the scientist to the soldier, "is not only badly hurt, but, I think, unused to the gravity of this planet; as you will note, the trail avoids any suggestion of a grade, winding between dunes rather than attempting to scale them. From the depth of the trough, I would estimate its weight to be about that of a man— perhaps a little less."

The soldier did not reply. He was bent under the weight of the rations and canteens taken from the dead men, and followed the scientist, walking in the track they were following. One of his arms was roughly bandaged, and he carried it thrust deep into the pocket of his overcoat.

The professor does not notice the difference in the air this afternoon, for he is unused to the deep Sahara; but I notice it, and I can tell that the sand-storm the desert is preparing for us is not one that two men on foot should face in the open. But I walk on behind him, saying nothing.

When the first gust of sand-laden wind buffets us, and the darkness covering the sun suddenly shrouds us in a roaring brown-yellow night, the professor is startled from his concentration. He turns to me in terror and I shout in his ear above the roar of the wind, It is a dust-storm, we must lie down and cover our heads. He throws himself full-length on the sand and covers his face with his hands.

It is then that I fall upon him in the shrieking darkness and smash his skull with a metal canteen. He makes not a sound as he dies, or if he does, it is carried away by the wind. I can no longer see for the sand in my eyes, cutting and stinging; I pull the revolver from his belt, and standing crouched over him, pull at his pockets for the compass and map. A gust of wind, heavy with flying sand, knocks me down and I roll over and over before the fury of it.

It is evening, and I am following the trail of the creature alone. Why? Because there is nowhere else for me to go. After the storm was over, I dug myself out and looked for the professor's body but it was useless. He is under at least a meter of sand—a better burial than he allowed Spinelli and the others—and all of the dunes have changed. It is hopeless to look for the body, and without the compass and map, there is little possibility of my finding my way back to a fort. But at least I will not die from slow thirst; I have five cartridges remaining in the lieutenant's revolver. So now I am more or less amusing myself until I decide that I have lived long enough.

I feel that I am very close to the creature now. The trail is obviously fresh; it was made after the sand-storm. It must have been very close, perhaps on the other side of the dune, when I killed the professor.

Its trail seems to curve around the end of this dune, perhaps to circle back again; the creature, fleeing from the Arabs as our little party distracted them from their sport, is as lost as I am. No, even more than I, for I at least stand on the planet and breathe the air native to my kind. But I can comprehend, now, a little of what it must feel, if it feels as we do at all. I decide to try to second-guess it by climbing over the dune.

It lies in the depression between two dunes, not moving at all. It is of a silvery color, like its craft, and is smaller but longer than a man, with many small legs or arms along its body. I half-walk, half-slide down the dune toward it. It begins to move spasmodically as I near it; I stop and wait for a moment. Its movements cease, but I can tell somehow that it is watching me.

I walk slowly toward it, and stop and crouch in the sand about a meter away. It is panting, breathing with a thin whistling sound. With each heave of its sides, small drops of fluid run from dozens of tiny slashes and wet the sand under it. I recognize the cuts. The Arabs had only started with this creature.

Then it moves again, and I look up; there they are atop the dune I have just crossed, a dozen or more dark, silent men in flowing white. They sit on their motionless camels, watching us.

My hand closes upon the revolver, and I glance back at the alien. For the savages I have three cartridges. But the last two are for me and my comrade.

Call it a favor from one stranger to another.

THE ECONOMICS OF WAR

by David Friedman, Ph.D

Editor's Introduction

My friend David Friedman is a remarkable man. He has no military experience, but he does have considerable background in military history.
He has also several times won the Crown of the East in the Society for
Creative Anachronism, that odd group that enjoys dressing in armor
and fighting tournaments. The tournament winner receives the Crown.

Dr. Friedman is an economist and a teacher of economics. He is
also what is often termed an "extreme libertarian," which is to say that
he considers freedom the highest of values and seeks ways whereby a
rational society might do away with coercion. Unlike many of that
persuasion, Dr. Friedman has given the subject no little thought, and
he does not avoid the hard questions. One may not agree with him,
but it is difficult not to be stimulated by him. At worst, one will better
understand why one disagrees.

Wars and armies are, by definition, coercive. They pose a real problem for the libertarian: How does a free society counter organized violence? Indeed, can that be done? Must there be taxation, conscription,
police and armies? Can there be a rule of rationality and contract?

Inter armes, silent leges; in the face of arms, the law is silent. So,
one might think, are contracts and voluntarism. Dr. Friedman seeks
insights into why men fight, and why they do not.

The cynic, it is said, knows the price of everything and the value of
nothing. One might say that Dr. Friedman's cool rationalism seeks

answers in places where they cannot be found.   Good soldiers are seldom paid in any coin that economists can quantify.

———————————

The science of war is moving live men like blocks.

—Stephen Vincent Benet, "John Brown's Body"

To most non-economists, economics has something to do with money, and the economics of war presumably has to do with how we pay for the bombs and bullets. Economists have different and broader ideas of what their field is; my own favorite definition is that economics is that approach to understanding human behavior which starts from the assumption that individuals have objectives and tend to choose the correct way to achieve them. From this standpoint, the potential subject matter is all of human behavior (some of my colleagues would include animal behavior as well) and the only test of whether behavior is or is not economic is the ability of our basic assumption to explain or predict it.

Given such a broad definition of economics, one might almost say that all of warfare reduces to the technical problem of making guns that will shoot and the economic problem of getting someone to shoot them, preferably in the right direction. Board games, strategic simulations and popular articles tend to emphasize the technical problems—how far a tank will shoot, what kind of armor it will go through and how many tanks (or knights or hoplites) each side has; they generally take it for granted that the playing pieces will go where they are moved. In real battles they frequently do not. The economic problem is why they do not and what can be done about it.

Economics assumes that individuals have objectives. We do not know all of the objectives that any individual has, but we do know that for most of us, staying alive is high on the list. The general commanding an army and the soldier in the front line have, in one sense, the same objectives. Both want their side to win, and both want both of them to survive the battle. The soldier, however, is likely to rank his own survival a good deal higher and the general's survival a good deal lower in importance than the general does. One consequence of that disagreement is that the general may rationally tell the soldier to do something and the soldier may rationally not do it. Neither is necessarily making a mistake; each may be correctly perceiving how to achieve his ends.

Consider a simple case. You are one of a line of men on foot with long spears; you are being charged by men on horses, also carrying spears (and swords and maces and...). You have a simple choice: You can stand and fight or you can run away. If everyone runs away, the line collapses and most of you get killed; if everyone stands, you have a good chance of stopping the charge and surviving the battle. Obviously you should stand.

It is not so obvious. I have described the consequences if everyone runs or everyone stands, but you are not everyone; all you control is whether you run or fight. If you are in a large army, your decision to run will only very slightly weaken it. If you run and everyone else fights and wins, some of them will be killed and you will not. If you run and everyone else fights and loses, at least they will slow down the attack—giving you some chance of getting away. If everyone runs and you stand to fight, you will certainly be killed; if everyone runs and you run first, you at least have a chance of getting away. It follows that whatever everyone else is going to do, unless you believe that your running away will have a significant effect on who wins (unlikely with large armies), you are better off running. Everyone follows this argument, everyone runs, the line collapses, you lose the battle and most of you get killed.

The conclusion seems paradoxical; I started by assuming that people want to live and correctly choose the means of doing so and ended by predicting that people will behave in a way that gets most of them killed. But rationality is an assumption about individuals, not about groups. Each individual, in my simple example of the economics of war, is making the correct decision about how he should act in order to keep himself alive. It so happens that the correct decision for me (running away) decreases the chance of being killed for me but increases it for everyone else on my side, and similarly for everyone else's correct decision; individually, each of us is better off (given what everyone else is doing) than if he stood and fought, but we are all worse off than we would be if each of us had failed to reach the correct conclusion and we had all stood and fought.

If this still seems paradoxical to you, consider a more homely example—an economic problem that occurs twice a day two blocks from where I am sitting. The scene is the intersection of Wilshire and Westwood, said to be the busiest in the world. The time is rush hour. As the light on Wilshire goes green, the traffic surges forward. As it turns yellow, a last few cars try to make it across. Since Wilshire is packed with cars, they fail and end up in the intersection, blocking the cars on Westwood, which now have a green light. Gradually the cars in the intersection make it across, allowing the traffic on Westwood to surge forward—just as the light changes again, trapping another batch of cars in the intersection.

If drivers on both streets refrained from entering an intersection unless there was clearly enough room for them on the far side, the jam would not occur, traffic would flow faster and they would all get where they are going sooner—which is presumably their objective. Yet each individual driver is behaving rationally. My aggressive driving on Wilshire benefits me (I may make it across before the light changes, and at worst I will get far enough into the intersection not to be blocked by cars going the other way at the next stage of the jam) and harms drivers on Westwood; your aggressive driving on Westwood benefits you and harms drivers (possibly including me) on Wilshire. The harm is much larger than the benefit, so on net we are all worse off. But I receive all of the benefit and none of the harm from the particular decision I control. I am correctly choosing the action that best achieves my objective—

but if we all made a mistake and drove less aggressively, we would all be better off.

I am not saying that rationality implies selfishness—that is a parody of economics. Drivers may value other people's time as well as their own, or they may value a self-image that requires them to act in a polite and considerate way; if so, rational behavior (in pursuit of those goals) may prevent the jam instead of causing it. The "paradox" is not that rational behavior always leads to undesirable results—it does not. In the two cases I have described, it does. What is paradoxical is that the results are undesirable in terms of precisely the same objectives (staying alive in the one case and getting home earlier in the other) that the individual behavior is correctly calculated to achieve.

Let us now return to the battlefield, replacing spears with guns. One of the less well-known facts about modern warfare is that in combat a substantial percentage of the soldiers (almost four-fifths, according to one source) do not fire their guns and those that do frequently do not aim them; this is one of the reasons that about 100,000 bullets are fired for every enemy killed. Such behavior seems irrational from the standpoint of the army—soldiers are given guns in order that they may shoot the enemy with them—but it may be entirely rational from the standpoint of the soldier. It is difficult to hide in a foxhole and take a carefully aimed shot at the enemy at the same time. If you can see him, he may be able to see you, and if you are taking the time to aim at him, you may be giving him, or his buddy, a chance to aim at you. If your objective is to stay alive, there is much to be said for climbing into a convenient hole and firing your gun, if at all, in the general direction of the enemy.

In discussing my first example, I pointed out that the desirability of running away depended, among other things, on how likely you thought your defection was to make your side lose the battle. The same argument applies here. At one extreme, consider a "battle" with one man on each side; hiding in a hole and firing random shots is not a sensible way of getting through it alive. At the other extreme, consider a battle with massed armies of tens of thousands of men, all shooting at each other at once. Whether you fight or hide is very unlikely to affect the outcome, so the sensible thing to do is to hide—assuming, as is usually the case, that the lives of your fellow soldiers are very much less valuable to you than your own.

Many real battles represent an intermediate situation. How hard you fight is unlikely to affect who wins the battle, but it may well affect the particular part of the battle immediately around you. In such a case, the soldier must decide which of his alternatives is less likely to get him killed. The more influence he believes his actions will have on the outcome of the fight, the more likely he is to shoot instead of hiding.

I recently came across an interesting fact that fits quite neatly into this economic prediction. A study of the behavior of G.I.s in World War II found that the soldiers most likely to fire their weapons were those carrying B.A.R.s (Browning Automatic Rifles). A B.A.R. is a substantially more powerful weapon than an ordinary rifle; the decision to fight or hide by the man carrying it is more likely to determine what happens on his part of the battlefield—and hence whether his position is overrun and he is killed—than the decision to fight or hide by other members of the squad.

So far I have discussed the economic problem of war without saying anything about solutions. Obviously I am not the first person in history to realize that soldiers sometimes run away, or even the first to suggest that they do so, not because they are struck with some mysterious panic, but as a sensible response to the circumstances they find themselves in. Commanders throughout history have been confronted with the problem and have come up with a variety of ways to make it in the interest of their soldiers to fight and, if possible, in the interest of the enemy soldiers to run away.

One solution has become proverbial. You march your army across a bridge, line it up for the battle with a river (hopefully unswimmable) behind it, then burn the bridge. Since there is now nowhere to run to, much of the argument for running away disappears. Of course, if you lose the battle, you all get killed. This is called burning your bridges behind you.

Another solution is to punish soldiers who run away. One way is to have a second line of soldiers whose job is to kill any member of the first line who runs. This unfortunately ties up quite a lot of your army; if the front line all gets killed, the second line runs away, unless there is a third line to kill them for doing so. A less expensive (but also less effective) solution is to keep track of who runs away and hang them after the battle. In order for this to work, you have to have a pretty good chance of winning the battle, or at least surviving it with your command structure intact; an army that has just been routed is unlikely to have time to punish the soldiers who ran first. This suggests one reason why some commanders are so much more successful than others; once a commander has won a few battles, his soldiers expect him to win the next one. If the battle is going to be won, it is prudent not to run away—and since nobody runs away, the battle is won. This is what is called a self-fulfilling prophecy. A French military theorist, Ardant du Pica, argued that the traditional picture of a charge, in which the charging column smashes into the defending line, is mythical. At some point in a real charge, either the column decides that the line is not going to run and stops, or the line decides that the column is not going to stop, and runs.

This brings me to the much-maligned British army of the eighteenth century, we all learn in elementary school about the foolish British, who dressed up their troops in bright scarlet uniforms and lined them up in rigid formations for the brave American revolutionaries to shoot at. The assumption (as in the nationalistic histories of most nations) is that we were smart and they were dumb and that explains it all. I am in no sense an expert in eighteenth-century military history, but I think I have a more plausible explanation. The British troops were armed with short-range muskets and bayonets, hence the relevant decision for them, as for the spearmen of a few centuries before, was to fight or to run. In order to make sure they fought, their commanders had to be able to see if someone was starting to run; rigid geometric formations and bright uniforms are a sensible way of doing so.

Bright uniforms serve the same purpose in another way as well—they make it more difficult for soldiers who run away to hide from the victorious enemy, and thus decrease the gain from running away. Of course the fugitive can always take off his uniform, assuming he has enough time (perhaps that was why they had so many buttons), but young men running around the countryside in their underwear are almost as conspicuous as soldiers in red uniforms.

Why does the range of weapons matter? With short-range weapons, the choice is fight or run; if you try to hide in a hole, someone will eventually come over and stick a spear in you. With long-range weapons, running away is hazardous, but warfare is much more likely to involve an extended exchange of fire from fixed positions, so if you hide (and enough other people on your side fight), the enemy may never get close enough to kill you.

So far all of the solutions I have discussed involve raising the cost of running away by penalizing it in one way or another. An alternative approach is to change the objectives of the fighters. If the most important thing to you is not surviving the battle but dying gloriously, the incentive to run away disappears—although it may be replaced by an incentive to die gloriously in some stupid attack that loses the battle for your side.

A set of objectives that ranks glory and heroism far above mere survival is a popular theme of heroic literature and frequently appears in descriptions of exotic foreign warriors, preferably "barbarian," but it is not very common in the real world. While I have no statistics on the subject, I do have an interesting anecdote. One of the most famous of heroic warrior cultures was the Norse; the ideals of Viking warriors certainly ranked heroic death far above cowardly survival. For the operation of those ideals in the real world, I give you the following story; the source (which tells it in somewhat more detail) is *Njal's Saga*:

Sigurd, the Jarl of the Orkneys, had a raven banner of which it was said that as long as it flew, the army would always advance, but whatever man carried it would die. At the battle of Clontarf, Sigurd led part of an army of Irish and Vikings against an Irish army commanded by the High King of Ireland. The fighting was heavy; Sigurd's forces advanced but the banner-carrier was killed. Another man took the banner; he too was killed. Sigurd told a third man to take the banner. The third man refused. Sigurd, after trying to get someone else to carry it, took the banner off the staff, tied it around his waist and led his army into battle. The army advanced, Sigurd was killed. No one would take up the banner, and the battle was lost.

So even in an army of Vikings, there were only three men (counting the Jarl) who were willing to give their lives for victory.

The desire for a hero's death is not the only objective that can keep soldiers from running away. If the soldier puts a high value on the cause he is fighting for or on the lives of his comrades, he may decide that even a small increase in the chance of losing the battle is too high a price to pay for an improved chance of his own survival. Alternatively, if the soldier puts a high value on his own reputation for courage, the shame of being seen to run away—even the shame of knowing he once ran away—may be sufficient to make him fight. Feelings of comradeship and an extraordinary emphasis on personal courage are sentiments traditionally associated with soldiers, and a wise commander will encourage them.

Perhaps the most famous historical example of this solution is a Theban military unit called the Sacred Band. It was said to consist of pairs of homosexual lovers. Since no man would abandon his lover or show cowardice in his presence, the Sacred Band never ran. Eventually they encountered Philip of Macedon and died to a man. This illustrates one disadvantage of courage as a solution; just as with burning your bridges behind you, the results are unpleasant when you lose.

So far I have discussed the problem from the point of view of the commander of the army that might run away. The conflict of interest between the individual soldier and the army of which he is a part is also a subject of considerable interest to the opposing commander. In playing a war game, one must actually destroy the other player's units. In fighting a war, it is sufficient to create a situation in which the members of a particular unit find it in their interest to run; having done so, one then goes on to the next unit. I conjecture that a considerable part of generalship is the ability to exploit the conflict of interest between the enemy soldiers and the army they make up.

One of my hobbies for many years has been the Society for Creative Anachronism, a group that does various medieval things for fun, including medieval hand-to-hand combat done as a rather rough sport. In order not to get anyone killed, we tend to use real armor and fake weapons; the latter are mostly made out of rattan, with reasonably realistic weight and balance but no cutting edge. The rules are supposed to define the winner as the person who would have survived the fight if both armor and weapons were real. In practice there are many difficulties, not the least being that nobody really knows how hard you have to hit chain mail with a medieval sword in order to kill the man wearing the mail.

We also do group fighting; the largest of the annual wars features armies of three or four hundred fighters on each side. The group fighting suffers from a fundamental flaw. Since being "killed" means at worst a bruise, everyone is a hero; units almost never surrender, and individual fighters never run away (except to find another fight elsewhere on the field). The battles are great fun, but considered as experimental archaeology, they are a failure; they omit one of the most essential features of real medieval battles.

There is one exception. I once participated in a melee tournament (a melee is a group fight) under rules that did, to some extent, recreate the conflict of interest between the individual and the army. The tournament consisted of a series of melees with randomly chosen teams. After each melee the fighters on the winning side received points according to their condition; an uninjured fighter received the most points, a fighter who died (but whose side won) received the fewest. At the end of the day, the fighter with the most points won. Under such a system, the fighter has an incentive to help his side win, but he also has an incentive to let someone else get killed in the front line while he bravely defends the rear. If we fought such tourneys more often, and if the winners received sufficiently valuable prizes, we might learn more about how medieval armies really worked.

This is supposed to be a book about the warfare of the future, but so far I have talked about the present and the past. My justification for doing so is that so far, at least, the economics of war—in the sense in which I use the term economics—has been much more stable than its technology. There has been enormous progress in weaponry over the last few millennia, but the economic problem is essentially the same, the only important change being the substitution of hiding for running as a result of the increased range of our weapons. It is possible that all this will change in the future; one can imagine a robot battlefield on which all of the problems are technical. In some respects we already have that; I presume that a soldier manning an ICBM is safer inside the silo firing the missile than running across the landscape as the warheads fall. But then, the same thing may well have been true eight hundred years ago for the soldier firing a trebuchet at a besieged castle. It remains the case now as then that a lot of soldiering involves a sharp conflict between the interest of the soldier and the interest of the soldiers, and it is likely to remain the case at least as long as the human brain continues to be a better weapons-control mechanism than anything else we can put in that small a box.

THAT DAY

by Rudyard Kipling

Editor's Introduction

C. Northcote Parkinson once said that the reply to rationalism is often not reasoned argument but banners and glory and the sounds of trumpets and drums.

Rudyard Kipling, like Dr. Friedman, inquired as to why men fight and win. There was a time when all Britons knew. A few know yet, as the Argentines learned to their sorrow.

It got beyond all orders an' it got beyond all 'ope;
　It got to shammin' wounded and retirin' from the 'alt.
'Ole companies was lookin' for the nearest road to slope;
　It were just a bloomin' knockout—an' our fault!

> *Now there ain't no chorus 'ere to give,*
> *　Nor there ain't no band to play;*
> *An' I wish I was dead 'fore I done what I did,*
> *　Or seen what I seed that day!*

We was sick o' bein' punished, an' we let 'em know it, too;
　An' a company-commander up an' 'it us with a sword,
'An some one shouted "'Ook it!" an' it come to sov-ki-poo,
　An' we chucked our rifles from us—O my Gawd!

There was thirty dead an' wounded on the ground we wouldn't keep—

No, there wasn't more than twenty when the front began to go—
But, Christ! along the line o' flight they cut us up like sheep,
    An' that was all we gained by doin' so!

I 'eard the knives be'ind me, but I dursn't face my man,
    Nor I don't know where I went to, 'cause I didn't 'alt to see,
Till I 'eard a beggar squealin' out for quarter as 'e ran,
    An' I thought I knew the voice an'—it was me!

We was 'idin' under beadsteads more than 'arf a march away:
    We was lyin' up like rabbits all about the countryside;
An' the Major cursed his Maker 'cause 'e'd lived to see that day,
    An' the Colonel broke 'is sword acrost, an' cried.

We was rotten 'fore we started—we was never disciplined;
    We made it out a favor if an order was obeyed.
Yes, every little drummer 'ad 'is rights and wrongs to mind,
    So we had to pay for teachin'—an' we paid!

The papers 'id it 'andsome, but you know the Army knows;
    We was put to groomin' camels till the regiments withdrew,
An' they gave us each a medal for subduin' England's foes,
    An' I 'ope you like my song—because it's true!

      An there ain't no chorus 'ere to give,
        Nor there ain't no band to play;
      But I wish I was dead 'fore I done what I did,
        Or seen what I seed that day!

THE MIRACLE-WORKERS

by Jack Vance

Editor's Introduction

It is a truism that Vietnam was a traumatic experience for the nation. We are generally less concerned about its effects on the Army—but we ignore those effects at our peril. Republics that bring home a defeated army have often regretted that action. Republics that betray both allies and army have more cause for regret.

While we were in Vietnam, there appeared a clutch of stories about primitive peoples victorious over sophisticated star folk. Generally, civilization was represented in those stories by one or more overbearing military people of no sensitivity. The fact that one seldom meets such people in real life—they wouldn't survive five minutes in combat even if the enemy were far away—did not prevent such stories from being nominated for, and winning, awards.

Then came our shameful withdrawal. Who can forget those terrible pictures of helicopters shoved over the sides of warships? There sprang up the curious myth that the United States had been defeated by the Viet Cong; that those stories of primitive peoples defeating sophisticated armies were all true. We so believe those myths that even those who know better speak as if something of the same sort is going on in Afghanistan.

The myths are dangerous. They are also not true.

South Vietnam did not fall to the Viet Cong. North Vietnam first attempted to take South Vietnam by main force, by maneuvering through "neutral" Cambodia. The result was their bloody defeat in November 1965 in the La Drang valley at the hands of the U.S. First Cavalry Division.

Two years later they tried again. This time their effort was timed to take advantage of the U.S. presidential elections. They used their regular North Vietnamese units to distract and extend U.S. forces in places like Khe San while employing the Viet Cong guerrillas against population centers such as Saigon and Hue.

The result was an unprecedented defeat.

The Viet Cong was destroyed during the 1968 Tet offensives. North Vietnam lost, by their own reckoning, over 100,000 troops—more than half their strength. The U.S. forces and their Army of the Republic of Vietnam (ARVN) allies won one of the most thorough victories in military history.

That victory was thrown away; indeed, in the United States it was not recognized as a victory. It was portrayed by the news media as a U.S. defeat.

After Nixon was elected, the U.S. sought to withdraw from Vietnam; at least to disengage our forces, leaving the protection of the nation to ARVN. This was a workable strategy, provided that ARVN faced nothing more than North Vietnamese regular forces operating as guerrillas. True, the Northern invaders had sanctuaries in Laos and Cambodia, and by using the Ho Chi Minh trail, had what amounted to interior lines; but even so, ARVN could handle the situation.

What ARVN couldn't handle was a massive invasion. On 29 March 1972, the North launched the Eastertide offensive. Naturally they massed their forces in the "demilitarized zone" (an area politically denied to U.S. and ARVN forces and used as both staging area and sanctuary by North Vietnam). Some twelve divisions, over 150,000 men, swept down from the North, supported by heavy armor and artillery. It was hardly a guerrilla effort.

They had miscalculated. ARVN was much better than the North had thought. Furthermore, the U.S. initiated a massive air attack on both the North Vietnam army and North Vietnam itself. U.S. Air Cavalry units struck at the invading armor. The result was a complete victory: Of 150,000 men sent south, fewer than 50,000 returned. The army of North Vietnam was utterly defeated. U.S. news media couldn't have cared less.

On January 27, 1973, Henry Kissinger and North Vietnamese Politburo member Le Duc Tho initialed "The Agreement on Ending the War and Restoring Peace in Vietnam." The agreement was broken even as it was signed: They had North Vietnamese regulars in the South; we knew that, and they knew that we knew it. The agreement would be kept only so long as North Vietnam feared U.S. retaliation.

The United States began the withdrawal of our combat forces. The war was to be "Vietnamized"; ARVN would have to defend South Vietnam in future. The nation breathed a sigh of relief; our boys were coming home. Of course the U.S. battle deaths in 1972 were only 300 (as compared to more than 20,000 young men of military age killed in traffic accidents in that year); but the news media were happy.

The Vietnam War, that evil and immoral war, was over. The Congress of the United States looked forward to the widely predicted "Vietnam bonus"—that is, a surplus of money no longer needed for the Vietnam War, and which could be spent on ever-expanding domestic programs.

In September, 1973, Ursula K. Le Guin's story, "The Word for World is Forest," won the Science Fiction Achievement Award (Hugo) for Best Novella. This is a story of how primitive but artistic and likable peoples defeat technologically sophisticated but loutish star men.

In 1973 the Arabs and Israelis fought another war. Congress, weary of military expenditures and desperate for more money—the "bonus" funds never materialized—cut the appropriations for ARVN. Not only were the Vietnamese to defend themselves without us, but they were to do it on the cheap. By mid-1974, ARVN hospitals were ordered to wash and re-use surgical dressings, since new ones were not obtainable.

In January, 1975, the Central Committee of North Vietnam decided the time was ripe, and on March 4, 1975, they attacked with some 5 to

1 superiority in men and 2 to 1 in artillery and armor. Four Army corps, employing about as much firepower and force as the United States massed on D-Day against the Germans, swept into the South.

Man for man, ARVN was superior, but they were outnumbered and outgunned. Even then they fought heroically: For example, at Xuan Loc the 18th ARVN Division stood and fought and destroyed three North Vietnamese divisions.

It was all to no avail. North Vietnam was plentifully supplied with munitions from Russia and the Warsaw Pact nations. The U.S. Congress's niggardly appropriations left ARVN with two grenades and some twenty rounds per soldier.

Nor had we made ARVN into a mobile army. Except for their marines and paratroops, ARVN was much like our National Guard, a militia stationed in hometowns with their families. Had the United States secured their borders, leaving ARVN to deal with internal security, Vietnam would never have been lost.

We were willing to secure the Korean border. We would not do it for Vietnam, even though it could be done with fewer troops employing high-technology weapons.

The war in Vietnam was not lost to guerrillas. That war was won. South Vietnam was lost to the failure of U.S. will. The president was occupied with Watergate. The Congress smelled the blood of political victory; it couldn't be bothered with a tiny nation so far away, even though we had left much American blood and treasure there.

American soldiers bought their Asian comrades some ten years of, if not freedom, then the absence of slavery. Then both the U.S. Army and the Republic of Vietnam were abandoned. The dominoes clatter down to this day.

Some of those whose stories contributed to our withdrawal from Vietnam remain proud to this day.

During the sixties, Poul Anderson circulated a petition among science fiction writers. It stressed the moral necessity for the U.S. to keep its pledged word in Vietnam. After our interference—it was, after all, with John F. Kennedy's personal approval that President Diem and his family were overthrown—many of us thought we had an obligation to finish what we had started: either to win or to persevere.

Jack Vance signed that petition.

I say all this lest someone inadvertently believe that Jack Vance's "The Miracle-Worker" was one of that clutch of stories intended as a Vietnam allegory.

It was not. "The Miracle-Worker" was written well before the war in Vietnam began to absorb U.S. attention. Jack Vance has long had the ability to create strange and wonderful worlds in which marvelous stories happen.

This is one of them.

_____

I

The war party from Faide Keep moved eastward across the downs; a column of a hundred armored knights, five hundred foot soldiers, a train of wagons. In the lead rode Lord Faide, a tall man in his early maturity, spare and catlike, with a sallow, dyspeptic face. He sat in the ancestral car of the Faides, a boat-shaped vehicle floating two feet above the moss, and carried, in addition to his sword and dagger, his ancestral side weapons.

An hour before sunset a pair of scouts came racing back to the column, their club-headed horses loping like dogs. Lord Faide braked the motion of his car. Behind him the Faide kinsmen, the lesser knights, the leather-capped foot soldiers halted; to the rear the baggage train and the high-wheeled wagons of the jinxmen creaked to a stop.

The scouts approached at breakneck speed, at the last instant flinging their horses sidewise. Long shaggy legs kicked out, padlike hooves plowed through the moss. The scouts jumped to the ground, ran forward. "The way to Ballant Keep is blocked!"

Lord Faide rose in his seat, stood staring eastward over the gray-green downs. "How many knights? How many men?"

"No knights, no men, Lord Faide. The First Folk have planted a forest between North and South Wildwood."

Lord Faide stood a moment in reflection, then seated himself, pushed the control knob. The car wheezed, jerked, moved forward. The knights touched up their horses; the foot soldiers resumed their slouching gait. At the rear the baggage train creaked into motion, together with the six wagons of the jinxmen.

The sun, large, pale and faintly pink, sank in the west. North Wildwood loomed down from the left, separated from South Wild wood by an area of stony ground, only sparsely patched with moss. As the sun passed behind the horizon, the new planting became visible: a frail new growth connecting the tracts of woodland like a canal between two seas.

Lord Faide halted his car, stepped down to the moss. He appraised the landscape, then gave the signal to make camp. The wagons were ranged in a circle, the gear unloaded. Lord Faide watched the activity for a moment, eyes sharp and critical, then turned and walked out across the downs through the lavender and green twilight. Fifteen miles to the east his last enemy awaited him: Lord Ballant of Ballant Keep. Contemplating tomorrow's battle, Lord Faide felt reasonably confident of the outcome. His troops had been tempered by a dozen campaigns; his kinsmen were loyal and single-hearted. Head Jinxman to Faide Keep was Hein Huss, and associated with him were three of the most powerful jinxmen of Pangborn: Isak Comandore, Adam McAdam and the remarkable Enterlin, together with their separate troupes of cabalmen, spell-binders and apprentices. Altogether, an impressive assemblage. Certainly there were obstacles to be overcome: Ballant Keep was strong; Lord Ballant would fight obstinately; Anderson Grimes, the Ballant jinxman, was efficient and highly respected. There was also this nuisance of the First Folk and the new planting which closed the gap between North and South Wildwood. The First Folk were a pale and feeble race, no match for human beings in single combat, but they guarded their forests with traps and deadfalls. Lord Faide cursed softly under his breath. To circle either North or South Wildwood meant a delay of three days, which could not be tolerated.

Lord Faide returned to the camp. Fires were alight, pots bubbled, orderly rows of sleep-holes had been dug into the moss. The knights groomed their horses within the corral of wagons; Lord Faide's own tent had been erected on a hummock, beside the ancient car.

Lord Faide made a quick round of inspection, noting every detail, speaking no word. The jinxmen were encamped a little distance apart from the troops. The apprentices and lesser spellbinders prepared food, while the jinxmen and cabalmen worked inside their tents, arranging cabinets and cases, correcting whatever disorder had been caused by the jolting of the wagons.

Lord Faide entered the tent of his Head Jinxman. Hein Huss was an enormous man, with arms and legs heavy as tree trunks, a torso like a barrel. His face was pink and placid, his eyes were water-clear; a stiff gray brush rose from his head, which was innocent of the cap jinxmen customarily wore against the loss of hair. Hein Huss disdained such precautions; it was his habit, showing his teeth in a face-splitting grin, to rumble, "Why should anyone hoodoo me, old Hein Huss? I am so inoffensive. Whoever tried would surely die, of shame and remorse."

Lord Faide found Huss busy at his cabinet. The doors stood wide, revealing hundreds of mannikins, each tied with a lock of hair, a bit of cloth, a fingernail clipping, daubed with grease, sputum, excrement, blood. Lord Faide knew well that one of these mannikins represented himself. He also knew that should he request it, Hein Huss would deliver it without hesitation. Part of Huss' *mana* derived from his enormous confidence, the effortless ease of his power. He glanced at Lord Faide and read the question in his mind. "Lord Ballant did not know of the new planting. Anderson Grimes has now informed him, and Lord Ballant expects that you will be delayed. Grimes has communicated with Gisborne Keep and Castle Cloud. Three hundred men march tonight to reinforce Ballant Keep. They will arrive in two days. Lord Ballant is much elated."

Lord Faide paced back and forth across the tent. "Can we cross this planting?"

Hein Huss made a heavy sound of disapproval. "There are many futures. In certain of these futures you pass. In others you do not pass. I cannot ordain these futures."

Lord Faide had long learned to control his impatience at what sometimes seemed to be pedantic obfuscation. He grumbled, "They are either very stupid or very bold, planting across the downs in this fashion. I cannot imagine what they intend."

Hein Huss considered, then grudgingly volunteered an idea. "What if they plant west from North Wildwood to Sarrow Copse? What if they plant west from South Wildwood to Old Forest?

Lord Faide stood stock-still, his eyes narrow and thoughtful. "Faide Keep would be surrounded by forest. We would be imprisoned... These plantings, do they proceed?"

"They proceed, so I have been told."

"What do they hope to gain?"

"I do not know. Perhaps they hope to isolate the keeps, to rid the planet of men. Perhaps they merely want secure avenues between the forests."

Lord Faide considered. Huss' final suggestion was reasonable enough. During the first centuries of human settlement, sportive young men had hunted the First Folk with clubs and lances, eventually had driven them from their native downs into the forests. "Evidently they are more clever than we realize. Adam McAdam asserts that they do not think, but it seems that he is mistaken."

Hein Huss shrugged. "Adam McAdam equates thought to the human cerebral process. He cannot telepathize with the First Folk, hence he deduced that they do not 'think.' But I have watched them at Forest Market, and they trade intelligently enough." He raised his head, appeared to listen, then reached into his cabinet, delicately tightened a noose around the neck of one of the mannikins. From outside the tent came a sudden cough and a whooping gasp for air. Huss grinned, twitched open the noose. "That is Isak Comandore's apprentice. He hopes to complete a Hein Huss mannikin. I must say he works diligently, going so far as to touch its feet into my footprints whenever possible."

Lord Faide went to the flap of the tent. "We break camp early. Be alert, I may require your help." Lord Faide departed the tent.

Hein Huss continued the ordering of the cabinet. Presently he sensed the approach of his rival, Jinxman Isak Comandore, who coveted the office of Head Jinxman with all-consuming passion. Huss closed the cabinet and hoisted himself to his feet.

Comandore entered the tent, a man tall, crooked and spindly. His wedge-shaped head was covered with coarse russet ringlets; hot red-brown eyes peered from under his red eyebrows. "I offer my complete rights to Keyril, and will include the masks, the headdress, and amulets. Of all the demons ever contrived he has won the widest public acceptance. To utter the name Keyril is to complete half the work of a possession. Keyril is a valuable property. I can give no more."

But Huss shook his head. Comandore's desire was the full simulacrum of Tharon Faide, Lord Faide's oldest son, complete with clothes, hair, skin, eyelashes, tears, excreta, sweat and sputum—the only one in existence, for Lord Faide guarded his son much more jealously than he did himself. "You offer convincingly," said Huss, "but my own demons suffice. The name Dant conveys fully as much terror as Keyril."

"I will add five hairs from the head of Jinxman Clarence Sears; they are the last, for he is now stark bald."

"Let us drop the matter; I will keep the simulacrum."

"As you please," said Comandore with asperity. He glanced out the flap of the tent. "That blundering apprentice. He puts the feet of the mannikin backwards into your prints."

Huss opened his cabinet, thumped a mannikin with his finger. From outside the tent came a grunt of surprise. Huss grinned. "He is young and earnest, and perhaps he is clever, who knows?" He went to the flap of the tent, called outside. "Hey, Sam Salazar, what do you do? Come inside."

Apprentice Sam Salazar came blinking into the tent, a thick-set youth with a round florid face, overhung with a rather untidy mass

of straw-colored hair. In one hand he carried a crude pot-bellied mannikin, evidently intended to represent Hein Huss.

"You puzzle both your master and myself," said Huss. "There must
be method in your folly, but we fail to perceive it. For instance, this
moment you place my simulacrum backwards into my track. I feel a
tug on my foot, and you pay for your clumsiness."

Sam Salazar showed small evidence of abashment. "Jinxman Comandore has warned that we must expect to suffer for our ambitions."

"If your ambition is jinxmanship," Comandore declared sharply,
"you had best mend your ways."

"The lad is craftier than you know," said Hein Huss. "Look now." He
took the mannikin, spit into its mouth, plucked a hair from his head,
thrust it into a convenient crevice. "He has a Hein Huss mannikin,
achieved at very small cost. Now, Apprentice Salazar, how will you
hoodoo me?"

"Naturally I would never dare. I merely want to fill the bare spaces
in my cabinet."

Hein Huss nodded his approval. "As good a reason as any. Of course
you own a simulacrum of Isak Comandore?"

Sam Salazar glanced uneasily side wise at Isak Comandore. "He
leaves none of his traces. If there is so much as an open bottle in the
room, he breathes behind his hand."

"Ridiculous!" exclaimed Hein Huss. "Comandore, what do you
fear?"

"I am conservative," said Comandore drily. "You make a fine gesture,
but some day an enemy may own that simulacrum; then you will regret
your bravado."

"Bah. My enemies are all dead, save one or two who dare not reveal
themselves." He clapped Sam Salazar a great buffet on the shoulder.
"Tomorrow, Apprentice Salazar, great things are in store for you."

"What manner of great things?"

"Honor, noble self-sacrifice. Lord Faide must beg permission to pass
Wildwood from the First Folk, which galls him. But beg he must.
Tomorrow, Sam Salazar, I will elect you to lead the way to the parley,

to deflect deadfalls, scythes and nettle-traps from the more important person who follows."

Sam Salazar shook his head and drew back. "There must be others more worthy; I prefer to ride in the rear with the wagons."

Comandore waved him from the tent. "You will do as ordered. Leave us; we have had enough apprentice talk."

Sam Salazar departed. Comandore turned back to Hein Huss.

"In connection with tomorrow's battle, Anderson Grimes is especially adept with demons. As I recall, he has developed and successfully publicized Font, who spreads sleep; Everid, a being of wrath; Deigne, a force of fear. We must take care that in countering these effects we do not neutralize each other."

"True," rumbled Huss. "I have long maintained to Lord Faide that a single jinxman—the Head Jinxman in fact—is more effective than a group at cross-purposes. But he is consumed by ambition and does not listen."

"Perhaps he wants to be sure that should advancing years overtake the Head Jinxman, other equally effective jinxmen are at hand."

"The future has many paths," agreed Hein Huss. "Lord Faide is well-advised to seek early for my successor, so that I may train him over the years. I plan to assess all the subsidiary jinxmen, and select the most promising. Tomorrow I relegate to you the demons of Anderson Grimes."

Isak Comandore nodded politely. "You are wise to give over responsibility. When I feel the weight of my years, I hope I may act with similar forethought. Good night, Hein Huss. I go to arrange my demon masks. Tomorrow Keyril must walk like a giant."

"Good night, Isak Comandore."

Comandore swept from the tent, and Huss settled himself on his stool. Sam Salazar scratched at the flap. "Well, lad?" growled Huss. "Why do you loiter?"

Sam Salazar placed the Hein Huss mannikin on the table. "I have no wish to keep this doll."

"Throw it in a ditch, then," Hein Huss spoke gruffly. "You must stop annoying me with stupid tricks. You efficiently obtrude yourself upon my attention, but you cannot transfer from Comandore's troupe without his express consent."

"If I gain his consent?"

"You will incur his enmity, he will open his cabinet against you. Unlike myself, you are vulnerable to a hoodoo. I advise you to be content. Isak Comandore is highly skilled and can teach you much."

Sam Salazar still hesitated. "Jinxman Comandore, though skilled, is intolerant of new thoughts."

Hein Huss shifted ponderously on his stool, examined Sam Salazar with his water-clear eyes. "What new thoughts are these? Your own?"

"The thoughts are new to me, and for all I know new to Isak Comandore. But he will say neither yes nor no."

Hein Huss sighed, settled his monumental bulk more comfortably. "Speak then, describe these thoughts, and I will assess their novelty."

"First, I have wondered about trees. They are sensitive to light, to moisture, to wind, to pressure. Sensitivity implies sensation. Might a man feel into the soul of a tree for these sensations? If a tree were capable of awareness, this faculty might prove useful. A man might select trees as sentinels in strategic sites, and enter into them as he chose."

Hein Huss was skeptical. "An amusing notion, but practically not feasible. The reading of minds, the act of possession, televoyance, similar interplay requires psychic congruence as a basic condition. The minds must be able to become identities at some particular stratum. Unless there is sympathy, there is no linkage. A tree is at opposite poles from a man; the images of tree and man are incommensurable. Hence, anything more than the most trifling flicker of comprehension must be a true miracle of jinxmanship."

Sam Salazar nodded mournfully. "I realize this, and at one time hoped to equip myself with the necessary identification."

"To do this you must become a vegetable. Certainly the tree will never become a man."

"So I reasoned," said Sam Salazar. "I went alone into a grove of trees, where I chose a tall conifer. I buried my feet in the mold, I stood silent and naked—in the sunlight, in the rain; at dawn, noon, dusk, midnight. I closed my mind to man-thoughts, I closed my eyes to vision, my ears to sound. I took no nourishment except from rain and sun. I sent roots forth from my feet and branches from my torso. Thirty hours I stood, and two days later, another thirty hours, and after two days another thirty hours. I made myself a tree, as nearly as possible to one of flesh and blood."

Hein Huss gave the great inward gurgle which signalized his amusement. "And you achieved sympathy?"

"Nothing useful," Sam Salazar admitted. "I felt something of the tree's sensations—the activity of light, the peace of dark, the coolness of rain. But visual and auditory experience—nothing. However, I do not regret the trial. It was a useful discipline."

"An interesting effort, even if inconclusive. The idea is by no means of startling originality, but the empiricism—to use an archaic word—of your method is bold, and no doubt antagonized Isak Comandore, who has no patience with the superstitions of our ancestors. I suspect that he harangued you against frivolity, metaphysics, and inspirationalism."

"True," said Sam Salazar. "He spoke at length."

"You should take the lesson to heart. Isak Comandore is sometimes unable to make the most obvious truth seem credible. However, I cite you the example of Lord Faide, who considers himself an enlightened man, free from superstition. Still, he rides in the feeble car, he carries a pistol sixteen hundred years old, he relies on Hellmouth to protect Faide Keep."

"Perhaps—unconsciously—he longs for the old magical times," suggested Sam Salazar thoughtfully.

"Perhaps," agreed Hein Huss. "And you do likewise?"

Sam Salazar hesitated. "There is an aura of romance, a kind of wild grandeur to the old days—but of course," he added quickly, "mysticism is no substitute for orthodox logic."

"Naturally not," agreed Hein Huss. "Now go; I must consider the events of tomorrow."

Sam Salazar departed, and Hein Huss, rumbling and groaning, hoisted himself to his feet. He went to the flap of his tent, surveyed the camp. All now was quiet. The fires were embers, the warriors lay in the pits they had cut into the moss. To the north and south spread the woodlands. Among the trees and out on the downs were faint flickering luminosities, where the First Folk gathered spore-pods from the moss.

Hein Huss became aware of a nearby personality. He turned his head and saw approaching the shrouded form of Jinxman Enterlin, who concealed his face, who spoke only in whispers, who disguised his natural gait with a stiff, stiltlike motion. By this means he hoped to reduce his vulnerability to hostile jinxmanship. The admission carelessly let fall of failing eyesight, of stiff joints, forgetfulness, melancholy, nausea might be of critical significance in controversy by hoodoo. Jinxmen therefore maintained the pose of absolute health and virility, even though they must grope blindly or limp doubled up from cramps.

Hein Huss called out to Enterlin, lifted back the flap to the tent. Enterlin entered; Huss went to the cabinet, brought forth a flask, poured liquor into a pair of stone cups. "A cordial only, free of covert significance."

"Good," whispered Enterlin, selecting the cup farthest from him. "After all, we jinxmen must relax into the guise of men from time to time." Turning his back on Huss, he introduced the cup through the folds of his hood, drank. "Refreshing," he whispered. "We need refreshment: tomorrow we must work."

Huss issued his reverberating chuckle. "Tomorrow Isak Comandore matches demons with Anderson Grimes. We others perform only subsidiary duties."

Enterlin seemed to make a quizzical inspection of Hein Huss through the black gauze before his eyes. "Comandore will relish this opportunity. His vehemence oppresses me, and his is a power which feeds on success. He is a man of fire, you are a man of ice."

"Ice quenches fire."

"Fire sometimes melts ice."

Hein Huss shrugged. "No matter. I grow weary. Time has passed all of us by. Only a moment ago a young apprentice showed me to myself."

"As a powerful jinxman, as Head Jinxman to the Faides, you have cause for pride."

Hein Huss drained the stone cup, set it aside. "No. I see myself at the top of my profession, with nowhere else to go. Only Sam Salazar the apprentice thinks to search for more universal lore: he comes to me for counsel, and I do not know what to tell him."

"Strange talk, strange talk!" whispered Enterlin. He moved to the flap of the tent. "I go now," he whispered. "I go to walk on the downs. Perhaps I will see the future."

"There are many futures."

Enterlin rustled away and was lost in the dark. Hein Huss groaned and grumbled, then took himself to his couch, where he instantly fell asleep.

II

The night passed. The sun, flickering with films of pink and green, lifted over the horizon. The new planting of the First Folk was silhouetted, a sparse stubble of saplings, against the green and lavender sky. The troops broke camp with practiced efficiency. Lord Faide marched to his car, leaped within; the machine sagged under his weight. He pushed a button, the car drifted forward, heavy as a waterlogged timber.

A mile from the new planting he halted, sent a messenger back to the wagons of the jinxmen. Hein Huss walked ponderously forward, followed by Isak Comandore, Adam McAdam, and Enterlin; Lord Faide spoke to Hein Huss. "Send someone to speak to the First Folk. Inform them we wish to pass, offering them no harm, but that we will react savagely to any hostility."

"I will go myself," said Hein Huss. He turned to Comandore. "Lend me, if you will, your brash young apprentice. I can put him to good use."

"If he unmasks a nettle trap by blundering into it, his first useful deed will be done," said Comandore. He signaled to Sam Salazar, who came reluctantly forward. "Walk in front of Head Jinxman Hein Huss that he may encounter no traps or scythes. Take a staff to probe the moss."

Without enthusiasm Sam Salazar borrowed a lance from one of the foot soldiers. He and Huss set forth, along the low rise that previously had separated North from South Wildwood. Occasionally outcroppings of stone penetrated the cover of moss; here and there grew bayberry trees, clumps of tarplant, ginger-tea, and rosewort.

A half mile from the planting Huss halted. "Now take care, for here the traps will begin. Walk clear of hummocks, these often conceal swing-scythes; avoid moss which shows a pale blue; it is dying or sickly and may cover a deadfall or a nettle trap."

"Why cannot you locate the traps by clairvoyance?" asked Sam Salazar in a rather sullen voice. "It appears an excellent occasion for the use of these faculties."

"The question is natural," said Hein Huss with composure. "However you must know that when a jinxman's own profit or security is at stake his emotions play tricks on him. I would see traps everywhere and would never know whether clairvoyance or fear prompted me. In this case, that lance is a more reliable instrument than my mind."

Sam Salazar made a salute of understanding and set forth, with Hein Huss stumping behind him. At first he prodded with care, uncovering two traps, then advanced more jauntily; so swiftly indeed that Huss called out in exasperation, "Caution, unless you court death!"

Sam Salazar obligingly slowed his pace. "There are traps all around us, but I detect the pattern, or so I believe."

"Ah, ha, you do? Reveal it to me, if you will. I am only Head Jinxmin, and ignorant."

"Notice. If we walk where the spore-pods have recently been harvested, then we are secure."

Hein Huss grunted. "Forward then. Why do you dally? We must do battle at Ballant Keep today."

Two hundred yards farther, Sam Salazar stopped short. "Go on, boy, go on!" grumbled Hein Huss.

"The savages threaten us. You can see them just inside the planting. They hold tubes which they point toward us."

Hein Huss peered, then raised his head and called out in the sibilant language of the First Folk.

A moment or two passed, then one of the creatures came forth, a naked humanoid figure, ugly as a demonmask. Foam-sacs bulged under its arms, orange-lipped foam-vents pointed forward. Its back was wrinkled and loose, the skin serving as a bellows to blow air through the foam-sacs. The fingers of the enormous hands ended in chisel-shaped blades, the head was sheathed in chitin. Billion-faceted eyes swelled from either side of the head, glowing like black opals, merging without definite limit into the chitin. This was a representative of the original inhabitants of the planet, who until the coming of man had inhabited the downs, burrowing in the moss, protecting themselves behind masses of foam exuded from the underarm sacs.

The creature wandered close, halted. "I speak for Lord Faide of Faide Keep," said Huss. "Your planting bars his way. He wishes that you guide him through, so that his men do not damage the trees, or spring the traps you have set against your enemies."

"Men are our enemies," responded the autochthon. "You may spring as many traps as you care to; that is their purpose." It backed away.

"One moment," said Hein Huss sternly. "Lord Faide must pass. He goes to battle Lord Ballant. He does not wish to battle the First Folk. Therefore it is wise to guide him across the planting without hindrance."

The creature considered a second or two. "I will guide him." He stalked across the moss toward the war party.

Behind followed Hein Huss and Sam Salazar. The autochthon, legs articulated more flexibly than a man's, seemed to weave and wander, occasionally pausing to study the ground ahead.

"I am puzzled," Sam Salazar told Hein Huss. "I cannot understand the creature's actions."

"Small wonder," grunted Hein Huss. "He is one of the First Folk, you are human. There is no basis for understanding."

"I disagree," said Sam Salazar seriously.

"Eh?" Hein Huss inspected the apprentice with vast disapproval. "You engage in contention with me, Head Jinxman Hein Huss?"

"Only in a limited sense," said Sam Salazar. "I see a basis for understanding with the First Folk in our common ambition to survive."

"A truism," grumbled Hein Huss. "Granting this community of interests with the First Folk, what is your perplexity?"

"The fact that it first refused, then agreed to conduct us across the planting."

Hein Huss nodded. "Evidently the information which intervened, that we go to fight at Ballant Keep, occasioned the change."

"This is clear," said Sam Salazar. "But think—"

"You exhort me to think?" roared Hein Huss.

"—here is one of the First Folk, apparently without distinction, who makes an important decision instantly. Is he one of their leaders? Do they live in anarchy?"

"It is easy to put questions," Hein Huss said gruffly. "It is not as easy to answer them."

"In short—"

"In short, I do not know. In any event, they are pleased to see us killing one another."

III

The passage through the planting was made without incident. A mile to the east the autochthon stepped aside and without formality returned to the forest. The war party, which had been marching in single file, regrouped into its usual formation. Lord Faide called Hein Huss and made the unusual gesture of inviting him up into the seat beside him. The ancient car dipped and sagged; the power-mechanism whined and chattered. Lord Faide, in high good spirits, ignored the noise. "I feared that we might be forced into a time-consuming wrangle. What of Lord Ballant? Can you read his thoughts?"

Hein Huss cast his mind forth. "Not clearly. He knows of our passage. He is disturbed."

Lord Faide laughed sardonically. "For excellent reason! Listen now, I will explain the plan of battle so that all may coordinate their efforts."

"Very well."

"We approach in a wide line. Ballant's great weapon is of course Volcano. A decoy must wear my armor and ride in the lead. The yellow-haired apprentice is perhaps the most expendable member of the party. In this way we will learn the potentialities of Volcano. Like our own Hellmouth, it was built to repel vessels from space and cannot command the ground immediately under the keep. Therefore we will advance in dispersed formation, to regroup two hundred yards from the keep. At this point the jinxmen will impel Lord Ballant forth from the keep. You no doubt have made plans to this end."

Hein Huss gruffly admitted that such was the case. Like other jinxmen, he enjoyed the pose that his power sufficed for extemporaneous control of any situation.

Lord Faide was in no mood for niceties and pressed for further information. Grudging each word, Hein Huss disclosed his arrangements. "I have prepared certain influences to discomfit the Ballant defenders and drive them forth. Jinxman Enterlin will sit at his cabinet, ready to retaliate if Lord Ballant orders a spell against you. Anderson Grimes undoubtedly will cast a demon—probably Everid—into the Ballant warriors; in return, Jinxman Comandore will possess an equal or a greater number of Faide warriors with the demon Keyril, who is even more ghastly and horrifying."

"Good. What more?"

"There is need for no more, if your men fight well."

"Can you see the future? How does today end?"

"There are many futures. Certain jinxmen—Enterlin for instance—profess to see the thread which leads through the maze; they are seldom correct."

"Call Enterlin here."

Hein Huss rumbled his disapproval. "Unwise, if you desire victory over Ballant Keep."

Lord Faide inspected the massive Jinxman from under his black saturnine brows. "Why do you say this?"

"If Enterlin foretells defeat, you will be dispirited and fight poorly. If he predicts victory, you become overconfident and likewise fight poorly."

Lord Faide made a petulant gesture. "The jinxmen are loud in their boasts until the test is made. Then they always find reasons to retract, to qualify."

"Ha, ha!" barked Hein Huss. "You expect miracles, not honest jinxmanship. I spit—" he spat. "I predict that the spittle will strike the moss. The probabilities are high. But an insect might fly in the way. One of the First Folk might raise through the moss. The chances are slight. In the next instant there is only one future. A minute hence there are four futures. Five minutes hence, twenty futures. A billion futures could not express all the possibilities of tomorrow. Of these billion, certain are more probable than others. It is true that these probable futures sometimes send a delicate influence into the jinxman's brain. But unless he is completely impersonal and disinterested, his own desires overwhelm this influence. Enterlin is a strange man. He hides himself, he has no appetites. Occasionally his auguries are exact. Nevertheless, I advise against consulting him. You do better to rely on the practical and real uses of jinxmanship."

Lord Faide said nothing. The column had been marching along the bottom of a low swale; the car had been sliding easily downslope. Now they came to a rise, and the power-mechanism complained so vigorously that Lord Faide was compelled to stop the car. He considered. "Once over the crest we will be in view of Ballant Keep. Now we must disperse. Send the least valuable man in your troupe forward—the apprentice who tested out the moss. He must wear my helmet and corselet and ride in the car."

Hein Huss alighted, returned to the wagons, and presently Sam Salazar came forward. Lord Faide eyed the round, florid face with distaste. "Come close," he said crisply. Sam Salazar obeyed. "You will now ride in my place," said Lord Faide. "Notice carefully. This rod impels a forward motion. This arm steers—to right, to left. To stop, return the rod to its first position."

Sam Salazar pointed to some of the other arms, toggles, switches, and buttons. "What of these?"

"They are never used."

"And these dials, what is their meaning?"

Lord Faide curled his lip, on the brink of one of his quick furies. "Since their use is unimportant to me, it is twenty times unimportant to you. Now. Put this cap on your head, and this helmet. See to it that you do not sweat."

Sam Salazar gingerly settled the magnificent black and green crest of Faide on his head, with a cloth cap underneath.

"Now this corselet."

The corselet was constructed of green and black metal sequins, with a pair of scarlet dragon-heads at either side of the breast.

"Now the cloak." Lord Faide flung the black cloak over Sam Salazar's shoulders. "Do not venture too close to Ballant Keep. Your purpose is to attract the fire of Volcano. Maintain a lateral motion around the keep, outside of dart range. If you are killed by a dart, the whole purpose of the deception is thwarted."

"You prefer me to be killed by Volcano?" inquired Sam Salazar.

"No. I wish to preserve the car and the crest. These are relics of great value. Evade destruction by all means possible. The ruse probably will deceive no one; but if it does, and if it draws the fire of Volcano, I must sacrifice the Faide car. Now—sit in my place."

Sam Salazar climbed into the car, settled himself on the seat.

"Sit straight," roared Lord Faide. "Hold your head up! You are simulating Lord Faide! You must not appear to slink!"

Sam Salazar heaved himself erect in the seat. "To simulate Lord Faide most effectively, I should walk among the warriors, with someone else riding in the car."

Lord Faide glared, then grinned sourly. "No matter. Do as I have commanded."

IV

Sixteen hundred years before, with war raging through space, a group of space captains, their home bases destroyed, had taken refuge on Pangborn. To protect themselves against vengeful enemies, they built great forts armed with weapons from the dismantled spaceships.

The wars receded, Pangborn was forgotten. The newcomers drove the First Folk into the forests, planted and harvested the river valleys. Ballant Keep, like Faide Keep, Gastle Cloud, Boghoten, and the rest, overlooked one of these valleys. Four squat towers of a dense black substance supported an enormous parasol roof, and were joined by walls two-thirds as high as the towers. At the peak of the roof a cupola housed Volcano, the weapon corresponding to Faide's Hell-mouth.

The Faide war party advancing over the rise found the great gates already secure, the parapets between the towers thronged with bow-men. According to Lord Faide's strategy, the war party advanced on a broad front. At the center rode Sam Salazar, resplendent in Lord Faide's armor. He made, however, small effort to simulate Lord Faide. Rather than sitting proudly erect, he crouched at the side of the seat, the crest canted at an angle. Lord Faide watched with disgust. Apprentice Salazar's reluctance to be demolished was understandable: if his imper-sonation failed to convince Lord Ballant, at least the Faide ancestral car might be spared. For a certainty Volcano was being manned; the

Ballant weapon-tender could be seen in the cupola, and the snout protruded at a menacing angle.

Apparently the tactic of dispersal, offering no single tempting target, was effective. The Faide war party advanced quickly to a point two hundred yards from the keep, below Volcano's effective field, without drawing fire; first the knights, then the foot soldiers, then the rumbling wagons of the magicians. The slow-moving Faide car was far outdistanced; any doubt as to the nature of the ruse must now be extinguished.

Apprentice Salazar, disliking the isolation, and hoping to increase the speed of the car, twisted one of the other switches, then another. From under the floor came a thin screeching sound; the car quivered and began to rise. Sam Salazar peered over the side, threw out a leg to jump. Lord Faide ran forward, gesturing and shouting. Sam Salazar hastily drew back his leg, returned the switches to their previous condition. The car dropped like a rock. He snapped the switches up again, cushioning the fall.

"Get out of that car!" roared Lord Faide. He snatched away the helmet, dealt Sam Salazar a buffet which toppled him head over heels. "Out of the armor; back to your duties!"

Sam Salazar hurried to the jinxmen's wagons where he helped erect Isak Comandore's black tent. Inside the tent a black carpet with red and yellow patterns was laid; Comandore's cabinet, his chair, and his chest were carried in, and incense set burning in a censer. Directly in front of the main gate Hein Huss superintended the assembly of a rolling stage, forty feet tall and sixty feet long, the surface concealed from Ballant Keep by a tarpaulin.

Meanwhile, Lord Faide had dispatched an emissary, enjoining Lord Ballant to surrender. Lord Ballant delayed his response, hoping to delay the attack as long as possible. If he could maintain himself a day and a half, reinforcements from Gisborne Keep and Castle Cloud might force Lord Faide to retreat.

Lord Faide waited only until the jinxmen had completed their preparations, then sent another messenger, offering two more minutes in which to surrender.

One minute passed, two minutes. The envoys turned on their heels, marched back to the camp.

Lord Faide spoke to Hein Huss. "You are prepared?"

"I am prepared," rumbled Hein Huss.

"Drive them forth."

Huss raised his arm; the tarpaulin dropped from the face of his great display, to reveal a painted representation of Ballant Keep.

Huss retired to his tent, and pulled the flaps together. Braziers burnt fiercely, illuminating the faces of Adam McAdam, eight cabalmen, and six of the most advanced spellbinders. Each worked at a bench supporting several dozen dolls and a small glowing brazier. The cabalmen and spellbinders worked with dolls representing Ballant men-at-arms; Huss and Adam McAdam employed simulacra of the Ballant knights. Lord Ballant would not be hoodooed unless he ordered a jinx against Lord Faide—a courtesy the keep-lords extended each other.

Huss called out: "Sebastian!"

Sebastian, one of Huss's spellbinders, waiting at the flap to the tent, replied, "Ready, sir."

"Begin the display."

Sebastian ran to the stage, struck fire to a fuse. Watchers inside Ballant Keep saw the depicted keep take fire. Flame erupted from the windows, the roof glowed and crumbled. Inside the tent the two jinxmen, the cabalmen, and the spellbinders methodically took dolls, dipped them into the heat of the braziers, concentrating, reaching out for the mind of the man whose doll they burnt. Within the keep men became uneasy. Many began to imagine burning sensations, which became more severe as their minds grew more sensitive to the idea of fire. Lord Ballant noted the uneasiness. He signaled to his chief jinxman Anderson Grimes. "Begin the counterspell."

Down the front of the keep unrolled a display even larger than Hein Muss's, depicting a hideous beast. It stood on four legs and was shown picking up two men in a pair of hands, biting off their heads. Grimes' cabalmen meanwhile took up dolls representing the Faide warriors, inserted them into models of the depicted beast, and closed the hinged

jaws, all the while projecting ideas of fear and disgust. And the Faide
warriors, staring at the depicted monster, felt a sense of horror and
weakness.

Inside Huss's tent, censers and braziers reeked and dolls smoked.
Eyes stared, brows glistened. From time to time one of the workers
gasped—signaling the entry of his projection into an enemy mind.
Within the keep warriors began to mutter, to slap at burning skin, to
eye each other fearfully, noting each other's symptoms. Finally one
cried out, and tore at his armor. "I burn! The cursed witches burn me!"
His pain aggravated the discomfort of the others; there was a growing
sound throughout the keep.

Lord Ballant's oldest son, his mind penetrated by Hein Huss himself,
struck his shield with his mailed fist. "They burn me! They burn us all!
Better to fight than burn!"

"Fight! Fight!" came the voices of the tormented men.

Lord Ballant looked around at the twisted faces, some displaying
blisters, scaldmarks. "Our own spell terrifies them; wait yet a moment!"
he pleaded.

His brother alled hoarsely, "It is not your belly that Hein Huss toasts
in the flames, it is mine! We cannot win a battle of hoodoos; we must
win a battle of arms!"

Lord Ballant cried desperately, "Wait, our own effects are working!
They will flee in terror; wait, wait!"

His cousin tore off his corselet. "It's Hein Huss! I feel him! My leg's
in the fire, the devil laughs at me. Next my head, he says. Fight, or I
go forth to fight alone!"

"Very well," said Lord Ballant in a fateful voice. "We go forth to
fight. First—the beast goes forth. Then we follow and smite them in
their terror."

The gates to the keep swung suddenly wide. Out sprang what appeared to be the depicted monster; legs moving, arms waving, eyes
rolling, issuing evil sounds. Normally the Faide warriors would have
seen the monster for what it was; a model carried on the backs of
three horses. But their minds had been influenced: they had been

infected with horror; they drew back with arms hanging flaccid. From behind the monster the Ballant knights galloped, followed by the Ballant foot soldiers. The charge gathered momentum, tore into the Faide center. Lord Faide bellowed orders; discipline asserted itself. The Faide knights disengaged, divided into three platoons, and engulfed the Ballant charge, while the foot soldiers poured darts into the advancing ranks.

There was the clatter and surge of battle; Lord Ballant, seeing that his sally had failed to overwhelm the Faide forces, and thinking to conserve his own forces, ordered a retreat. In good order the Ballant warriors began to back up toward the keep. The Faide knights held close contact, hoping to win to the courtyard. Close behind came a heavily loaded wagon pushed by armored horses, to be wedged against the gate.

Lord Faide called an order; a reserve platoon of ten knights charged from the side, thrust behind the main body of Ballant horsemen, rode through the foot soldiers, fought into the keep, cut down the gate-tenders.

Lord Ballant bellowed to Anderson Grimes, "They have won inside; quick with your cursed demon! If he can help us, let him do so now!"

"Demon-possession is not a matter of an instant," muttered the jinxman. "I need time."

"You have no time! Ten minutes and we're all dead!"

"I will do my best. Everid, Everid, come swift!"

He hastened into his workroom, donned his demonmask, tossed handful after handful of incense into the brazier. Against one wall stood a great form: black, slit-eyed, noseless. Great white fangs hung from its upper palate; it stood on heavy bent legs, arms reached forward to grasp. Anderson Grimes swallowed a cup of syrup, paced slowly back and forth. A moment passed.

"Grimes!" came Ballant's call from outside. "Grimes!"

A voice spoke. "Enter without fear."

Lord Ballant, carrying his ancestral side arm, entered. He drew back with an involuntary sound. "Grimes!" he whispered.

"Grimes is not here," said the voice. "I am here. Enter."

Lord Ballant came forward stiff-legged. The room was dark except for the feeble glimmer of the brazier. Anderson Grimes crouched in a corner, head bowed under his demonmask. The shadows twisted and pulsed with shapes and faces, forms struggling to become solid. The black image seemed to vibrate with life.

"Bring in your warriors," said the voice. "Bring them in five at a time, bid them look only at the floor until commanded to raise their eyes."

Lord Ballant retreated; there was no sound in the room.

A moment passed; then five limp and exhausted warriors filed into the room, eyes low.

"Look slowly up," said the voice. "Look at the orange fire. Breathe deeply. Then look at me. I am Everid, Demon of Hate. Look at me. Who am I?"

"You are Everid, Demon of Hate," quavered the warriors.

"I stand all around you, in a dozen forms... I come closer. Where am I?"

"You are close."

"Now I am you. We are together."

There was a sudden quiver of motion. The warriors stood straighter, their faces distorted.

"Go forth," said the voice. "Go quietly into the court. In a few minutes we march forth to slay."

The five stalked forth. Five more entered.

Outside the wall, the Ballant knights had retreated as far as the gate; within, seven Faide knights still survived, and with their backs to the wall held the Ballant warriors away from the gate mechanism.

In the Faide camp, Huss called to Comandore, "Everid is walking. Bring forth Keyril."

"Send the men," came Comandore's voice, low and harsh. "Send the men to me. I am Keyril."

Within the keep twenty warriors came marching into the courtyard. Their steps were cautious, tentative, slow. Their faces had lost individuality, they were twisted and distorted, curiously alike.

"Bewitched!" whispered the Ballant soldiers, drawing back. The seven Faide knights watched with sudden fright. But the twenty warriors, paying them no heed, marched out the gate. The Ballant knights parted; for an instant there was a lull in the fighting. The twenty sprang like tigers. Their swords glistened, twinkling in water-bright arcs. They crouched, jerked, jumped; Faide arms, legs, heads were hewed off. The twenty were cut and battered, but the blows seemed to have no effect.

The Faide attack faltered, collapsed. The knights, whose armor was no protection against the demoniac swords, retreated. The twenty possessed warriors raced out into the open toward the foot soldiers, running with great strides, slashing and rending. The Faide foot soldiers fought for a moment, then they too gave way and turned to flee.

From behind Comandore's tent appeared thirty Faide warriors, marching stiffly, slowly. Like the Ballant twenty, their faces were alike—but between the Everid-possessed and the Keyril-possessed was the difference between the face of Everid and the face of Keyril.

Keyril and Everid fought, using the men as weapons, without fear, retreat, or mercy. Hack, chop, cut. Arms, legs, sundered torsos. Bodies fought headless for moments before collapsing.

Only when a body was minced, hacked to bits, did the demoniac vitality depart. Presently there were no more men of Everid, and only fifteen men of Keyril. These hopped and limped and tumbled toward the keep where Faide knights still held the gate. The Ballant knights met them in despair, knowing that now was the decisive moment. Leaping, leering from chopped faces, slashing from tireless arms, the warriors cut a hole into the iron. The Faide knights, roaring victory cries, plunged after. Into the courtyard surged the battle, and now there was no longer doubt of the outcome. Ballant Keep was taken.

Back in his tent Isak Comandore took a deep breath, shuddered, flung down his demonmask. In the courtyard the twelve remaining warriors dropped in their tracks, twitched, gasped, gushed blood and died.

Lord Ballant, in the last gallant act of a gallant life, marched forth brandishing his ancestral side arm. He aimed across the bloody field at

Lord Faide, pulled the trigger. The weapon spewed a brief gout of light; Lord Faide's skin prickled and hair rose from his head. The weapon crackled, turned cherry-red, and melted. Lord Ballant threw down the weapon, drew his sword, marched forth to challenge Lord Faide.

Lord Faide, disinclined to unnecessary combat, signaled to his soldiers. A flight of darts ended Lord Ballant's life, saving him the discomfort of formal execution.

There was no further resistance. The Ballant defenders threw down their arms and marched grimly out to kneel before Lord Faide, while inside the keep the Ballant women gave themselves to mourning and grief.

V

Lord Faide had no wish to linger at Ballant Keep, for he took no relish in his victories. Inevitably, a thousand decisions had to be made. Six of the closest Ballant kinsmen were summarily stabbed and the title declared defunct. Others of the clan were offered a choice: an oath of lifelong fealty together with a moderate ransom, or death. Eyes blazing hate, two chose death and were stabbed.

Lord Faide had now achieved his ambition. For over a thousand years the keep-lords had struggled for power; now one, now another gaining ascendancy. None before had ever extended his authority across the entire continent—which meant control of the planet, since all other land was either sun-parched rock or eternal ice. Ballant Keep had long thwarted Lord Faide's drive to power; now—success, total and absolute. It still remained to chastise the lords of Castle Cloud and Gisborne, both of whom, seeing opportunity to overwhelm Lord Faide, had ranged themselves behind Lord Ballant. But these were matters that might well be assigned to Hein Huss.

Lord Faide, for the first time in his life, felt a trace of uncertainty. Now what? No real adversaries remained. The First Folk must be whipped back, but here was no great problem: they were numerous, but no more than savages. He knew that dissatisfaction and controversy would ultimately arise among his kinsmen and allies. Inaction and boredom would breed irritability; idle minds would calculate the pros and cons of mischief. Even the most loyal would remember the campaigns with nostalgia and long for the excitement, and release, the license, of warfare. Somehow he must find means to absorb the energy of so many active and keyed-up men. How and where, this was the problem. The construction of roads? New farmland claimed from the downs? Yearly tournaments-at-arms? Lord Faide frowned at the inadequacy of his solutions, but his imagination was impoverished by the lack of tradition. The original settlers of Pangborn had been warriors, and had brought with them a certain amount of practical rule-of-thumb knowledge, but little else. The tales they passed down the generations described the great spaceships which moved with magic speed and certainty, the miraculous weapons, the wars in the void, but told nothing of human history or civilized achievement. And so Lord Faide, full of power and success, but with no goal toward which to turn his strength, felt more morose and saturnine than ever.

He gloomily inspected the spoils from Ballant Keep. They were of no great interest to him. Ballant's ancestral car was no longer used, but displayed behind a glass case. He inspected the weapon Volcano, but this could not be moved. In any event it was useless, its magic lost forever. Lord Faide now knew that Lord Ballant had ordered it turned against the Faide car, but that it had refused to spew its vaunted fire. Lord Faide saw with disdainful amusement that Volcano had been sadly neglected. Corrosion had pitted the metal, careless cleaning had twisted the exterior tubing, undoubtedly diminishing the potency of the magic. No such neglect at Faide Keep! Jambart the weapon-tender cherished Hellmouth with absolute devotion. Elsewhere were other ancient devices, interesting but useless—the same sort of curios that cluttered shelves and cases at Faide Keep. (Peculiar, these ancient men! thought Lord Faide: at once so clever, yet so primitive and impractical. Conditions had changed: there had been enormous advances since the dark ages sixteen hundred years ago. For instance, the ancients had used intricate fetishes of metal and glass to communicate with each other. Lord Faide need merely voice his needs; Hein Huss could project his mind a hundred miles to see, to hear, to relay Lord Faide's words.) The ancients had contrived dozens of such objects, but the old magic had worn away and they never seemed to function. Lord Ballant's side arm had melted, after merely stinging Lord Faide. Imagine a troop armed thus trying to cope with a platoon of demon-possessed warriors! Slaughter of the innocents!

Among the Ballant trove Lord Faide noted a dozen old books and several reels of microfilm. The books were worthless, page after page of incomprehensible jargon; the microfilm was equally undecipherable. Again Lord Faide wondered skeptically about the ancients. Clever of course, but to look at the hard facts, they were little more advanced than the First Folk: neither had facility with telepathy or voyance or demon-command. And the magic of the ancients: might there not be a great deal of exaggeration in the legends? Volcano, for instance. A joke. Lord Faide wondered about his own Hellmouth. But no—surely Hellmouth was more trustworthy; Jambart cleaned and polished the weapon daily and washed the entire cupola with vintage wine every month. If human care could induce faithfulness, then Hellmouth was ready to defend Faide Keep!

Now there was no longer need for defense. Faide was supreme. Considering the future. Lord Faide made a decision. There should no longer be keep-lords on Pangborn; he would abolish the appellation. Habitancy of the keeps would gradually be transferred to trusted bailiffs on a yearly basis. The former lords would be moved to comfortable but indefensible manor houses, with the maintenance of private troops forbidden. Naturally they must be allowed jinxmen, but these would be made accountable to himself—perhaps through some sort of licensing provision. He must discuss the matter with Hein Huss. A matter for the future, however. Now he merely wished to settle affairs and return to Faide Keep.

There was little more to be done. The surviving Ballant kinsmen he sent to their homes after Huss had impregnated fresh dolls with their essences. Should they default on their ransoms, a twinge of fire, a few stomach cramps would more than set them right. Ballant Keep itself Lord Faide would have liked to burn, but the material of the ancients was proof to fire. But in order to discourage any new pretenders to the Ballant heritage Lord Faide ordered all the heirlooms and relics brought forth into the courtyard, and then, one at a time, in order of rank, he bade his men choose. Thus the Ballant wealth was distributed. Even the jinxmen were invited to choose, but they despised the ancient trinkets as works of witless superstition. The lesser spellbinders and apprentices rummaged through the leavings, occasionally finding an overlooked bauble or some anomalous implement. Isak Comandore was irritated to find Sam Salazar staggering under a load of the ancient books. "And what is your purpose with these?" he barked. "Why do you burden yourself with rubbish?"

Sam Salazar hung his head. "I have no definite purpose. Undoubtedly there was wisdom—or at least knowledge—among the ancients: perhaps I can use these symbols of knowledge to sharpen my own understanding."

Comandore threw up his hands in disgust. He turned to Hein Huss, who stood nearby. "First he fancies himself a tree and stands in the mud; now he thinks to learn jinxmanship through a study of ancient symbols."

Huss shrugged. "They were men like ourselves, and, though limited, they were not entirely obtuse. A certain simian cleverness is required to fabricate these objects."

"Simian cleverness is no substitute for sound jinxmanship," retorted Isak Comandore. "This is a point hard to overemphasize; I have drummed it into Salazar's head a hundred times. And now, look at him."

Huss grunted noncommitally. "I fail to understand what he hopes to achieve."

Sam Salazar tried to explain, fumbling for words to express an idea that did not exist. "I thought perhaps to decipher the writing, if only to understand what the ancients thought, and perhaps to learn how to perform one or two of their tricks."

Comandore rolled up his eyes. "What enemy bewitched me when I consented to take you as apprentice? I can cast twenty hoodoos in an hour, more than any of the ancients could achieve in a lifetime."

"Nevertheless," said Sam Salazar, "I notice that Lord Faide rides in his ancestral car, and that Lord Ballant sought to kill us with Volcano."

"I notice," said Comandore with feral softness, "that my demon Keyril conquered Lord Ballant's Volcano, and that riding on my wagon I can outdistance Lord Faide in his car."

Sam Salazar though better of arguing further. "True, Jinxman Comandore, very true. I stand corrected."

"Then discard that rubbish and make yourself useful. We return to Faide Keep in the morning."

"As you wish, Jinxman Comandore." Sam Salazar threw the books back into the trash.

VI

The Ballant clan had been dispersed, Ballant Keep was despoiled. Lord Faide and his men banqueted somberly in the great hall, tended by silent Ballant servitors.

Ballant Keep had been built on the same splendid scale as Faide Keep. The great hall was a hundred feet long, fifty feet wide, fifty feet high, paneled in planks sawn from pale native hardwood, rubbed and waxed to a rich honey color. Enormous black beams supported the ceiling; from these hung candelabra, intricate contrivances of green, purple, and blue glass, knotted with ancient but still bright light-motes. On the far wall hung portraits of all the lords of Ballant Keep—105 grave faces in a variety of costumes. Below, a genealogical chart ten feet high detailed the descent of the Ballants and their connections with the other noble clans. Now there was a desolate air to the hall, and the 105 dead faces were meaningless and empty.

Lord Faide dined without joy, and cast dour side glances at those of his kinsmen who revelled too gladly. Lord Ballant, he thought, had conducted himself only as he himself might have done under the same circumstances; coarse exultation seemed in poor taste, almost as if it were disrespect for Lord Faide himself. His followers were quick to catch his mood, and the banquet proceeded with greater decorum.

The jinxmen sat apart in a smaller room to the side. Anderson Grimes, erstwhile Ballant Head Jinxman, sat beside Hein Huss, trying to put a good face on his defeat. After all, he had performed creditably against four powerful adversaries, and there was no cause to feel a diminution of *mana*. The five jinxmen discussed the battle, while the cabalmen and spellbinders listened respectfully. The conduct of the demon-possessed troops occasioned the most discussion. Anderson Grimes readily admitted that his conception of Everid was a force absolutely brutal and blunt, terrifying in its indomitable vigor. The other jinxmen agreed that he undoubtedly succeeded in projecting these qualities; Hein Huss however pointed out that Isak Comandore's Keyril, as cruel and vigorous as Everid, also combined a measure of crafty malice, which tended to make the possessed soldier a more effective weapon.

Anderson Grimes allowed that this might well be the case, and that in fact he had been considering such an augmentation of Everid's characteristics.

"To my mind," said Huss, "the most effective demon should be swift enough to avoid the strokes of the brute demons, such as Keyril and Everid. I cite my own Dant as example. A Dant-possessed warrior can easily destroy a Keyril or an Everid, simply through his agility. In an encounter of this sort the Keyrils and Everids presently lose their capacity to terrify, and thus half the effect is lost."

Isak Comandore pierced Huss with a hot russet glance. "You state a presumption as if it were fact. I have formulated Keyril with sufficient craft to counter any such displays of speed. I firmly believe Keyril to be the most fearsome of all demons."

"It may well be," rumbled Hein Huss thoughtfully. He beckoned to a steward, gave instructions. The steward reduced the light a trifle. "Behold," said Hein Huss. "There is Dant. He comes to join the banquet." At the side of the room loomed the tiger-striped Dant, a creature constructed of resilient metal, with four terrible arms, and a squat black head which seemed all gaping jaw.

"Look," came the husky voice of Isak Comandore. "There is Keyril." Keyril was rather more humanoid and armed with a cutlass. Dant spied Keyril. The jaws gaped wider, it sprang to the attack.

The battle was a thing of horror; the two demons rolled, twisted, bit, frothed, uttered soundless shrieks, tore each other apart. Suddenly Dant sprang away, circled Keyril with dizzying speed, faster, faster; became a blur, a wild coruscation of colors that seemed to give off a high-pitched wailing sound, rising higher and higher in pitch. Keyril hacked brutally with his cutlass, then seemed to grow feeble and wan. The light that once had been Dant blazed white, exploded in a mental shriek; Keyril was gone and Isak Comandore lay moaning.

Hein Huss drew a deep breath, wiped his face, looked about him with a complacent grin. The entire company sat rigid as stones, staring, all except the apprentice Sam Salazar, who met Hein Huss's glance with a cheerful smile.

"So," growled Huss, panting from his exertion, "you consider yourself superior to the illusion; you sit and smirk at one of Hein Huss's best efforts."

"No, no," cried Sam Salazar, "I mean no disrespect! I want to learn, so I watched you rather than the demons. What could they teach me? Nothing!"

"Ah," said Huss, mollified. "And what did you learn?"

"Likewise, nothing," said Sam Salazar, "but at least I do not sit like a fish."

Comandore's voice came soft but crackling with wrath. "You see in me the resemblance to a fish?"

"I except you, Jinxman Comandore, naturally," Sam Salazar explained.

"Please go to my cabinet, Apprentice Salazar, and fetch me the doll that is your likeness. The steward will bring a basin of water, and we shall have some sport. With your knowledge of fish you perhaps can breathe under water. If not—you may suffocate."

"I prefer not, Jinxman Comandore," said Sam Salazar. "In fact, with your permission, I now resign your service."

Comandore motioned to one of his cabalmen. "Fetch me the Salazar doll. Since he is no longer my apprentice, it is likely indeed that he will suffocate."

"Come now, Comandore," said Hein Huss gruffly. "Do not torment the lad. He is innocent and a trifle addled. Let this be an occasion of placidity and ease."

"Certainly, Hein Huss," said Comandore. "Why not? There is ample time in which to discipline this upstart."

"Jinxman Huss," said Sam Salazar, "since I am now relieved of my duties to Jinxman Comandore, perhaps you will accept me into your service."

Hein Huss made a noise of vast distaste. "You are not my responsibility."

"There are many futures, Hein Huss," said Sam Salazar. "You have said as much yourself."

Hein Huss looked at Sam Salazar with his water-clear eyes. "Yes, there are many futures. And I think that tonight sees the full amplitude of jinxmanship... I think that never again will such power and skill gather at the same table. We shall die one by one and there shall be none to fill our shoes... Yes, Sam Salazar, I will take you as apprentice. Isak Comandore, do you hear? This youth is now of my company."

"I must be compensated," growled Comandore.

"You have coveted my doll of Tharon Faide, the only one in existence. It is yours."

"Ah, ha!" cried Isak Comandore, leaping to his feet. "Hein Huss, I salute you! You are generous indeed! I thank you and accept!"

Hein Huss motioned to Sam Salazar. "Move your effects to my wagon. Do not show your face again tonight."

Sam Salazar bowed with dignity and departed the hall.

The banquet continued, but now something of melancholy filled the room. Presently a messenger from Lord Faide came to warn all to bed, for the party returned to Faide Keep at dawn.

VII

The victorious Faide troops gathered on the heath before Ballant Keep. As a parting gesture, Lord Faide ordered the great gate torn off the hinges, so that ingress could never again be denied him. But even after sixteen hundred years the hinges were proof to all the force the horses could muster, and the gates remained in place.

Lord Faide accepted the fact with good grace and bade farewell to his cousin Renfroy, whom he had appointed bailiff. He climbed into his car, settled himself, snapped the switch. The car groaned and moved forward. Behind came the knights and the foot soldiers, then the baggage train, laden with booty, and finally the wagons of the jinxmen.

Three hours the column marched across the mossy downs. Ballant Keep dwindled behind; ahead appeared North and South Wild wood, darkening all the sweep of the western horizon. Where once the break had existed, the First Folk's new planting showed a smudge lower and less intense than the old woodlands.

Two miles from the woodlands Lord Faide called a halt and signaled up his knights. Hein Huss laboriously dismounted from his wagon, came forward.

"In the event of resistance," Lord Faide told the knights, "do not be tempted into the forest. Stay with the column and at all times be on your guard against traps."

Hein Huss spoke. "You wish me to parley with the First Folk once more?"

"No," said Lord Faide. "It is ridiculous that I must ask permission of savages to ride over my own land. We return as we came; if they interfere, so much the worse for them."

"You are rash," said Huss with simple candor.

Lord Faide glanced down at him with black eyebrows raised. "What damage can they do if we avoid their traps? Blow foam at us?"

"It is not my place to advise or to warn," said Hein Huss. "However, I point out that they exhibit a confidence which does not come from conscious weakness; also, that they carried tubes, apparently hollow grasswood shoots, which imply missiles."

Lord Faide nodded. "No doubt. However, the knights wear armor, the soldiers carry bucklers. It is not fit that I, Lord Faide of Faide Keep, choose my path to suit the whims of the First Folk. This must be made clear, even if the exercise involves a dozen or so First Folk corpses."

"Since I am not a fighting man," remarked Hein Huss, "I will keep well to the rear, and pass only when the way is secure."

"As you wish." Lord Faide pulled down the visor of his helmet. "Forward."

The column moved toward the forest, along the previous track, which showed plain across the moss. Lord Faide rode in the lead, flanked by his brother, Gethwin Faide, and his cousin, Mauve Dermont-Faide.

A half-mile passed, and another. The forest was only a mile distant. Overhead the great sun rode at zenith; brightness and heat poured down; the air carried the oily scent of thorn and tarbush. The column moved on, more slowly; the only sounds the clanking of armor, the muffled thud of hooves in the moss, the squeal of wagon wheels.

Lord Faide rose up in his car, watching for any sign of hostile preparation. A half-mile from the planting the forms of the First Folk, waiting in the shade along the forest's verge, became visible. Lord Faide ignored them, held a steady pace along the track they had traveled before.

The half-mile became a quarter-mile. Lord Faide turned to order the troops into single file and was just in time to see a hole suddenly open into the moss and his brother, Gethwin Faide, drop from sight. There was a rattle, a thud, the howling of the impaled horse; Gethwin's wild calls as the horse kicked and crushed him into the stakes. Mauve

Dermont-Faide, riding beside Gethwin, could not control his own horse, which leaped aside from the pit and blundered upon a trigger. Up from the moss burst a tree trunk studded with foot-long thorns. It snapped, quick as a scorpion's tail; the thorns punctured Mauve Dermont-Faide's armor, his chest, and whisked him from his horse to carry him suspended, writhing and screaming. The tip of the scythe pounded into Lord Faide's car, splintered against the hull. The car swung groaning through the air. Lord Faide clutched at the windscreen to prevent himself from falling.

The column halted; several men ran to the pit, but Gethwin Faide lay twenty feet below, crushed under his horse. Others took Mauve Dermont-Faide down from the swaying scythe, but he, too, was dead.

Lord Faide's skin tingled with a gooseflesh of hate and rage. He looked toward the forest. The First Folk stood motionless. He beckoned to Bernard, sergeant of the foot soldiers. "Two men with lances to try out the ground ahead. All others ready with darts. At my signal spit the devils."

Two men came forward, and marching before Lord Faide's car, probed at the ground. Lord Faide settled in his seat. "Forward."

The column moved slowly toward the forest, every man tense and ready. The lances of the two men in the vanguard presently broke through the moss, to disclose a nettle trap—a pit lined with nettles, each frond ripe with globes of acid. Carefully they probed out a path to the side, and the column filed around, each man walking in the other's tracks.

At Lord Faide's side now rode his two nephews, Scolford and Edwin. "Notice," said Lord Faide in a voice harsh and tight. "These traps were laid since our last passage; an act of malice."

"But why did they guide us through before?"

Lord Faide smiled bitterly. "They were willing that we should die at Ballant Keep. But we have disappointed them."

"Notice, they carry tubes," said Scolford.

"Blowguns possibly," suggested Edwin.

Scolford disagreed. "They cannot blow through their foam-vents."

"No doubt we shall soon learn," said Lord Faide. He rose in his seat, called to the rear. "Ready with the darts!"

The soldiers raised their crossbows. The column advanced slowly, now only a hundred yards from the planting. The white shapes of the First Folk moved uneasily at the forest's edges. Several of them raised their tubes, seemed to-sight along the length. They twitched their great hands.

One of the tubes was pointed toward Lord Faide. He saw a small black object leave the opening, flit forward, gathering speed. He heard a hum, waxing to a rasping, clicking flutter. He ducked behind the windscreen; the projectile swooped in pursuit, struck the windscreen like a thrown stone. It fell crippled upon the forward deck of the car—a heavy black insect like a wasp, its broken proboscis oozing ocher liquid, horny wings beating feebly, eyes like dumbbells fixed on Lord Faide. With his mailed fist, he crushed the creature.

Behind him other wasps struck knights and men; Corex Faide-Battaro took the prong through his visor into the eye, but the armor of the other knights defeated the wasps. The foot soldiers, however, lacked protection; the wasps half buried themselves in flesh. The soldiers called out in pain, clawed away the wasps, squeezed the wounds. Corex Faide-Battaro toppled from his horse, ran blindly out over the heath, and after fifty feet fell into a trap. The stricken soldiers began to twitch, then fell on the moss, thrashed, leaped up to run with flapping arms, threw themselves in wild somersaults, foaming and thrashing.

In the forest, the First Folk raised their tubes again. Lord Faide bellowed, "Spit the creatures! Bowmen, launch your darts!"

There came the twang of crossbows, darts snapped at the quiet white shapes. A few staggered and wandered aimlessly away; most, however, plucked out the darts or ignored them. They took capsules from small sacks, put them to the end of their tubes.

"Beware the wasps!" cried Lord Faide. "Strike with your bucklers! Kill the cursed things in flight!"

The rasp of horny wings came again; certain of the soldiers found courage enough to follow Lord Faide's orders, and battered down the wasps. Others struck home as before; behind came another flight. The column became a tangle of struggling, crouching men.

"Footmen, retreat!" called Lord Faide furiously. "Footmen back! Knights to me!"

The soldiers fled back along the track, taking refuge behind the baggage wagons. Thirty of their number lay dying, or dead, on the moss.

Lord Faide cried out to his knights in a voice like a bugle. "Dismount, follow slow after me! Turn your helmets, keep the wasps from your eyes! One step at a time, behind the car! Edwin, into the car beside me, test the footing with your lance. Once in the forest there are no traps! Then attack!"

The knights formed themselves into a line behind the car. Lord Faide drove slowly forward, his kinsman Edwin prodding the ground ahead. The First Folk sent out a dozen more wasps, which dashed themselves vainly against the armor. Then there was silence… cessation of sound, activity. The First Folk watched impassively as the knights approached, step by step.

Edwin's lance found a trap, the column moved to the side. Another trap—and the column was diverted from the planting toward the forest. Step by step, yard by yard—another trap, another detour, and now the column was only a hundred feet from the forest. A trap to the left, a trap to the right: the safe path led directly toward an enormous heavy-branched tree. Seventy feet, fifty feet, then Lord Faide drew his sword.

"Prepare to charge, kill till your arms tire!"

From the forest came a crackling sound. The branches of the great tree trembled and swayed. The knights stared, for a moment frozen into place. The tree toppled forward, the knights madly tried to flee—to the rear, to the sides. Traps opened; the knights dropped upon sharp stakes. The tree fell; boughs cracked armored bodies like nuts; there was the hoarse yelling of pinned men, screams from the traps, the crackling subsidence of breaking branches. Lord Faide had been battered down into the car, and the car had been pressed groaning into the moss. His first instinctive act was to press the switch to rest position; then he staggered erect, clambered up through the boughs. A pale unhuman face peered at him; he swung his fist, crushed the faceted eyebulge, and roaring with rage scrambled through the branches. Others of his knights were working themselves free, although almost a third were either crushed or impaled.

The First Folk came scrambling forward, armed with enormous thorns, long as swords. But now Lord Faide could reach them at close quarters. Hissing with vindictive joy, he sprang into their midst, swinging his sword with both hands, as if demon-possessed. The surviving knights joined him and the ground became littered with dismembered First Folk. They drew back slowly, without excitement. Lord Faide reluctantly called back his knights. "We must succor those still pinned, as many as still are alive."

As well as possible branches were cut away, injured knights drawn forth. In some cases the soft moss had cushioned the impact of the tree. Six knights were dead, another four crushed beyond hope of recovery. To these Lord Faide himself gave the *coup de grace*. Ten minutes further hacking and chopping freed Lord Faide's car, while the First Folk watched incuriously from the forest. The knights wished to charge once more, but Lord Faide ordered retreat. Without interference they returned the way they had come, back to the baggage train.

Lord Faide ordered a muster. Of the original war party, less than two-thirds remained. Lord Faide shook his head bitterly. Galling to think how easily he had been led into a trap! He swung on his heel, strode to the rear of the column, to the wagons of the magicians. The jinxmen sat around a small fire, drinking tea. "Which of you will hoodoo these white forest vermin? I want them dead—stricken with sickness, cramps, blindness, the most painful afflictions you can contrive!"

There was general silence. The jinxmen sipped their tea. "Well?" demanded Lord Faide. "Have you no answer? Do I not make myself plain?"

Hein Huss cleared his throat, spat into the blaze. "Your wishes are plain. Unfortunately we cannot hoodoo the First Folk."

"And why?"

"There are technical reasons."

Lord Faide knew the futility of argument. "Must we slink home around the forest? If you cannot hoodoo the First Folk, then bring out your demons! I will march on the forest and chop out a path with my sword!"

"It is not for me to suggest tactics," grumbled Hein Huss.

"Go on, speak! I will listen."

"A suggestion has been put to me, which I will pass to you. Neither I nor the other jinxmen associate ourselves with it, since it recommends the crudest of physical principles."

"I await the suggestion," said Lord Faide.

"It is merely this. One of my apprentices tampered with your car, as you may remember."

"Yes, and I will see he gets the hiding he deserves."

"By some freak he caused the car to rise high into the air. The suggestion is this: that we load the car with as much oil as the baggage train affords, that we send the car aloft and let it drift over the planting. At a suitable moment, the occupant of the car will pour the oil over the trees, then hurl down a torch. The forest will burn. The First Folk will be at least discomfited; at best a large number will be destroyed."

Lord Faide slapped his hands together. "Excellent! Quickly, to work!" He called a dozen soldiers, gave them orders; four kegs of cooking oil, three buckets of pitch, six demijohns of spirit were brought and lifted into the car. The engines grated and protested, and the car sagged almost to the moss.

Lord Faide shook his head sadly. "A rude use of the relic, but all in good purpose. Now, where is that apprentice? He must indicate which switches and which buttons he turned."

"I suggest," said Hein Huss, "that Sam Salazar be sent up with the car."

Lord Faide looked sidewise at Sam Salazar's round, bland countenance. "An efficient hand is needed, a seasoned judgment. I wonder if he can be trusted?"

"I would think so," said Hein Huss, "inasmuch as it was Sam Salazar who evolved the scheme in the first place."

"Very well. In with you, Apprentice! Treat my car with reverence! The wind blows away from us; fire this edge of the forest, in as long a strip as you can manage. The torch, where is the torch?"

The torch was brought and secured to the side of the car.

"One more matter," said Sam Salazar. "I would like to borrow the armor of some obliging knight, to protect myself from the wasps. Otherwise—"

"Armor!" bawled Lord Faide. "Bring armor!"

At last, fully accoutered and with visor down, Sam Salazar climbed into the car. He seated himself, peered intently at the buttons and switches. In truth he was not precisely certain as to which he had manipulated before... He considered, reached forward, pushed, turned. The motors roared and screamed; the car shuddered, sluggishly rose into the air. Higher, higher, twenty feet, forty feet, sixty feet—a hundred, two hundred. The wind eased the car toward the forest; in the shade the First Folk watched. Several of them raised tubes, opened the shutters. The onlookers saw wasps dart through the air to dash against Sam Salazar's armor.

The car drifted over the trees; Sam Salazar began ladling out the oil. Below, the First Folk stirred uneasily. The wind carried the car too far over the forest; Sam Salazar worked the controls, succeeded in guiding himself back. One keg was empty, and another; he tossed them out, presently emptied the remaining two, and the buckets of pitch. He soaked a rag in spirit, ignited it, threw it over the side, poured the spirit after.

The flaming rag fell into leaves. A crackle; fire blazed and sprang. The car now floated at a height of five hundred feet. Salazar poured over the remaining spirits, dropped the demijohns, guided the car back over the heath, and fumbling nervously with the controls, dropped the car in a series of swoops back to the moss.

Lord Faide sprang forward, clapped him on the shoulder. "Excellently done! The forest blazes like tinder!"

The men of Faide Keep stood back, rejoicing to see the flames soar and lick. The First Folk scurried back from the heat, waving their arms; foam of a peculiar purple color issued from their vents as they ran, small useless puffs discharged as if by accident or through excitement. The flames ate through first the forest, then spread into the new planting, leaping through the leaves.

"Prepare to march!" called Lord Faide. "We pass directly behind the flames, before the First Folk return."

Off in the forest the First Folk perched in the trees, blowing out foam in great puffs and billows, building a wall of insulation. The flames had eaten half across the new planting, leaving behind smoldering saplings.

"Forward! Briskly!"

The column moved ahead. Coughing in the smoke, eyes smarting, they passed under still blazing trees and came out on the western downs.

Slowly the column moved forward, led by a pair of soldiers prodding the moss with lances. Behind followed Lord Faide with the knights, then came the foot soldiers, then the rumbling baggage train, and finally the six wagons of the jinxmen.

A thump, a creak, a snap. A scythe had broken up from the moss; the soldiers in the lead dropped flat; the scythe whipped past, a foot from Lord Faide's face. At the same time a plaintive cry came from the rear guard. "They pursue! The First Folk come!"

Lord Faide turned to inspect the new threat. A clot of First Folk, two hundred or more, came across the moss, moving without haste or urgency. Some carried wasp tubes, others thorn-rapiers.

Lord Faide looked ahead. Another hundred yards should bring the army out upon safe ground; then he could deploy and maneuver. "Forward!"

The column proceeded, the baggage train and the jinxmen's wagons pressing close up against the soldiers. Behind and to one side came the First Folk, moving casually and easily.

At last Lord Faide judged they had reached secure ground. "Forward, now! Bring the wagons out, hurry now!"

The troops needed no urging; they trotted out over the heath, the wagons trundling after. Lord Faide ordered the wagons into a close double line, stationed the soldiers between, with the horses behind them protected from the wasps. The knights, now dismounted, waited in front.

The First Folk came listlessly, formlessly forward. Blank white faces stared; huge hands grasped tubes and thorns; traces of the purplish foam showed at the lips of their underarm orifices.

Lord Faide walked along the line of knights. "Swords ready. Allow them as close as they care to come. Then a quick charge." He motioned to the foot soldiers. "Choose a target...!" A volley of darts whistled overhead, to plunge into white bodies. With chisel-bladed fingers the First Folk plucked them out, discarded them with no evidence of vexation. One or two staggered, wandered confusedly across the line of approach. Others raised their tubes, withdrew the shutter. Out flew the insects, homy wings rasping, prongs thrust forward. Across the moss they flickered, to crush themselves against the armor of the knights, to drop to the ground, to be stamped upon. The soldiers cranked their crossbows back into tension, discharged another flight of darts, caused several more First Folk casualties.

The First Folk spread into a long line, surrounding the Faide troops. Lord Faide shifted half his knights to the other side of the wagons.

The First Folk wandered closer. Lord Faide called for a charge. The knights stepped smartly forward, swords swinging. The First Folk advanced a few more steps, then stopped short. The flaps of skin at their back swelled, pulsed; white foam gushed through their vents; clouds and billows rose up around them. The knights halted uncertainly, prodding and slashing into the foam but finding nothing. The foam piled higher, rolling in and forward, pushing the knights back toward the wagons. They looked questioningly toward Lord Faide.

Lord Faide waved his sword. "Cut through to the other side! Forward!" Slashing two-handed with his sword, he sprang into the foam. He struck something solid, hacked blindly at it, pushed forward. Then his legs were seized; he was upended and fell with a spine-rattling jar. Now he felt the grate of a thorn searching his armor. It found a crevice under his corselet and pierced him. Cursing, he raised on his hands and knees, and plunged blindly forward. Enormous hard hands grasped him, heavy forms fell on his shoulders. He tried to breathe, but the foam clogged his visor; he began to smother. Staggering to his feet he half ran, half fell out into the open air, carrying two of the First Folk with him. He had lost his sword, but managed to draw his dagger. The First Folk released him and stepped back into the foam. Lord Faide sprang to his feet. Inside the foam came the sounds of combat; some of his knights burst into the open; others called for help. Lord Faide motioned to the knights. "Back within; the devils slaughter our kinsmen! In and on to the center!"

He took a deep breath. Seizing his dagger, he thrust himself back into the foam. A flurry of shapes came at him; he pounded with his fists, cut with his dagger, stumbled over a mass of living tissue. He kicked the softness, and stepped on metal. Bending, he grasped a leg but found it limp and dead. First Folk were on his back, another thorn found its mark; he groaned and thrust himself forward, and once again fell out into the open air.

A scant fifty of his knights had won back into the central clearing. Lord Faide cried out, "To the center; mount your horses!" Abandoning his car, he himself vaulted into a saddle. The foam boiled and billowed closer. Lord Faide waved his arm. "Forward, all; at a gallop! After us the wagons—out into the open!"

They charged, thrusting the frightened horses into the foam. There was white blindness, the feel of forms underneath, then the open air once again. Behind came the wagons, and the foot soldiers, running along the channel cut by the wagons. All won free—all but the knights who had fallen under the foam.

Two hundred yards from the great white clot of foam, Lord Faide halted, turned, looked back. He raised his fist, shook it in a passion. "My knights, my car, my honor! I'll burn your forests, I'll drive you into the sea, there'll be no peace till all are dead!" He swung around.

"Come," he called bitterly to the remnants of his war party. "We have been defeated. We retreat to Faide Keep."

VIII

Faide Keep, like Ballant Keep, was constructed of a black, glossy substance, half metal, half stone, impervious to heat, force, and radiation. A parasol roof, designed to ward off hostile energy, rested on five squat outer towers, connected by walls almost as high as the lip of the overhanging roof.

The homecoming banquet was quiet and morose. The soldiers and knights ate lightly and drank much, but instead of becoming merry, lapsed into gloom. Lord Faide, overcome by emotion, jumped to his feet. "Everyone sits silent, aching with rage. I feel no differently. We shall take revenge. We shall put the forests to the torch. The cursed white savages will smother and burn. Drink now with good cheer; not a moment will be wasted. But we must be ready. It is no more than idiocy to attack as before. Tonight I take council with the jinxmen, and we will start a program of affliction."

The soldiers and knights rose to their feet, raised their cups and drank a somber toast. Lord Faide bowed and left the hall.

He went to his private trophy room. On the walls hung escutcheons, memorials, deathmasks, clusters of swords like many-petaled flowers; a rack of side arms, energy pistols, electric stilettos; a portrait of the original Faide, in ancient spacefarer's uniform, and a treasured, almost unique, photograph of the great ship that had brought the first Faide to Pangborn.

Lord Faide studied the ancient face for several moments, then summoned a servant. "Ask the Head Jinxman to attend me."

Hein Huss presently stumped into the room. Lord Faide turned away from the portrait, seated himself, motioned to Hein Huss to do likewise. "What of the keep-lords?" he asked. "How do they regard the setback at the hands of the First Folk?"

"There are various reactions," said Hein Huss. "At Boghoten, Candelwade, and Havve there is distress and anger."

Lord Faide nodded. "These are my kinsmen."

"At Ginsbome, Graymar, Castle Cloud, and Alder there is satisfaction, veiled calculation."

"To be expected," muttered Lord Faide. "These lords must be humbled; irt spite of oaths and undertakings, they still think rebellion."

"At Star Home, Julian-Douray, and Oak Hall I read surprise at the abilities of the First Folk, but in the main disinterest."

Lord Faide nodded sourly. "Well enough. There is no actual rebellion in prospect; we are free to concentrate on the First Folk. I will tell you what is in my mind. You report that new plantings are in progress between Wildwood, Old Forest, Sarrow Copse, and elsewhere—possibly with the intent of surrounding Faide Keep." He looked inquiringly at Hein Huss, but no comment was forthcoming. Lord Faide continued. "Possibly we have underestimated the cunning of the savages. They seem capable of forming plans and acting with almost human persistence. Or, I should say, more than human persistence, for it appears that after sixteen hundred years they still consider us invaders and hope to exterminate us."

"That is my own conclusion," said Hein Huss.

"We must take steps to strike first. I consider this a matter for the jinxmen. We gain no honor dodging wasps, falling into traps, or groping through foam. It is a needless waste of lives. Therefore, I want you to assemble your jinxmen, cabalmen, and spellbinders; I want you to formulate your most potent hoodoos–

"Impossible!"

Lord Faide's black eyebrows rose high. "*Impossible?*" Hein Huss seemed vaguely uncomfortable.

"I read the wonder in your mind. You suspect me of disinterest, irresponsibility. Not true. If the First Folk defeat you, we suffer likewise."

"Exactly," said Lord Faide dryly. "You will starve."

"Nevertheless, the jinxmen cannot help you." He hoisted himself to his feet, started for the door.

"Sit," said Lord Faide. "It is necessary to pursue this matter." Hein Huss looked around with his bland, water-clear eyes. Lord Faide met his gaze. Hein Huss sighed deeply. "I see I must ignore the precepts of my trade, break the habits of a lifetime. I must explain." He took his bulk to the wall, fingered the side arms in the rack, studied the portrait of the ancestral Faide. "These miracle-workers of the old times—unfortunately we cannot use their magic! Notice the bulk of the spaceship! As heavy as Faide Keep." He turned his gaze on the table, teleported a candelabra two or three inches. "With considerably less effort they gave that spaceship enormous velocity, using ideas and forces they knew to be imaginary and irrational. We have advanced since then, of course. We no longer employ mysteries, arcane constructions, wild nonhuman forces. We are rational and practical—but we cannot achieve the effects of the ancient magicians."

Lord Faide watched Hein Huss with saturnine eyes. Hein Huss gave his deep rumbling laugh. "You think that I wish to distract you with talk? No, this is not the case. I am preparing to enlighten you." He returned to his seat, lowered his bulk with a groan. "Now I must talk at length, to which I am not accustomed. But you must be given to understand what we jinxmen can do and what we cannot do.

"First, unlike the ancient magicians, we are practical men. Naturally there is difference in our abilities. The best jinxman combines great telepathic facility, implacable personal force, and intimate knowledge of his fellow humans. He knows their acts, motives, desires, and fears; he understands the symbols that most vigorously represent these qualities. Jinxmanship in the main is drudgery—dangerous, difficult, and unromantic—with no mystery except that which we employ to confuse our enemies." Hein Huss glanced at Lord Faide to encounter the same saturnine gaze.

"Ha! I still have told you nothing; I still have spent many words talking around my inability to confound the First Folk. Patience."

"Speak on," said Lord Faide.

"Listen then. What happens when I hoodoo a man? First I must enter into his mind telepathically. There are three operational levels: the conscious, the unconscious, the cellular. The most effective jinxing is done if all three levels are influenced. I feel into my victim, I learn as much as possible, supplementing my previous knowledge of him, which is part of my stock in trade. I take up his doll, which carries his traces. The doll is highly useful but not indispensable. It serves as a focus for my attention; it acts as a pattern, or a guide, as I fix upon the mind of the victim, and he is bound by his own telepathic capacity to the doll which bears his traces.

"So! Now! Man and doll are identified in my mind, and at one or more levels in the victim's mind. Whatever happens to the doll the victim feels to be happening to himself. There is no more to simple hoodooing than that, from the standpoint of the jinxmen. But naturally the victims differ greatly. Susceptibility is the key idea here. Some men are more susceptible than others. Fear and conviction breed susceptibility. As a jinxman succeeds, he becomes ever more feared, and consequently the more efficacious he becomes. The process is self-generative.

"Demon-possession is a similar technique. Susceptibility is again essential; again conviction creates susceptibility. It is easiest and most dramatic when the characteristics of the demon are well known, as in the case of Comandore's Keyril. For this reason, demons can be exchanged or traded among jinxmen. The commodity actually traded is public acceptance and familiarity with the demon."

"Demons then do not actually exist?" inquired Lord Faide half-incredulously.

Hein Huss grinned vastly, showing enormous yellow teeth. "Telepathy works through a superstratum. Who knows what is created in this superstratum? Maybe the demons live on after they have been conceived; maybe they now are real. This of course is speculation, which we jinxmen shun.

"So much for demons, so much for the lesser techniques of jinxmanship. I have explained sufficient to serve as background to the present situation."

"Excellent," said Lord Faide. "Continue."

"The question, then, is: How does one cast a hoodoo into a creature of an alien race?" He looked inquiringly at Lord Faide. "Can you tell me?"

"I?" asked Lord Faide, surprised. "No."

"The method is basically the same as in the hoodooing of men. It is necessary to make the creature believe, in every cell of his being, that he suffers or dies. This is where the problems begin to arise. Does the creature think—that is to say, does he arrange the processes of his life in the same manner as men? This is a very important distinction. Certain creatures of the universe use methods other than the human nerve-node system to control their environments. We call the human system 'intelligence'—a word which properly should be restricted to human activity. Other creatures use different agencies, different systems, arriving sometimes at similar ends. To bring home these generalities, I cannot hope to merge my mind with the corresponding capacity in the First Folk. The key will not fit the lock. At least, not altogether. Once or twice when I watched the First Folk trading with men at Forest Market, I felt occasional weak significances. This implies that the First Folk mentality creates something similar to human telepathic impulses. Nevertheless, there is no real sympathy between the two races.

"This is the first and the least difficulty. If I were able to make complete telephatic contact—what then? The creatures are different from us. They have no words for 'fear,' 'hate,' 'rage,' 'pain,' 'bravery,' 'cowardice.' One may deduce that they do not feel these emotions. Undoubtedly they know other sensations, possibly as meaningful. Whatever these may be, they are unknown to me, and therefore I cannot either form or project symbols for these sensations."

Lord Faide stirred impatiently. "In short, you tell me that you cannot efficiently enter these creatures' minds; and that if you could, you do not know what influences you could plant there to do them harm."

"Succinct," agreed Hein Huss. "Substantially accurate."

Lord Faide rose to his feet. "In that case you must repair these deficiencies. You must learn to telepathize with the First Folk;

you must find what influences will harm them. As quickly as possible."

Hein Huss stared reproachfully at Lord Faide. "But I have gone to great lengths to explain the difficulties involved! To hoodoo the First Folk is a monumental task! It would be necessary to enter Wildwood, to live with the First Folk, to become one of them, as my apprentice thought to become a tree. Even then an effective hoodoo is improbable! The First Folk must be susceptible to conviction! Otherwise there would be no bite to the hoodoo! I could guarantee no success. I would predict failure. No other jinxman would dare tell you this, no other would risk his *mana*. I dare because I am Hein Huss, with life behind me."

"Nevertheless we must attempt every weapon at hand," said Lord Faide in a dry voice. "I cannot risk my knights, my kinsmen, my soldiers against these pallid half-creatures. What a waste of good flesh and blood to be stuck by a poison insect! You must go to Wildwood; you must learn how to hoodoo the First Folk."

Hein Huss heaved himself erect. His great round face was stony; his eyes were like bits of water-worn glass. "It is likewise a waste to go on a fool's errand. I am no fool and I will not undertake a hoodoo which is futile from the beginning."

"In that case," said Lord Faide, "I will find someone else." He went to the door, summoned a servant. "Bring Isak Comandore here."

Hein Huss lowered his bulk into the chair. "I will remain during the interview, with your permission."

"As you wish."

Isak Comandore appeared in the doorway, tall, loosely articulated, head hanging forward. He darted a glance of swift appraisal at Lord Faide, at Hein Huss, then stepped into the room.

Lord Faide crisply explained his desires. "Hein Huss refuses to undertake the mission. Therefore I call you."

Isak Comandore calculated. The pattern of his thinking was clear: he possibly could gain much *mana*, there was small risk of diminution, for had not Hein Huss already dodged away from the project? Comandore nodded. "Hein Huss has made clear the difficulties; only a very clever and very lucky jinxman can hope to succeed. But I accept the challenge. I will go."

"Good," said Hein Huss, "I will go, too." Isak Comandore darted him a sudden hot glance. "I wish only to observe. To Isak Comandore goes the responsibility and whatever credit may ensue."

"Very well," said Comandore presently. "I welcome your company. Tomorrow morning we leave. I go to order our wagon."

Late in the evening Apprentice Sam Salazar came to Hein Huss, where he sat brooding in his workroom. "What do you wish?" growled Huss.

"I have a request to make of you, Head Jinxman Huss."

"Head Jinxman in name only," grumbled Hein Huss. "Isak Comandore is about to assume my position."

Sam Salazar blinked, laughed uncertainly. Hein Huss fixed wintry-pale eyes on him. "What do you wish?"

"I have heard that you go on an expedition to Wildwood, to study the First Folk."

"True, true. What then?"

"Surely they will now attack all men?"

Hein Huss shrugged. "At Forest Market they trade with men. At Forest Market men have always entered the forest. Perhaps there will be change, perhaps not."

"I would go with you, if I may," said Sam Salazar.

"This is no mission for apprentices."

"An apprentice must take every opportunity to learn," said Sam Salazar. "Also, you will need extra hands to set up tents, to load and unload cabinets, to cook, to fetch water, and other such matters."

"Your argument is convincing," said Hein Huss. "We depart at dawn; be on hand."

IX

As the sun lifted over the heath, the jinxmen departed Faide Keep. The high-wheeled wagon creaked north over the moss. Hein Huss and Isak Comandore riding the front seat, Sam Salazar with his legs hanging over the tail. The wagon rose and fell with the dips and mounds of the moss, wheels wobbling, and presently passed out of sight behind Sky watcher's Hill.

Five days later, an hour before sunset, the wagon reappeared. As before, Hein Huss and Isak Comandore rode the front seat, with Sam Salazar perched behind. They approached the keep, and without giving so much as a sign or a nod, drove through the gate into the courtyard.

Isak Comandore unfolded his long legs, stepped to the ground like a spider; Hein Huss lowered himself with a grunt. Both went to their quarters, while Sam Salazar led the wagon to the jinxmen's warehouse.

Somewhat later Isak Comandore presented himself to Lord Faide, who had been waiting in his trophy room, forced to a show of indifference through considerations of position, dignity, and protocol. Isak Comandore stood in the doorway, grinning like a fox. Lord Faide eyed him with sour dislike, waiting for Comandore to speak. Hein Huss might have stationed himself an entire day, eyes placidly fixed on Lord Faide, awaiting the first word; Isak Comandore lacked the absolute serenity. He came a step forward. "I have returned from Wildwood."

"With what results?"

"I believe that it is possible to hoodoo the First Folk."

Hein Huss spoke from behind Comandore. "I believe that such an undertaking, if feasible, would be useless, irresponsible, and possibly dangerous." He lumbered forward.

Isak Comandore's eyes glowed hot red-brown; he turned back to Lord Faide. "You ordered me forth on a mission; I will render a report."

"Seat yourselves. I will listen."

Isak Comandore, nominal head of the expedition, spoke. "We rode along the river bank to Forest Market. Here was no sign of disorder or of hostility. A hundred First Folk traded timber, planks, posts, and poles for knife blades, iron wire, and copper pots. When they returned to their barge, we followed them aboard, wagon, horses, and all. They showed no surprise—"

"Surprise," said Hein Huss heavily, "is an emotion of which they have no knowledge."

Isak Comandore glared briefly. "We spoke to the barge-tenders, explaining that we wished to visit the interior of Wildwood. We asked if the First Folk would try to kill us to prevent us from entering the forest. They professed indifference as to either our well-being or our destruction. This was by no means a guarantee of safe conduct; however, we accepted it as such, and remained aboard the barge." He spoke on with occasional emendations from Hein Huss.

They had proceeded up the river, into the forest, the First Folk poling against the slow current. Presently they put away the poles; nevertheless the barge moved as before. The mystified jinxmen discussed the possibility of teleportation, or symbological force, and wondered if the First Folk had developed jinxing techniques unknown to men. Sam Salazar, however, noticed that four enormous water beetles, each twelve feet long with oil-black carapaces and blunt heads, had risen from the river bed and pushed the barge from behind—apparently without direction or command. The First Folk stood at the bow, turning the nose of the barge this way or that to follow the winding of the river. They ignored the jinxmen and Sam Salazar as if they did not exist.

The beetles swam tirelessly; the barge moved for four hours as fast as a man could walk. Occasionally, First Folk peered from the forest shadows, but none showed interest or concern in the barge's unusual cargo. By midafternoon the river widened, broke into many channels and became a marsh; a few minutes later the barge floated out into the open water of a small lake. Along the shore, behind the first line of trees, appeared a large settlement. The jinxmen were interested and surprised. It had always been assumed that the First Folk wandered at random through the forest, as they had originally lived in the moss of the downs.

The barge grounded; the First Folk walked ashore, the Men followed with the horses and wagon. Their immediate impressions were

of swarming numbers, of slow but incessant activity, and they were
attacked by an overpoweringly evil smell.

Ignoring the stench, the men brought the wagon in from the shore,
paused to take stock of what they saw. The settlement appeared to
be a center of many diverse activities. The trees had been stripped of
lower branches, and supported blocks of hardened foam three hundred
feet long, fifty feet high, twenty feet thick, with a space of a man's
height intervening between the underside of the foam and the ground.
There were a dozen of these blocks, apparently of cellular construction.
Certain of the cells had broken open and seethed with small white
fishlike creatures—the First Folk young.

Below the blocks masses of First Folk engaged in various occupations,
in the main unfamiliar to the jinxmen. Leaving the wagon in the care of
Sam Salazar, Hein Huss and Isak Comandore moved forward among
the First Folk, repelled by the stench and the pressure of alien flesh,
but drawn by curiosity. They were neither heeded nor halted; they
wandered everywhere about the settlement. One area seemed to be an
enormous zoo, divided into a number of sections. The purpose of one
of these sections—a kind of range two hundred feet long—was all too
clear. At one end a human corpse hung on a rope—a Faide casualty
from the battle at the new planting. Certain of the wasps flew straight
at the corpse; just before contact they were netted and removed. Others
flew up and away or veered toward the First Folk who stood along the
side of the range. These latter also were netted and killed at once.

The purpose of the business was clear enough. Examining some of
the other activity in this new light, the jinxmen were able to interpret
much that had hitherto puzzled them.

They saw beetles tall as dogs with heavy saw-toothed pincers attacking objects resembling horses; pens of insects even larger, long,
narrow, segmented, with dozens of heavy legs and nightmare heads.
All these creatures—wasps, beetles, centipedes—in smaller and less
formidable form were indigenous to the forest; it was plain that the First
Folk had been practicing selective breeding for many years, perhaps
centuries.

Not all the activity was warlike. Moths were trained to gather nuts, worms to gnaw straight holes through timber; in another section caterpillars chewed a yellow mash, molded it into identical spheres. Much of the evil odor emanated from the zoo; the jinxmen departed without reluctance, and returned to the wagon. Sam Salazar pitched the tent and built a fire, while Hein Huss and Isak Comandore discussed the settlement.

Night came; the blocks of foam glowed with imprisoned light; the activity underneath proceeded without cessation. The jinxmen retired to the tent and slept, while Sam Salazar stood guard.

The following day Hein Huss was able to engage one of the First Folk in conversation; it was the first attention of any sort given to them.

The conversation was long; Hein Huss reported only the gist of it to Lord Faide. (Isak Comandore turned away, ostentatiously disassociating himself from the matter.)

Hein Huss first of all had inquired as to the purpose of the sinister preparations: the wasps, beetles, centipedes, and the like.

"We intend to kill men," the creature had reported ingenuously. "We intend to return to the moss. This has been our purpose ever since men appeared on the planet."

Huss had stated that such an ambition was shortsighted, that there was ample room for both men and First Folk on Pangborn. "The First Folk," said Hein Huss, "should remove their traps and cease their efforts to surround the keeps with forest."

"No," came the response. "Men are intruders. They mar the beautiful moss. All will be killed."

Isak Comandore returned to the conversation. "I noticed here a significant fact. All the First Folk within sight had ceased their work; all looked toward us, as if they, too, participated in the discussion. I reached the highly important conclusion that the First Folk are not complete individuals but components of a larger unity, joined to a greater or less extent by a telepathic phase not unlike our own."

Hein Huss continued placidly, "I remarked that if we were attacked, many of the First Folk would perish. The creature showed no concern, and in fact implied much of what Jinxman Comandore had already induced: 'There are always more in the cells to replace the elements which die. But if the community becomes sick, all suffer. We have been forced into the forests, into a strange existence. We must arm ourselves and drive away the men, and to this end we have developed the methods of men to our own purposes!'"

Isak Comandore spoke. "Needless to say, the creature referred to the ancient men, not ourselves."

"In any event," said Lord Faide, "they leave no doubt as to their intentions. We should be fools not to attack them at once, with every weapon at our disposal."

Hein Huss continued imperturbably. "The creature went on at some length. 'We have learned the value of irrationality.' 'Irrationality' of course was not his word or even his meaning. He said something like 'a series of vaguely motivated trials'—as close as I can translate. He said, 'We have learned to change our environment. We use insects and trees and plants and waterslugs. It is an enormous effort for us who would prefer a placid life in the moss. But you men have forced this life on us, and now you must suffer the consequences.' I pointed out once more that men were not helpless, that many First Folk would die. The creature seemed unworried. 'The community persists.' I asked a delicate question, 'If your purpose is to kill men, why do you allow us here?' He said, 'The entire community of men will be destroyed.' Apparently they believe the human society to be similar to their own, and therefore regard the killing of three wayfaring individuals as pointless effort."

Lord Faide laughed grimly. "To destroy us, they must first win past Hellmouth, then penetrate Faide Keep. This they are unable to do."

Isak Comandore resumed his report. "At this time I was already convinced that the problem was one of hoodooing not an individual but an entire race. In theory this should be no more difficult than hoodooing one. It requires no more effort to speak to twenty than to one. With this end in view, I ordered the apprentice to collect substances associated with the creatures. Skinflakes, foam, droppings, all other exudations obtainable. While he did so, I tried to put myself in rapport with the creatures. It is difficult, for their telepathy works across a different stratum from ours. Nevertheless, to a certain extent I have succeeded."

"Then you can hoodoo the First Folk?" asked Lord Faide.

"I vouchsafe nothing until I try. Certain preparations must be made."

"Go then; make your preparations."

Comandore rose to his feet and with a sly side glance for Hein Huss left the room. Huss waited, pinching his chin with heavy fingers. Lord Faide looked at him coldly. "You have something to add?"

Huss grunted, hoisted himself to his feet. "I wish that I did. But my thoughts are confused. Of the many futures, all seem troubled and angry. Perhaps our best is not good enough."

Lord Faide looked at Hein Huss with surprise; the massive Head Jinxman had never before spoken in terms so pessimistic and melancholy. "Speak then; I will listen."

Hein Huss said gruffly, "If I knew any certainties, I would speak gladly. But I am merely beset by doubts. I fear that we can no longer depend on logic and careful jinxmanship. Our ancestors were miracle workers, magicians. They drove the First Folk into the forest. To put us to flight in our turn, the First Folk have adopted the ancient methods: random trial and purposeless empiricism. I am dubious. Perhaps we must turn our backs on sanity and likewise return to the mysticism of our ancestors."

Lord Faide shrugged. "If Isak Comandore can hoodoo the First Folk, such a retreat may be unnecessary."

"The world changes," said Hein Huss. "Of so much I feel sure: The old days of craft and careful knowledge are gone. The future is for men of cleverness, and imagination untroubled by discipline; the unorthodox Sam Salazar may become more effective than I. The world changes."

Lord Faide smiled his sour, dyspeptic smile. "When that day comes, I will appoint Sam Salazar Head Jinxman and also name him Lord Faide, and you and I will retire together to a hut on the downs."

Hein Huss made a heavy, fateful gesture and departed.

X

Two days later Lord Faide, coming upon Isak Comandore, inquired as to his progress. Comandore took refuge in generalities. After another two days, Lord Faide inquired again and this time insisted on particulars. Comandore grudgingly led the way to his workroom, where a dozen cabalmen, spellbinders, and apprentices worked around a large table, building a model of the First Folk settlement in Wildwood.

"Along the lakeshore," said Comandore, "I will range a great number of dolls, daubed with First Folk essences. When this is complete I will work up a hoodoo and blight the creatures."

"Good. Perform well." Lord Faide departed the workroom, mounted to the topmost pinnacle of the keep, to the cupola where the ancestral weapon Hellmouth was housed. "Jambart! Where are you?"

Weapon-tender Jambart, short, blue-jowled, red-nosed and big-bellied, appeared. "My lord?"

"I come to inspect Hellmouth. It is prepared for instant use?"

"Prepared, my lord, and ready. Oiled, greased, polished, scraped, burnished, tended—every part smooth as an egg."

Lord Faide made a scowling examination of Hellmouth—a heavy cylinder six feet in diameter, twelve feet long, studded with half-domes interconnected with tubes of polished copper. Jambart undoubtedly had been diligent. No trace of dirt or rust or corrosion showed; all was gleaming metal. The snout was covered with a heavy plate of metal and tarred canvas; the ring upon which the weapon swiveled was well greased.

Lord Faide surveyed the four horizons. To the south was fertile Faide Valley; to the west, open downs; to north and east, the menacing loom of Wildwood.

He turned back to Hellmouth and pretended to find a smear of grease. Jambart boiled with expostulations and protestations; Lord Faide uttered a grim warning, enjoining less laxity, then descended to the workroom of Hein Huss. He found the Head Jinxman reclining on a couch, staring at the ceiling. At a bench stood Sam Salazar surrounded by bottles, flasks, and dishes.

Lord Faide stared balefully at the confusion. "What are you doing?" he asked the apprentice.

Sam Salazar looked up guiltily. "Nothing in particular, my lord."

"If you are idle, go then and assist Isak Comandore."

"I am not idle, Lord Faide."

"Then what do you do?"

Sam Salazar gazed sulkily at the bench. "I don't know."

"Then you are idle!"

"No, I am occupied. I pour various liquids on this foam. It is First Folk foam. I wonder what will happen. Water does not dissolve it, nor spirits. Heat chars and slowly burns it, emitting a foul smoke."

Lord Faide turned away with a sneer. "You amuse yourself as a child might. Go to Isak Comandore; he can find use for you. How do you expect to become a jinxman, dabbling and prattling like a baby among pretty rocks?"

Hein Huss gave a deep sound; a mingling of sigh, snort, grunt, and clearing of the throat. "He does no harm, and Isak Comandore has hands enough. Salazar will never become a jinxman; that has been clear a long time."

Lord Faide shrugged. "He is your apprentice, and your responsibility. Well, then. What news from the keeps?"

Hein Huss, groaning and wheezing, swung his legs over the edge of the couch. "The lords share your concern, to greater or lesser extent. Your close allies will readily place troops at your disposal; the others likewise if pressure is brought to bear."

Lord Faide nodded in dour satisfaction. "For the moment there is no urgency. The First Folk hold to their forests. Faide Keep of course is impregnable, although they might ravage the valley..." he paused thoughtfully. "Let Isak Comandore cast his hoodoo. Then we will see."

From the direction of the bench came a hiss, a small explosion, a whiff of acrid gas. Sam Salazar turned guiltily to look at them, his eyebrows singed. Lord Faide gave a snort of disgust and strode from the room.

"What did you do?" Hein Huss inquired in a colorless voice.

"I don't know."

Now Hein Huss likewise snorted in disgust. "Ridiculous. If you wish to work miracles, you must remember your procedures. Miracle working is not jinxmanship, with established rules and guides. In matters so complex, it is well that you take notes, so that the miracles may be repeated."

Sam Salazar nodded in agreement and turned back to the bench.

XI

Late during the day, news of new First Folk truculence reached Faide Keep. On Honeymoss Hill, not far west of Forest Market, a camp of shepherds had been visited by a wandering group of First Folk, who began to kill the sheep with thorn-swords. When the shepherds protested, they, too, were attacked, and many were killed. The remainder of the sheep were massacred.

The following day came other news: four children swimming in Brastock River at Gilbert Ferry had been seized by enormous water-beetles and cut into pieces. On the other side of Wildwood, in the foothills immediately below Castle Cloud, peasants had cleared several hillsides and planted them to vines. Early in the morning they had discovered a horde of black disklike flukes devouring the vines—leaves, branches, trunks, and roots. They set about killing the flukes with spades and at once were stung to death by wasps.

Adam Me Adam reported the incidents to Lord Faide, who went to Isak Comandore in a fury. "How soon before you are prepared?"

"I am prepared now. But I must rest and fortify myself. Tomorrow morning I work the hoodoo."

"The sooner the better! The creatures have left their forest; they are out killing men!"

Isak Comandore pulled his long chin. "That was to be expected; they told us as much."

Lord Faide ignored the remark. "Show me your tableau."

Isak Comandore took him into his workroom. The model was now complete, with the masses of simulated First Folk properly daubed and sensitized, each tied with a small wad of foam. Isak Comandore pointed to a pot of dark liquid. "I will explain the basis of the hoodoo. When I visited the camp, I watched everywhere for powerful symbols. Undoubtedly there were many at hand, but I could not discern them. However, I remembered a circumstance from the battle at the planting; when the creatures were attacked, threatened with fire and about to die, they spewed foam of dull purple color. Evidently this purple foam is associated with death. My hoodoo will be based upon this symbol."

"Rest well, then, so that you may hoodoo to your best capacity."

The following morning Isak Comandore dressed in long robes of black and set a mask of the demon Nard on his head to fortify himself. He entered his workroom, closed the door.

An hour passed, two hours. Lord Faide sat at breakfast with his kin, stubbornly maintaining a pose of cynical unconcern. At last he could contain himself no longer and went out into the courtyard, where Comandore's underlings stood fidgeting and uneasy. "Where is Hein Huss?" demanded Lord Faide. "Summon him here."

Hein Huss came stumping out of his quarters. Lord Faide motioned to Comandore's workshop. "What is happening? Is he succeeding?"

Hein Huss looked toward the workshop. "He is casting a powerful hoodoo. I feel confusion, anger–"

"In Comandore, or in the First Folk?"

"I am not in rapport. I think he has conveyed a message to their minds. A very difficult task, as I explained to you. In this preliminary aspect he has succeeded."

" 'Preliminary?' What else remains?"

"The two most important elements of the hoodoo: the susceptibility of the victim and the appropriateness of the symbol."

Lord Faide frowned. "You do not seem optimistic."

"I am uncertain. Isak Comandore may be right in his assumption. If so, and if the First Folk are highly susceptible, today marks a great victory, and Comandore will achieve tremendous *mana!*"

Lord Faide stared at the door to the workshop. "What now?"

Hein Huss's eyes went blank with concentration. "Isak Comandore is near death. He can hoodoo no more today."

Lord Faide turned, waved his arm to the cabalmen. "Enter the workroom! Assist your master!"

The cabalmen raced to the door, flung it open. Presently they emerged supporting the limp form of Isak Comandore, his black robe spattered with purple foam. Lord Faide pressed close. "What did you achieve? Speak!"

Isak Comandore's eyes were half closed, his mouth hung loose and wet. "I spoke to the First Folk, to the whole race. I sent the symbol into their minds—" His head fell limply side wise.

Lord Faide moved back. "Take him to his quarters. Put him on his couch." He turned away, stood indecisively, chewing at his drooping lower lip. "Still we do not know the measure of his success."

"Ah," said Hein Huss, "but we do!"

Lord Faide jerked around. "What is this? What do you say?"

"I saw into Comandore's mind. He used the symbol of the purple foam; with tremendous effort he drove it into their minds. Then he learned that purple foam means not death—purple foam means fear for the safety of the community, purple foam means desperate rage."

"In any event," said Lord Faide after a moment, "there is no harm done. The First Folk can hardly become more hostile."

Three hours later a scout rode furiously into the courtyard, threw himself off his horse, ran to Lord Faide. "The First Folk have left the forest! A tremendous number! Thousands! They are advancing on Faide Keep!"

"Let them advance!" said Lord Faide. "The more the better! Jambart, where are you?"

"Here, sir."

"Prepare Hellmouth! Hold all in readiness!"

"Hellmouth is always ready, sir!"

Lord Faide struck him across the shoulders. "Off with you! Bernard!"

The sergeant of the Faide troops came forward. "Ready, Lord Faide."

"The First Folk attack. Armor your men against wasps, feed them well. We will need all our strength."

Lord Faide turned to Hein Huss. "Send to the keeps, to the manor houses, order our kinsmen to join us, with all their troops and all their armor. Send to Bellgard Hall, to Boghoten, Camber, and Candelwade. Haste, haste, it is only hours from Wildwood."

Huss held up his hand. "I have already done so. The keeps are warned. They know your need."

"And the First Folk—can you feel their minds?"

"No."

Lord Faide walked away. Hein Huss lumbered out the main gate, walked around the keep, casting appraising glances up the black walls of the squat towers, windowless and proof even against the ancient miracle-weapons. High on top of the great parasol roof, Jambart the weapon-tender worked in the cupola, polishing that which already glistened, greasing surfaces already heavy with grease.

Hein Huss returned within. Lord Faide approached him, mouth hard, eyes bright. "What have you seen?"

"Only the keep, the walls, the towers, the roof, and Hellmouth."

"And what do you think?"

"I think many things."

"You are noncommittal; you know more than you say. It is best that you speak, because if Faide Keep falls to the savages, you die with the rest of us."

Hein Huss's water-clear eyes met the brilliant black gaze of Lord Faide. "I know only what you know. The First Folk attack. They have proved they are not stupid. They intend to kill us. They are not jinxmen; they cannot afflict us or force us out. They cannot break in the walls. To burrow under, they must dig through solid rock. What are their plans? I do not know. Will they succeed? Again, I do not know. But the day of the jinxman and his orderly array of knowledge is past. I think that we must grope for miracles, blindly and foolishly, like Salazar pouring liquids on foam."

A troop of armored horsemen rode in through the gates: warriors from nearby Bellgard Hall. And as the hours passed, contingents from other keeps came to Faide Keep, until the courtyard was dense with troops and horses.

Two hours before sunset the First Folk were sighted across the downs. They seemed a very large company, moving in an undisciplined clot with a number of stragglers, forerunners and wanderers out on the flanks.

The hotbloods from outside keeps came clamoring to Lord Faide, urging a charge to cut down the First Folk; they found no seconding voices among the veterans of the battle at the planting. Lord Faide, however, was pleased to see the dense mass of First Folk. "Let them approach only a mile more—and Hellmouth will take them! Jambart!"

"At your call, Lord Faide."

"Come, Hellmouth speaks!" He strode away with Jambart after. Up to the cupola they climbed.

"Roll forth Hellmouth, direct it against the savages!"

Jambart leaped to the glistening array of wheels and levers. He hesitated in perplexity, then tentatively twisted a wheel. Hellmouth responded by twisting slowly around on its radial track, to the groan and chatter of long-frozen bearings. Lord Faide's brows lowered into a menacing line. "I hear evidence of neglect."

"Neglect, my lord, never! Find one spot of rust, a shadow of grime, you may have me whipped!"

"What is that sound?"

"That is internal and invisible—none of my responsibility."

Lord Faide said nothing. Hellmouth now pointed toward the great pale tide from Wild wood. Jambart twisted a second wheel and Hellmouth thrust forth its heavy snout. Lord Faide, in a voice harsh with anger, cried, "The cover, fool!"

"An oversight, my lord, easily repaired." Jambart crawled out along the top of Hellmouth, clinging to the protuberances for dear life, with below only the long, smooth sweep of roof. With considerable difficulty he tore the covering loose, then, grunting and cursing, inched himself back, jerking with his knees, rearing his buttocks.

The First Folk had slowed their pace a trifle, the main body only a half-mile distant.

"Now," said Lord Faide in high excitement, "before they disperse, we exterminate them!" He sighted through a telescopic tube, squinting through the dimness of internal films and incrustations, signaled to Jambart for the final adjustments. "Now! Fire!"

Jambart pulled the firing lever. Within the great metal barrel came a sputter of clicking sounds. Hellmouth whined, roared. Its snout glowed red, orange, white, and out poured a sudden gout of blazing purple radiation—which almost instantly died. Hellmouth's barrel quivered with heat, fumed, seethed, hissed. From within came a faint pop. Then there was silence.

A hundred yards in front of the First Folk a patch of moss burnt black where the bolt had struck. The aiming device was inaccurate. Hellmouth's bolt had killed perhaps twenty of the First Folk vanguard.

Lord Faide made feverish signals. "Quick! Raise the barrel. Now! Fire again!"

Jambart pulled the firing arm, to no avail. He tried again, with the same lack of success. "Hellmouth evidently is tired."

"Hellmouth is dead," cried Lord Faide. "You have failed me. Hellmouth is extinct."

"No, no," protested Jambart. "Hellmouth rests! I nurse it as my own child! It is polished like glass! Whenever a section wears off or breaks loose, I neatly remove the fracture, and every trace of cracked glass."

Lord Faide threw up his arms, shouted in vast, inarticulate grief, ran below. "Huss! Hein Huss!"

Hein Huss presented himself. "What is your will?"

"Hellmouth has given up its fire. Conjure up more fire for Hellmouth, and quickly!"

"Impossible."

"Impossible!" cried Lord Faide. "That is all I hear from you! Impossible, useless, impractical! You have lost your ability. I will consult Isak Comandore."

"Isak Comandore can put no more fire into Hellmouth than can I."

"What sophistry is this? He puts demons into men, surely he can put fire into Hellmouth!"

"Come, Lord Faide, you are overwrought. You know the difference between jinxmanship and miracle-working."

Lord Faide motioned to a servant. "Bring Isak Comandore here to me!"

Isak Comandore, face haggard, skin waxy, limped into the courtyard. Lord Faide waved preemptorily. "I need your skill. You must restore fire to Hellmouth."

Comandore darted a quick glance at Hein Huss, who stood solid and cold. Comandore decided against dramatic promises that could not be fulfilled. "I cannot do this, my lord."

"What! You tell me this, too?"

"Remark the difference, Lord Faide, between man and metal. A man's normal state is something near madness; he is at all times balanced on a knife-edge between hysteria and apathy. His senses tell him far less of the world than he thinks they do. It is a simple trick to deceive a man, to possess him with a demon, to drive him out of his mind, to kill him. But metal is insensible; metal reacts only as its shape and condition dictates, or by the working of miracles."

"Then you must work miracles!"

"Impossible."

Lord Faide drew a deep breath, collected himself. He walked swiftly across the court. "My armor, my horse. We attack."

The column formed, Lord Faide at the head. He led the knights through the portals, with armored footmen behind.

"Beware the foam!" called Lord Faide. "Attack, strike, cut, draw back. Keep your visors drawn against the wasps! Each man must kill a hundred! Attack!"

The troop rode forth against the horde of First Folk, knights in the lead. The hooves of the horses pounded softly over the thick moss; in the west the large pale sun hung close to the horizon.

Two hundred yards from the First Folk the knights touched the club-headed horses into a lope. They raised their swords, and shouting, plunged forward, each man seeking to be first. The clotted mass of First Folk separated; black beetles darted forth and after them long, seg-mented centipede creatures. They dashed among the horses, mandibles clicking, snouts slashing. Horses screamed, reared, fell over backwards; beetles cut open armored knights as a dog cracks a bone. Lord Faide's horse threw him and ran away; he picked himself up, hacked at a nearby beetle, lopped off its front leg. It darted forward, he lopped off the leg opposite; the heavy head dipped, tore up the moss. Lord Faide cut off the remaining legs, and it lay helpless.

"Retreat," he bellowed. "Retreat!"

The knights moved back, slashing and hacking at beetles and cen-tipedes, killing or disabling all which attacked.

"Form into a double line, knights and men. Advance slowly, sup-porting each other!"

The men advanced. The First Folk dispersed to meet them, armed with their thorn-swords and carrying pouches. Ten yards from the men, they reached into the pouches, brought forth dark balls which they threw at the men. The balls broke and spattered on the armor.

"Charge!" bawled Lord Faide. The men sprang forward into the mass of First Folk, cutting, slashing, killing. "Kill!" called Lord Faide in exultation. "Leave not one alive!"

A pang struck him, a sting inside his armor, followed by another and another. Small things crawled inside the metal, stinging, biting, crawling. He looked about: On all sides were harassed expressions, faces working in anguish. Sword arms fell limp as hands beat on the metal, futilely trying to scratch, rub. Two men suddenly began to tear off their armor.

"Retreat," cried Lord Faide. "Back to the keep!"

The retreat was a rout, the soldiers shedding articles of armor as they ran. After them came a flight of wasps—a dozen or more, and half as many men cried out as the poison prongs struck into their backs.

Inside the keep stormed the disorganized company, casting aside the last of their armor, slapping their skin, scratching, rubbing, crushing the ferocious red mites that infested them.

"Close the gates," roared Lord Faide.

The gates slid shut. Faide Keep was besieged.

XII

During the night the First Folk surrounded the keep, forming a ring fifty yards from the walls. All night there was motion, ghostly shapes coming and going in the starlight.

Lord Faide watched from a parapet until midnight, with Hein Huss at his side. Repeatedly, he asked, "What of the other keeps? Do they send further reinforcements?" to which Hein Huss each time gave the same reply: "There is confusion and doubt. The keep-lords are anxious to help but do not care to throw themselves away. At this moment they consider and take stock of the situation."

Lord Faide at last left the parapet, signaling Hein Huss to follow. He went to his trophy room, threw himself into a chair, motioned Hein Huss to be seated. For a moment he fixed the jinxman with a cool, calculating stare. Hein Huss bore the appraisal without discomfort.

"You are Head Jinxman," said Lord Faide finally. "For twenty years you have worked spells, cast hoodoos, performed auguries—more effectively than any other jinxman of Pangborn. But now I find you inept and listless. Why is this?"

"I am neither inept or listless. I am unable to achieve beyond my abilities. I do not know how to work miracles. For this you must consult my apprentice Sam Salazar, who does not know either, but who earnestly tries every possibility and many impossibilities."

"You believe in this nonsense yourself! Before my very eyes you become a mystic!"

Hein Huss shrugged. "There are limitations to my knowledge. Miracles occur—that we know. The relics of our ancestors lie everywhere. Their methods were supernatural, repellent to our own mental processes—but think! Using these same methods, the First Folk threaten to destroy us. In the place of metal they use living flesh—but the result is similar. The men of Pangborn, if they assemble and accept casualties, can drive the First Folk back to Wildwood—but for how long? A year? Ten years? The First Folk plant new trees, dig more traps—and presently come forth again, with more terrible weapons: flying beetles, large as a horse, wasps strong enough to pierce armor, lizards to scale the walls of Faide Keep."

Lord Faide pulled at his chin. "And the jinxmen are helpless?"

"You saw for yourself. Isak Comandore intruded enough into their consciousness to anger them, no more."

"So then—what must we do?"

Hein Huss held out his hands. "I do not know. I am Hein Huss, jinxman. I watch Sam Salazar with fascination. He learns nothing, but he is either too stupid or too intelligent to be discouraged. If this is the way to work miracles, he will work them."

Lord Faide rose to his feet. "I am deathly tired. I cannot think, I must sleep. Tomorrow we will know more."

Hein Huss left the trophy room, returned to the parapet. The ring of First Folk seemed closer to the walls, almost within dart-range. Behind them and across the moors stretched a long pale column of marching

First Folk. A little back from the keep a pile of white material began to grow, larger and larger as the night proceeded.

Hours passed, the sky lightened; the sun rose in the east. The First Folk tramped the downs like ants, bringing long bars of hardened foam down from the north, dropping them into piles around the keep, returning into the north once more.

Lord Faide came up on the parapet, haggard and unshaven. "What is this? What do they do?"

Bernard the sergeant responded. "They puzzle us all, my lord."

"Hein Huss! What of the other keeps?"

"They have armed and mounted; they approach cautiously."

"Can you communicate our urgency?"

"I can, and I have done so. I have only accentuated their caution."

"Bah!" cried Lord Faide in disgust. "Warriors they call themselves! Loyal and faithful allies!"

"They know of your bitter experience," said Hein Huss. "They ask themselves, reasonably enough, what they can accomplish which you who are already here cannot do first."

Lord Faide laughed sourly. "I have no answer for them. In the meantime we must protect ourselves against the wasps. Armor is useless; they drive us mad with mites... Bernard!"

"Yes, Lord Faide."

"Have each of your men construct a frame two-feet square, fixed with a short handle. To these frames should be sewed a net of heavy mesh. When these frames are built, we will sally forth, two soldiers to guard one half-armored knight on foot."

"In the meantime," said Hein Huss, "the First Folk proceed with their plans."

Lord Faide turned to watch. The First Folk came close up under the walls carrying rods of hardened foam. "Bernard! Put your archers to work! Aim for the heads!"

Along the walls bowmen cocked their weapons. Darts spun down into the First Folk. A few were affected, turned and staggered away;

others plucked away the bolts without concern. Another flight of bolts, a few more First Folk were disabled. The others planted the rods in the moss, exuded foam in great gushes, their back-flaps vigorously pumping air. Other First Folk brought more rods, pushed them into the foam. Entirely around the keep, close under the walls, extended the mound of foam. The ring of First Folk now came close and all gushed foam; it bulked up swiftly. More rods were brought, thrust into the foam, reinforcing and stiffening the mass.

"More darts!" barked Lord Faide. "Aim for the heads! Bernard—your men, have they prepared the wasp nets?"

"Not yet, Lord Faide. The project requires some little time."

Lord Faide became silent. The foam, now ten feet high, rapidly piled higher. Lord Faide turned to Hein Huss. "What do they hoped to achieve?"

Hein Huss shook his head. "For the moment I am uncertain."

The first layer of foam had hardened; on top of this the First Folk spewed another layer, reinforcing again with the rods, crisscrossing, horizontal and vertical. Fifteen minutes later, when the second layer was hard, the First Folk emplaced and mounted rude ladders to raise a third layer. Surrounding the keep now was a ring of foam thirty feet high and forty feet thick at the base.

"Look," said Hein Huss. He pointed up. The parasol roof overhanging the walls ended only thirty feet above the foam. "A few more layers and they will reach the roof."

"So then?" asked Lord Faide. "The roof is as strong as the walls."

"And we will be sealed within."

Lord Faide studied the foam in the light of this new thought. Already the First Folk, climbing laboriously up ladders along the outside face of their wall of foam, were preparing to lay on a fourth layer. First—rods, stiff and dry, then great gushes of white. Only twenty feet remained between roof and foam.

Lord Faide turned to the sergeant. "Prepare the men to sally forth."

"What of the wasp nets, sir?"

"Are they almost finished?"

"Another ten minutes, sir."

"Another ten minutes will see us smothering. We must force a passage through the foam."

Ten minutes passed, and fifteen. The First Folk created ramps behind their wall: first dozens of the rods, then foam, and on top, to distribute the weight, reed mats.

Bernard the sergeant reported to Lord Faide. "We are ready."

"Good." Lord Faide descended into the courtyard. He faced the men, gave them their orders. "Move quickly, but stay together; we must not lose ourselves in the foam. As we proceed, slash ahead and to the sides. The First Folk see through the foam; they have the advantage of us. When we break through, we use the wasp nets. Two foot soldiers must guard each knight. Remember, quickly through the foam, that we do not smother. Open the gates."

The gates slid back, the troops marched forth. They faced an unbroken blank wall of foam. No enemy could be seen.

Lord Faide waved his sword. "Into the foam." He strode forward, pushed into the white mass, now crisp and brittle and harder than he had bargained for. It resisted him; he cut and hacked. His troops joined him, carving a way into the foam. First Folk appeared above them, crawling carefully on the mats. Their back flaps puffed, pumped; foam issued from their vents, falling in a cascade over the troops.

Hein Huss sighed. He spoke to Apprentice Sam Salazar. "Now they must retreat, otherwise they smother. If they fail to win through, we all smother."

Even as he spoke, the foam, piling up swiftly, in places reached the roof. Below, bellowing and cursing, Lord Faide backed out from under, wiped his face clear. Once again, in desperation, he charged forward, trying at a new spot.

The foam was friable and cut easily, but the chunks detached still blocked the opening. And again down tumbled a cascade of foam, covering the soldiers.

Lord Faide retreated, waved his men back into the keep. At the same moment, First Folk, crawling on mats on the same level as the parapet over the gate, laid rods up from the foam to rest against the projecting edge of the roof. They gushed foam; the view of the sky was slowly blocked from the view of Hein Huss and Sam Salazar.

"In an hour, perhaps two, we will die," said Hein Huss. "They have now sealed us in. There are many men here in the keep, and all will now breathe deeply."

Sam Salazar said nervously, "There is a possibility we might be able to survive—or at least not smother."

"Ah?" inquired Hein Huss with heavy sarcasm. "You plan to work a miracle?"

"If a miracle, the most trivial sort. I observed that water has no effect on the foam, nor a number of other liquids: milk, spirits, wine, or caustic. Vinegar, however, instantly dissolves the foam."

"Aha," said Hein Huss. "We must inform Lord Faide."

"Better that you do so," said Sam Salazar. "He will pay me no heed."

XIII

Half an hour passed. Light filtered into Faide Keep only as a dim gray gloom. Air tasted flat, damp, and heavy. Out from the gates sallied the troops. Each carried a crock, a jug, a skin, or a pan containing strong vinegar.

"Quickly now," called Lord Faide, "but careful! Spare the vinegar, don't throw it wildly. In close formation now—forward."

The soldiers approached the wall, threw ladles of vinegar ahead. The foam crackled, melted.

"Waste no vinegar," shouted Lord Faide, "Forward, quickly now; bring forward the vinegar!"

Minutes later they burst out upon the downs. The First Folk stared at them, blinking.

"Charge," croaked Lord Faide, his throat thick with fumes. "Mind now, wasp nets! Two soldiers to each knight! Charge, double-quick. Kill the white beasts."

The men dashed ahead. Wasp tubes were leveled. "Halt!" yelled Lord Faide. "Wasps!"

The wasps came, wings rasping. Nets rose up; wasps struck with a thud. Down went the nets; hard feet crushed the insects. The beetles and the lizard-centipedes appeared, not so many as of the last evening, for a great number had been killed. They darted forward, and a score of men died, but the insects were soon hacked into chunks of reeking brown flesh. Wasps flew, and some struck home; the agonies of the dying men were unnerving. Presently the wasps likewise decreased in number, and soon there were no more.

The men faced the First Folk, armored only with thorn-swords and their foam, which now came purple with rage.

Lord Faide waved his sword: The men advanced and began to kill the First Folk, by dozens, by hundreds.

Hein Huss came forth and approached Lord Faide. "Call a halt."

"A halt? Why? Now we kill these bestial things."

"Far better not. Neither need kill the other. Now is the time to show great wisdom."

"They have besieged us, caught us in their traps, stung us with their wasps! And you say halt?"

"They nourish a grudge sixteen hundred years old. Best not to add another one."

Lord Faide stared at Hein Huss. "What do you propose?"

"Peace between the two races, peace and cooperation."

"Very well. No more traps, no more plantings, no more breeding of deadly insects."

"Call back your men. I will try."

Lord Faide cried out, "Men, fall back. Disengage."

Reluctantly the troops drew back. Hein Huss approached the huddled mass of purple-foaming First Folk. He waited a moment. They watched him intently. He spoke in their language.

"You have attacked Faide Keep; you have been defeated. You planned well, but we have proved stronger. At this moment we can kill you. Then we can go on to fire the forest, starting a hundred blazes. Some of the fires you can control. Others not. We can destroy Wild Wood. Some First Folk may survive, to hide in the thickets and breed new plans to kill men. This we do not want. Lord Faide has agreed to peace, if you likewise agree. This means no more death traps. Men will freely approach and pass through the forests. In your turn you may freely come out on the moss. Neither race shall molest the other. Which do you choose? Extinction—or peace?"

The purple foam no longer dribbled from the vents of the First Folk. "We choose peace."

"There must be no more wasps, beetles. The death traps must be disarmed and never replaced."

"We agree. In our turn we must be allowed freedom of the moss."

"Agreed. Remove your dead and wounded, haul away the foam rods."

Hein Huss returned to Lord Faide. "They have chosen peace."

Lord Faide nodded. "Very well. It is for the best." He called to his men. "Sheathe your weapons. We have won a great victory." He ruefully surveyed Faide Keep, swathed in foam and invisible except for the parasol roof. "A hundred barrels of vinegar will not be enough."

Hein Huss looked off into the sky. "Your allies approach quickly. Their jinxmen have told them of your victory."

Lord Faide laughed his sour laugh. "To my allies will fall the task of removing the foam from Faide Keep."

XIV

In the hall of Faide Keep, during the victory banquet, Lord Faide called jovially across to Hein Huss. "Now, Head Jinxman, we must deal with your apprentice, the idler and the waster Sam Salazar."

"He is here, Lord Faide. Rise, Sam Salazar, take cognizance of the honor being done you."

Sam Salazar rose to his feet, bowed.

Lord Faide proffered him a cup. "Drink, Sam Salazar, enjoy yourself. I freely admit that your idiotic tinkerings saved the lives of us all. Sam Salazar, we salute you, and thank you. Now, I trust that you will put frivolity aside, apply yourself to your work, and learn honest jinxmanship. When the time comes, I promise that you shall find a lifetime of employment at Faide Keep."

"Thank you," said Sam Salazar modestly. "However, I doubt if I will become a jinxman."

"No? You have other plans?"

Sam Salazar stuttered, grew faintly pink in the face, then straightened himself and spoke as clearly and distinctly as he could. "I prefer to continue what you call my frivolity. I hope I can persuade others to join me."

"Frivolity is always attractive," said Lord Faide. "No doubt you can find other idlers and wasters, runaway farm boys and the like."

Sam Salazar said staunchly, "This frivolity might become serious. Undoubtedly the ancients were barbarians. They used symbols to control entities they were unable to understand. We are methodical and rational; why can't we systematize and comprehend the ancient miracles?"

"Well, why can't we?" asked Lord Faide. "Does anyone have an answer?"

No one responded, although Isak Comandore hissed between his teeth and shook his head.

"I personally may never be able to work miracles; I suspect it is more complicated than it seems," said Sam Salazar. "However, I hope that you will arrange for a workshop where I and others who might share my views can make a beginning. In this matter I have the encouragement and the support of Head Jinxman Hein Huss."

Lord Faide lifted his goblet. "Very well, Apprentice Sam Salazar. Tonight I can refuse you nothing. You shall have exactly what you wish, and good luck to you. Perhaps you will produce a miracle during my lifetime."

Isak Comandore said huskily to Hein Huss, "This is a sad event! It signalizes intellectual anarchy, the degradation of jinxmanship, the prostitution of logic. Novelty has a way of attracting youth; already I see apprentices and spellbinders whispering in excitement. The jinx-men of the future will be sorry affairs. How will they go about demon-possession? With a cog, a gear, and a push-button. How will they cast a hoodoo? They will find it easier to strike their victim with an axe."

"Times change," said Hein Huss. "There is now the one rule of Faide on Pangborn, and the keeps no longer need to employ us. Perhaps I will join Sam Salazar in his workshop."

"You depict a depressing future," said Isak Comandore with a sniff of disgust.

"There are many futures, some of which are undoubtedly depressing."

Lord Faide raised his glass. "To the best of your many futures, Hein Huss. Who knows? Sam Salazar may conjure a spaceship to lead us back to home planet."

"Who knows?" said Hein Huss. He raised his goblet. "To the best of the futures!"

THE DEFENSE OF EUROPE

by Stefan T. Possony

Editor's Introduction

Dr. Stefan T. Possony received his Ph.D. from the University of Vienna in the early thirties. He worked for the anti-Nazi government of Austria until German forces occupied the country, and fled just ahead of the Gestapo. After many adventures, he came to the United States, where he was during World War II and for many years after that an intelligence specialist in the Pentagon. He then became a Senior Fellow at the Hoover Institution for War, Revolution, and Peace.

Dr. Possony and I have co-authored *The Strategy of Technology* and a number of shorter papers. He has been an invaluable contributor to the various reports and papers of the Citizens' Advisory Council on National Space Policy, and we are at present working on a new book, *The Strategy of Progress*.

I think of few people more competent to examine the knotty problem of the defense of Europe.

Introduction

During 1981–82, West German Chancellor Helmuth Schmidt's dying administration provoked a quarrel with U.S. General Bernard Rogers, Supreme Commander of NATO in Europe. Rogers had proposed that the modernization of NATO armaments was long overdue and that it would be feasible to neutralize the Soviet threat against Western Europe at affordable costs. He was not thinking that "Buck Rogers," his namesake, should design weapons of a totally new type, and he made no specific proposals. But he knew from his experiences in the U.S. Army that virtually all weapons were going to be altered by electronics. He was hinting that the Allies should stop limping behind in electronics, electronic countermeasures, sensors and computers.

Schmidt and his incompetent defense minister did not know what Rogers was talking about. The German military who were advising the government knew a part of what Rogers had been calling to their attention. After all, they must have heard of the interest in the "hyper-technology" that was preoccupying France's Aerospatiale, Britain's British Aerospace and West Germany's own Dornier Werke.

But they failed to understand General Rogers because their thinking was not preoccupied with hyper-technology in weapons. They were far more worried that Rogers was upsetting their budget and that, in his alleged naiveté, he was helping the anti-NATO "peace movement."

After Schmidt's departure, the quarrel stopped, but at this writing, it is too early to say that Rogers' point finally got through to the military brains of West Germany.

A Bit of Early History

The ancient Greeks went to battle on a chariot. The Romans were masters of road building. At the turn of the twentieth century, railroads—and since 1914, automobiles—have been moving the soldiers into battle. During two World Wars, tanks, later supplemented by armored personnel carriers and jeeps, were decisive. Rommel and Patton ran the battle from tanks equipped with radio communications.

What do modern weapons designers think is the battle chariot of the future? A small truck carrying a detachable container in which there stands a microprocessor loaded with software, modems and wireless communications.

The computer-on-a-truck is the ridiculous new weapon that military staffs and budgeteers have been slow in discovering and which they began to notice only after the military events in Falkland and in Lebanon.

Did a sudden and entirely unexpected technological revolution burst upon the world in 1982? Not quite.

The significance of strategic and tactical warning has been recognized since the 1950s. A first and improvised use of remotely piloted reconnaissance aircraft occurred as early as 1962, to collect intelligence from Cuba. In 1964, the Chinese shot down three American RPVs over Vietnam. During the early 1970s, "smart weapons" were used for highly accurate bombing attacks in Vietnam in the form of laser-guided bombs and jets riding on laser beams. Their precision was so unprecedented and "impossible" that the report of the U.S. Air Force on collateral casualties was simply disbelieved. (Note 1). In 1973, the Israelis suffered heavy aircraft losses and improvised the use in combat of target drones. In Falkland, radar guidance, including terminal guidance, and computers installed in the aircraft tail for flight control demonstrated new combinations.

Of course computers began their military career during World War II, when they were used to design the ULTRA code-breaking system and enabled physicists to build the atom bomb.

Missiles, in particular ICBMs, and telemetric tests and flight controls are forerunners of robots. Space satellites, especially recent versions, can be regarded as robots.

By 1984 the electronic revolution in defense is just beginning. Hence it is not practical to forecast where it will lead. Every day brings surprises. However, it is feasible to sketch how some of the new and upcoming capabilities might be incorporated into existing arsenals and how they might be utilized to solve some of the difficulties that are hampering current military missions.

Alternative Assumptions

How might the new electronic technology strengthen the defense of Europe against Soviet attack? In line with NATO tradition, this problem may first be discussed on the assumption that the Soviets would not use conventional, chemical or biological weapons. Thereupon the discussion may be resumed on the alternate assumption that the aggression would be executed with nuclear and other weapons of "mass destruction."

Right at this point trouble arises: The old dichotomy between "conventional" and "nuclear" war smacks of obsoleteness. The indispensable and meaningful question is this: Will the space systems be left untouched except perhaps for jamming, or will they be attacked prior to, or simultaneously with, the ground attack? This question is rarely asked.

Targets in space can be struck with conventional weapons like ASATS, which the Soviets have been testing. They also are subject to attack by historical forms of nuclear firepower like fusion. They are really vulnerable to nuclear weapons involving beams, or "directed energy," which are not yet ready for deployment. Under both the current conventional and nuclear dispensations, a space attack presumably would have to precede attack on the ground. Such an overture would abandon the asset of surprise. Considering the various difficulties of space attack, it is most logical to assume that in a conflict during the proximate future, the space systems will remain intact on both sides.

Accordingly, we will examine two different cases: Case 1, aggression without ABC and space weapons; and Case 2, aggression with ABC and space weapons. Note that space sensors and communications, as well as the entire C3 capability, lack the power to destroy. Therefore they are not considered to be "weapons."

Case 1

Ground aggression, schematically speaking, requires mobilization; forward moves to start and cover positions; force concentrations; crossing of the border; initial hostilities and penetrations; formation of a center of gravity; seizure and occupation of territory; decisive battle; establishment of technological and quantitative superiority on the battlefield; victory, occupation or imposed disarmament and change of government.

This scheme can be made more realistic by various complications, detours and prolongations, but in our discussion, simplicity is all that is needed.

If the aggression is waged against an opponent of approximately equivalent strength, success is dependent on some or all of the following factors: a substantial lead in mobilization; secrecy of the forward deployment; deception on the center of gravity; the location of follow-on echelons and reserves; and the preservation of technological, tactical and operational secrets. Abbreviated version: Success depends on concealment and deception.

Now, if the defender—the target of the aggression—is operating an up-to-date and properly deployed space-warning system of the appropriate size, the aggressor's mobilization will be noticed and so will his troop and arms concentrations, and his forward deployments. Aggression can no longer be prepared secretly. In addition, the space system will produce the aggressor's battle order together with its geographic locations, and it will indicate the movements of the attacking force, the approximate size of each column as well as the points of the attack and the locations of the reserves. Concealment and deception would succeed only if the opposing space system were inefficiently operated.

True, space intelligence may be reduced by weather, technical insufficiencies and defects, and limits of coverage. Moreover, the aggressor may be partially successful with his ruses and deception measures. Finally, if the victim does not react and does not increase and move his forces, the warning may be in vain.

Normally, if a victim state acquires a warning capability, it would be for the purpose of using it and acting on the information. European NATO's warning capability is rudimentary, and the members of the alliance must rely on U.S. signals. The manner by which the European NATO states plan to utilize American space warnings is as yet far from being optimized. At this writing, NATO has merely the potential to benefit from warning.

Nevertheless, the would-be aggressor, though he may hope to confuse the defender through countermeasures, must assume that the aggression will be detected from its first steps onward. If despite such a handicap he wishes to go through with his project, he must estimate that he possesses strength and operational superiority adequate to defeat the opponent. Under current circumstances, a Soviet planner would presumably assume that the USSR's numerical superiority in divisions, artillery, tanks, troop carriers and aircraft negates the warning and provides high odds for success in battle.

Shortly before crossing the border, the aggressor is likely to launch air strikes, mainly to cripple the defending air force. Since the flight from the border to the targets is a matter of minutes, the aggressor may have a chance to catch the defending air force on the ground. If so, the experience from World War II would suggest that the defender will be more or less unable to recover.

But let us assume the warning system includes sensors that detect air movements before the attacking aircraft reach the border and that a space warning of the air strike reaches the defending command in near real time. It also may be assumed that the defending air force was alerted to the coming danger hours, or even days, ahead of time. In this case, a substantial portion of the defender's aircraft should succeed in starting before they are hit on the ground. Also, anti-air defenses would be ready for action. This implies that the defender can save a percentage of his bombers, which may redeploy to temporarily secure airfields or else proceed to execute a strike of their own. It implies also that an air battle would ensue, resulting in heavy losses for the aggressor, perhaps spelling failure of the aggressor's air plan.

Whether the defender's tactics would be partially or fully successful depends on unpredictable circumstances. The point is that the existence of an efficient warning system, paired to preparations for instant reaction upon warning, compels the planner of the aggression to anticipate a low probability of a successful air operation.

How would the conditions affecting the advance of an invading ground force be changed by the new technology? If history serves as a guide, the army planner would assume either that he will succeed in overrunning the defender's forces that are deployed near the border or that he will encounter only token resistance and therefore, if he is able to move with great speed, he will execute a deep penetration. He also might assume that while the defender has been warned, he lacks the capability to carry out an effective counter-deployment in time; nor could he possibly know where the counterforce would be optimally deployed.

For the defender, the battle at the frontier has always been an almost insoluble problem. The defender may have known that an attack was impending, but in most cases he lacked this knowledge, and he never knew the precise time and the precise direction of the assault. In addition, for reasons of operations, logistics, mobilization schedules and the need to maintain strategic reserves, the defender usually found it impractical, or even impossible, to deploy a strong force forward and engage battle in an orderly, planned fashion. Accordingly, defenders rarely tried to win the battle at the frontier, and if they attempted to stop the invasion immediately, they hardly ever succeeded and often paid a high price for their failure. (Example: the French in 1914 and 1940.)

What new capabilities are emerging that might enhance the power of the defender?

Let us look at robotics, cruise missiles, targeting, battlefield intelligence, C3I, accuracy and fire control.

Without wasting time on debating class operational models, battlefield robotics should be viewed as information-collectors and transmitters, as command relays, as specialized command posts, as ground weapons, and as air weapons.

When the U.S. Army was dragging its feet for more than ten years, Congress got into the act and insisted on an RPV program. Thereupon the army approved two major missions for remotely piloted vehicles: meterology and electronic support to the ground force.

The latter mission includes ELINT collection, ground-based radar jamming, communications jamming and battlefield surveillance linked with C3 in space. It is also planned to use RPVs for target acquisition, artillery fire direction and target designation. The system, together with data terminals and ground-control stations, and with anti-jam data links for reconnaissance, is scheduled to be deployed by 1985.

For the time being, merely the use of mini RPVs is envisaged, but the small robots will have interesting characteristics, to wit, real-time information through video and zoom video, long flight endurance, high survivability and short training time, as well as net, parachute and automatic recovery. Thus the RPVs are no longer viewed as "drones," and they are assigned to important missions. But no combat mission was approved.

Whether or not RPVs should be used as an "independent" weapons system is debatable. In their Beka Valley operation, the Israelis used missiles to knock out radars, and they jammed interceptors, which they also attacked with missiles using heat-seeking (infrared) guidance. In combination with AWACS-type command aircraft, and with propeller-driven planes carrying radar detection and analysis equipment, the Israelis were using RPVs. They went all out for electronic techniques and electronic countermeasures, and in particular they utilized the frequencies that their opponent employed to track the Israeli RPVs, to knock out the surface-to-air missiles of the Syrians.

Those tactics required RPVs as a major link in the combination. But bigger and more "independent" missions can be envisaged, especially if electronic warfare and anti-radar operations should grow in significance.

RPVs are usable for telecommunications relay, photo and radar recce, for SIGINT, ELINT and COMINT, for ECM such as jamming, saturation and deception, for target locating, target marking, fire control, air attack, and also for suppression and destruction, provided they are linked into space-based navigation systems and weapons-control systems and are equipped with special ammunition. The RPVs are divided into recoverable and non-recoverable equipment, the latter being chiefly cheap minis.

The combination of RPVs with helicopters for fast deployment and firepower could prove to be very potent.

The vulnerability of RPVs against interception must be reduced: They already offer a low radar profile and a weak IR signature, and they are flying very low. Presumably they can be built from non-reflecting materials. For missions requiring many sorties, RPVs probably will be more cost-effective than manned aircraft, especially since the Soviets must be expected to make excessive use of anti-air weapons. It is important to remember that a loss quota of 3 percent per sortie may result in the destruction of half an entire air force within a week.

Armed RPVs could carry out many jobs. However, numerous jobs must be accomplished without firepower. It is primarily important that there are plenty of RPVs with diversified capabilities. With their endurance of something like seven hours, they should be doing plenty of flying, close to the ground.

In comparison with RPVs, ground robots, including self-propelled vehicles, are lagging in development. There is no doubt, however, that they can make great contributions to defense.

As a minimum, the ground robots would discharge four major missions: in connection with the C3I system, collection of battlefield intelligence; exercise of mobility or the holding of territory; combat actions against selected stationary and mobile targets; on-the-spot tactical operations analysis.

Accordingly, a robot unit needs leadership groups equipped with a vehicle carrying computers, software and communications materiel plus vehicles transporting various sensors; plus manned and unmanned electronic support vehicles, including RPVs. Depending on its mission, the unit would also have weapons and ammunition. In fact, unless the robot unit is entirely stationary and mainly engages in passive tasks like surveillance, it requires firepower to protect the equipment and the crews, if any.

The intelligence would be secured by electronic means, also by photography and by observation, and much information would be received from higher command.

The mobile control station would be housed in a container mounted on the ground or on a truck, and its computer would be tied to plotting devices, teleprinter, display, communications, mappers, link interfaces, countermeasures and equipment to support air, land and sea operations.

Main targets include radars, tanks and apes (with troops), artillery and aircraft. Logistics and other targets may be added to the list. Enemy jammers and other ECM capabilities, some of which are mobile and accompany the invading force, are necessarily high-priority targets.

Anti-tank weapons may use line-of-sight guidance like wires and fiber optics, gun sights, range finders and accuracy devices. In good weather and during daylight, such devices would be aimed by lasers; in bad weather and during the night, other beams must be used, e.g., microwave and IR. Tank targets may be laser-illuminated by a soldier on the ground. For that matter, projectile-firing guns, in particular anti-tank guns, may be replaced by ruby lasers. The laser family is growing, and the lasers are becoming increasingly versatile due to tunability of frequency and color so that the acuity of various sensors will be enhanced.

A key anti-tank weapon may be a robotic tank-destroyer carrying a gun, possibly a laser gun, or a rocket with real accuracy, a good range and fire-control links.

A robotic tank could be built for employment against "dismounted" infantry.

Battlefield C3I is based on microprocessors and special software. To be usable by robots or an infantry squad, such systems weigh less than fifty pounds and require not more than two hundred watts. They can be combined with a display system that handles all types of sensors, including photography. The "superposition" of the several images produced by different sensors is a key for really useful battlefield intelligence.

The control station of a robot unit must be assisted by a computer that can transmit commands. The computer systems that will be used in connection with robotics defense will be those of the future—ten years from now—and they might incorporate artificial intelligence features for the anticipation of enemy moves and the identification of alternate courses of action.

Such ground facilities will in due time be connected to positioning systems operating in space. Positioning systems can spot with high accuracy the location both of the weapon and the target, thus increasing the accuracy that can be achieved from ground fire. This means robot units, through their computers and communications, need to provide tactical fire control from advanced positions. The fire that is brought to bear from distant bases, by missiles and bombs, would be equipped with lasers or equivalent target-seekers and guidance devices.

Whereas radars can be easily hit and damaged, small enemy units like guerrilla bands remain difficult to locate. The robot units may lack the firepower to eliminate them. But they can call in and direct fire from distant bases using missiles or aircraft-launching missiles or dropping bombs. Small or guerrilla units would not be important in the context of a large Soviet attack. In the case of a sizable invasion, the robot units on the ground would not look for a few soldiers; instead, they would report on tanks, radars and large units which, presumably, they will spot before they are spotted themselves and which might be delayed by robot-controlled mine fields.

The new characteristics spell a new dimension of accuracy. The probability of hitting targets has grown, and targets can be hit at longer ranges and with higher speeds. Moreover, the invader may lose a large portion of his radars, in which case the effectiveness of his force would be degraded. At the same time, weapons are smaller and therefore harder to see and more difficult to shoot down by the infantry. This in turn means that fewer weapons are needed to knock out targets, offsetting some of the costs of the new equipment. Not to overlook is the probability that the risks to military personnel and platforms will decline. Whatever the details, the growing lethality of precision weapons must cause changes in the structure of combat and in the organization of the forces.

What does it all signify? First of all, it is obvious that the old concept of a "land battle" is obsolete. The U.S. Army has been operating for some time under the concept of the air-land war. Today's and tomorrow's reality is, however, that of a land-airspace or, since naval elements may be used in some geographies, a surface-air-space conflict. The space element includes synchronous orbiters and low-earth-orbiting satellites for reconnaissance, low-level photography, ferret operations and ocean surveillance, as well as synthetic aperture radar observation.

The second fact is that all military operations and movements, as well as strategic and tactical decisions and actions, are dependent on electronics such as sensors, command, control and communication links, computer memories, processing and analysis, and intelligence, as well as electronics embedded in the weapons.

The third fact is that robots will supplement and partially replace troops and manned aircraft. For example, anti-tank rockets, which need not weigh more than twenty pounds and which have a range of more than four hundred meters and fire a shaped charge, can be handled by a single soldier. This sounds as though one soldier who is well-trained and armed with a modern antitank weapon is the equivalent of a tank. If this equation depicted only an approximation, and if it were impractical to concentrate more than a few hundred tanks in one operational sector, a small number of well-prepared soldiers should be able to stop a tank attack. Precisely this capability of the soldier was assumed by Ludendorff in 1918, when his assumption was crazy. It may turn out to be correct after a time lag of seventy years. Whether this means that robots can take over the initial defense of forward areas and that this would free troops for maneuver and counterattack deployment may be left open until we know better what robots can do and what their limitations are. In any event, this much is clear: There will be many crucial locations where it is infeasible to deploy troops in adequate strength. Such locations can be "occupied" by robots with self-defense capabilities. It is also clear that in places where friendly troops are outnumbered by the enemy, robots may be used to cover the deficit.

The fourth fact is that robot weapons allow a vast improvement of tactics, e.g., they are necessarily employing kamikaze tactics. As another example, robots can quickly clear a mine field or, for that matter, lay one down.

The fifth fact is that an invading force and virtually all of its elements are henceforth subject to near real-time surveillance. As a result, they can be attacked at any time with long-range weapons, such as cruise missiles.

The sixth fact is that embedded computers can be reprogrammed within a very short time. In Falkland, British naval weapons were adjusted to the Exocet threat within twenty-four hours, a unique occurrence in military history. This capability of quickly updating weapons technology will be improved as the progress of computer hardware technology and software design continues.

Naturally it is to be expected that the technological revolution in the "land battle" will not be restricted to one side. The new technology will be bilateral. But it is also to be expected that qualitative differences will be large. The prospect that electronics will equalize military strengths is not impressive. There is a better chance that the computers that are now middle-aged have rendered the array of Soviet tanks potentially obsolete. This does not preclude a Soviet attack on Western Europe: The Soviets may rely on crude quantitative superiority and NATO may not modernize fast enough.

Still, the new technology is unquestionably strengthening the deterrence of a Soviet conventional attack. It also reinvigorates the defensive that, for some thirty years, was being overpowered by the offensive.

Case 2

In looking at ground defense in nuclear conflict, do we consider a conflict that is restricted to the European theater or is the battle for the control of Europe merely a segment of a worldwide struggle, in particular of a contest between the USSR and the U.S., which is overarching the European encounter?

It is generally assumed that nuclear attack by the USSR in Europe would be risked only if and when the Kremlin is ready to take on the U.S. at the same time. Furthermore, difficulties in the European battle might create unmanageable complications in the main contest. Hence the usual scenario ascribes top priority to a first strike by the Soviets against the American Triad.

This means that: 1. Soviet surprise against the U.S. is more important than surprise against Europe; 2. the strike against Europe must not precede the strike against the U.S.; 3. a strike against nuclear and strategic U.S. capabilities in Europe would be delayed until the main blow against the U.S. mainland had been launched.

This scheme is too neat if the Soviet strategists feel they must include a strike against U.S. facilities in space. This problem may remain insoluble for as long as the Soviets either don't have a space platform whence the U.S. facilities can be neutralized or else they have directed energy weapons that can be fired effectively from the ground.

In the proximate future they may disregard the space problem and rely mainly on brute missile and high-yield power. Thus they could enact the old scenario of a surprise attack: Schematically, the ICBMs attack the U.S. ICBMs; the SLBMs go after the U.S. bombers on the airbases; and nuclear-attack submarines fire torpedoes to sink American submarines carrying SLBMs.

This strategy could result in a full American defeat, with two aspects: The Triad would be significantly reduced; and the Administration would be knocked out, or else it would capitulate. If the U.S. were defeated militarily and politically, it would be useless to worry about the defense of Europe.

Alternatively, suppose the Soviet first-strike strategy fails. In this case, the U.S. would retaliate and Soviet military power operating against Europe would be significantly reduced.

If the Soviets started their European attack before the outcome of its first strike were known, the battle for Europe would be underway and would continue. Depending on the American strengths that are remaining, the U.S. could force the Soviets to desist, or it could help Europe. If the Soviet attack against Europe had not been started, U.S. success in surviving the first strike might deter the Soviets from any adventures against Europe.

The American presence in Europe would couple the U.S. in either eventuality: The American forces overseas either would be involved by the Soviets or they would be legally at war with the USSR.

To simplify this complex, we might discuss the defense of Europe against a Soviet nuclear attack in isolation from the broader problem. We can postulate that the U.S. continues as a military factor, either because it was not attacked or because the first strike failed. It may also be postulated that if the U.S. were attacked and retaliated, the effects of the American counterattack would impair Soviet capabilities against Europe. Finally, it may be postulated that the USSR will not attack Europe with nuclear weapons for so long as the U.S. is strong enough and fully dedicated to continue with an effective strategy of deterrence. But a Soviet attack would become increasingly probable as American deterrence weakens and as European NATO separates itself from the U.S., or collapses as an effective alliance.

The assumption that the U.S. is uncoupled from Europe includes the further assumption that U.S. forces in Europe are withdrawn or stay out of the conflict.

There is no point to argue about the realism of such assumptions or about the assumption that the USSR still has the option to launch a first strike without first eliminating the American presence in space. The purpose of our intellectual experiment is merely to determine what needs to be done to render the defense of Europe militarily effective.

If the USSR deems it fairly safe to tackle offensively what it regards as its European task, it may first pick a quarrel with one or the other European states. If, for one reason or the other, it does not want to stick to conventional weapons, it may resort to nuclear blackmail. This means that it could limit itself to threats or it could fire a psycho-nuke, e.g., a demonstration shot against an unpopulated or evacuated spot. The psycho-nuke approach might facilitate the enthronement of a Communist regime. Thus it holds out the prospect of a maximal victory at no cost of blood.

If the state refuses, the USSR could place nuclear firepower on a few targets, either minimizing or maximizing population losses. If the victim state possesses a token nuclear force, it may retaliate, and if so, his weapons either may hit targets in the USSR or they may be intercepted. If the victim state estimates that it will remain in isolation and will be unable to match Soviet firepower, it may resort to some hocus-pocus, or it will surrender.

A similarly hopeless development would occur if the USSR were to pick its quarrel with the whole set of European states. It could employ psycho-nukes against some of those states, devastation nukes against others and a disarming strike against a third group. This strategy can be varied in many different ways. In such a cat-and-mouse game, the Soviets could, for example, replace the devastation nukes by chemical munitions—maybe even by biological ones—and they could employ their airborne divisions to occupy one or two capitals and implant a Communist regime from the air. The USSR has a vast quantitative and qualitative superiority; it possesses powerful weapons the Europeans are lacking and against which they have no defenses; it has a mature space deployment, and it has little to fear from a European military riposte.

European politicians shy away from such a conclusion, not because they overestimate the military strength of their countries, but because they are unable to visualize nuclear war except to cry about "holocaust." The fact is that after thirty-odd years of NATO military policies in most European countries remain obsolete.

To break away from the tradition of loving ancient weapons, let us make the bold assumption that the Europeans realize they can't continue to put the real burdens of security on the U.S. Henceforth they want to ensure their self-preservation, not by breaking up NATO, but by doing most of the job themselves.

So what is to be done?

Most of the key tasks appear to be obvious. European NATO is not particularly lacking in tanks, anti-tank weapons, wing aircraft, helicopters, anti-aircraft, etc. Unfortunately, the force does not exist—several forces exist, qualitatively different in many respects. Those forces are difficult to deploy geographically so that they would oppose maximal defense against Soviet invasion. This problem may not have a "solution," but it has been unjustifiably downgraded.

It is more critical that upon receipt of strategic warning, the forces may not be mobilized in a fully coordinated and optimal manner: The timing problems of mobilization and concentration are not solved. This insufficiency is in part due to obstacles like traffic congestion and to backwardness in staff organization and practices. The chief trouble is, on the one hand, that warning cannot be handled efficiently within NATO—too many security problems remain unsolved. On the other hand, difficulties like traffic congestion versus mobilization and force concentrations cannot be managed until electronic capabilities like computers and robots are introduced on a large scale. Those devices cannot be bought from the shelf but presuppose a think-tank effort to design a "system" for mobilization and concentration.

Thus the first job to be done is to assemble the NATO forces on the battlefields in time. The second job is to reequip the combat forces with modern technology as adumbrated in Case 1.

Thereupon the third job looms large: It is to acquire defense capabilities against nuclear missile, air and ground attack.

The Europeans could go all out in producing nuclear weapons for deterrence. No doubt the nuclear imbalance calls for correction. This necessitates the liquidation of industrial lags and political obstacles, like out-of-date treaties. It is another question whether the Europeans should aim at a retaliatory strategy: Such an approach would risk devastating counterblows. A nuclear exchange would be to Europe's disadvantage. Since deterrence based on retaliation was unavoidable only during the initial phase of the high-technology age and is now being modified by the U.S., this model is not suitable.

The slogan that Europe should increase its "conventional" forces is silly. Which conventional system can prevent nuclear blackmail or a missile attack? To be sure, the tank and helicopter forces should be increased to balance the size of the Soviet tank force more effectively. But the Soviets deploy several types of missiles that are destined for use in land war and that have a dual nuclear-conventional capability. The obvious and urgent requirement is to counter those missiles, the SS-21, 22, and 23, which are reported to exist in truly large numbers. A dual capability can be countered only by a dual capability, unless an electronic capability exists to shoot down the missiles with a high kill probability.

The Soviets regard the tank and the heavy helicopter, which they conceive of as a flying tank, as the key weapons of ground warfare, helped by numerous missiles, many of which can be fitted with nuclear explosives. A large effort in military robots would be an appropriate counter, provided manned weapons are available to counter the survivors, of which there will be plenty; and provided also the nuclear impacts can be prevented effectively.

Since the British acquired the *Seawolf* missile to intercept missiles attacking surface ships, defense missiles can be built to intercept missiles attacking troops and targets on the ground.

The same argument applies, other things being equal, to the need to intercept IRBMs and MRBMs, and especially—at this time—the SS-20.

A short while ago the notion that missiles can be intercepted was completely incomprehensible. It is now realized that through modern electronics, missile-interception is becoming feasible.

It is granted that the required technology may not be attainable very quickly. However, a crash program would seem to be in order, precisely because estimates on the required time are utterly unreliable. In any event, whether progress must be slow or can be fast, one needs to know where one is going.

Furthermore, it should be realized that the requisite electronic equipment can be designed and built by the leading European firms, which, of course, can pool resources with American firms.

Once there is clarity on those points, it may be possible to revitalize NATO, both in Europe and in North America, by centering it on a joint technological program to acquire the needed anti-missile capability. This would be a better and faster solution than to pursue modem defense on a bicontinental, let alone on a national, basis.

From there on, it should be feasible to acquire and share NATO-wide the various electronic equipment that is becoming practical, such as robots and RPVs, and to push the embedding of computers in weapons.

It also would be necessary to build a joint accuracy system to improve warning and tracking and to obtain a NATO C3 capability.

There is little doubt that the NATO forces, precisely because they have a defensive mission, must increase the numbers of their battlefield missiles and modern weapons like laser guns.

If the alliance stays together, defensive strength on the ground could be drastically increased by nuclear mines combined with robot controls, and by American neutron weapons. Chemical and biological weapons could be held in reserve to deter their employment by the Soviets.

So much for the requirements, and the potential, of a successful defense of Europe.

Unfortunately, as things stand early in 1984, the NATO forces in Europe are suffering from severe quantitative deficiencies, lack nuclear weapons (with the U.S. forces overseas being armed mainly by obsolescent nuclear devices), are threatened by massive surprise attack and are improperly equipped to tie their tactics to space sensors. The new technology cannot be effectively utilized unless it is based on space and is integrated by a C3 and correlated intelligence system.

Conclusion

The deficiency problems can be solved, but it is utterly impossible for "conventional" (i.e., obsolete) forces to survive for as long as they are unable to react to warning with timely mobilization, are pitted against across-the-board superiority, are vulnerable to surprise blows and lack the crucial technological capabilities of the epoch.

Note: The main operation that was carried out in Vietnam with smart weapons was called Linebacker II (December 18–29, 1972). More than 15,000 tons of bombs resulted in 1,318 civilian deaths, or .08 fatalities per one ton of bombs. The notorious bombing of Guernica (1937), where 40.5 tons were dropped, or 1/370th of the Linebacker II bomb load, cost 1,654 lives. Thus per ton of bombs, 500 times more people were killed during one afternoon in Guernica than during the major air assault in Vietnam, which lasted eleven days. In the Battle of Britain (June-December 1940), the civilian deaths per one ton of bombs were seven times larger than those caused by Linebacker II. The combined average of Guernica, Battle of Britain, Coventry (1940), Hamburg (July 1943), Dresden (February 1945) and Tokyo (March 1945) was 260 times more lethal, while in Tokyo, 629 times more fatalities were produced than during the Vietnam operation twenty-seven years later. (Statistical data from *Air University Review*, January-February 1983, p. 24.)

Hide and Seek

by Arthur C. Clarke

Editor's Introduction

I am reminded of this story nearly every morning.

For more than a dozen years I have been the chief provisioner for a family of California jays. This is not entirely generosity: The cocky birds settle outside my study window and raise such a fuss that I can either feed them, shoot them or abandon my work.

They're too tame to shoot. When we first moved into this house, one was already accustomed to people: My neighbor, actor John Agar, had so tamed one of the jays that he would come to your shoulder in search of peanuts and sunflower seeds. The next summer that jay brought his mate and one of his brood to my window, and since that time, several generations of jays have been taught to come annoy me whenever they are hungry.

For the past two years, though, they haven't had it all their way. One fall there appeared on the jays' feeding platform an obviously pregnant squirrel. After a moment's confrontation the leader of the flock of jays was driven away; after all, a squirrel is larger than a jay, has big teeth, and is much stronger.

There began a period of guerrilla warfare. The jays may be smaller, but they're airborne. One will distract the squirrel, while another attacks from behind, dealing painful if not injurious blows with his beak, then quickly flying away. When the squirrel turns, the first jay darts in to seize a peanut.

After the initial period of warfare, they began a new phase: The squirrel tore holes in the wire screen so that she could come into the office and help herself. It wasn't long before the largest jay followed, until my very desk became a battleground. That ended only when I replaced the screens with wire strong enough to withstand squirrel teeth.

Then this spring the squirrel came no more. She may have been victim of an automobile, or perhaps age, or she may have been plucked from an overhead wire by the red-tailed hawks who live on the hill above us. The jays' peace was short-lived, though: Last week a new squirrel has come. She looks to be less than a year old, and I suppose she was taught the way by her mother...

Arthur C. Clarke, Fellow of the British Interplanetary Society and Fellow of the Royal Astronomical Society, lives in Sri Lanka, a nation formerly known as Ceylon. He is considered a national treasure, and is also the Rector of one of their national universities. Every few years, Arthur swears he will never write another book, or indeed leave his beloved adopted land. However, some years ago I helped induce him to buy a computer, making it easier for him to write books; and the need for publicity tours brings him willy-nilly to the United States. On his last trip I held a party for him and explained the strange warfare outside and how it reminded me of his story, which, once thought of, would obviously fit into this book.

––––––––––––––––––

We were walking back through the woods when Kingman saw the gray squirrel. Our bag was a small but varied one—three grouse, a couple of pigeons and four rabbits—one, I am sorry to say, an infant in arms. And contrary to certain dark forecasts, both the dogs were still alive.

The squirrel saw us at the same moment. It knew that it was marked for immediate execution as a result of the damage it had done to the trees on the estate, and perhaps it had lost close relatives to Kingman's gun. In three leaps it had reached the base of the nearest tree and vanished behind it in a flicker of gray. We saw its face once more, appearing for a moment round the edge of its shield a dozen feet from the ground; but though we waited, with guns leveled hopefully at various branches, we never saw it again.

Kingman was very thoughtful as we walked back across the lawn to the magnificent old house. He said nothing as we handed our victims to the cook—who received them without much enthusiasm—and only emerged from his reverie when we were sitting in the smoking room and he remembered his duties as a host.

"That tree-rat," he said suddenly—he always called them "tree-rats," on the grounds that people were too sentimental to shoot the dear little squirrels—"it reminded me of a very peculiar experience that happened shortly before I retired. Very shortly indeed, in fact."

"I thought it would," said Carson dryly. I gave him a glare; he'd been in the Navy and had heard Kingman's stories before, but they were still new to me.

"Of course," Kingman remarked, slightly nettled, "if you'd rather I didn't—"

"Do go on," I said hastily. "You've made me curious. What connection there can possibly be between a gray squirrel and the Second Jovian War I can't imagine."

Kingman seemed mollified.

"I think I'd better change some names," he said thoughtfully, "but I won't alter the places. The story begins about a million kilometers sunwards of Mars—"

K.15 was a military intelligence operator. It gave him considerable pain when unimaginative people called him a spy, but at the moment he had much more substantial grounds for complaint. For some days now a fast cruiser had been coming up astern, and though it was flattering to have the undivided attention of such a fine ship and so many highly-trained men, it was an honor that K.15 would willingly have forgone.

What made the situation doubly annoying was the fact that his friends would be meeting him off Mars in about twelve hours, aboard a ship quite capable of dealing with a mere cruiser—from which you will gather that K.15 was a person of some importance. Unfortunately, the most optimistic calculation showed that the pursuers would be within accurate gun range in six hours. In some six hours five minutes, therefore, K.15 was likely to occupy an extensive and still expanding volume of space.

There might just be time for him to land on Mars, but that would be one of the worst things he could do. It would certainly annoy the aggressively neutral Martians, and the political complications would be frightful. Moreover, if his friends *had* to come down to the planet to rescue him, it would cost them more than ten kilometers a second in fuel—most of their operational reserve.

He had only one advantage, and that a very dubious one. The commander of the cruiser might guess that he was heading for a rendezvous, but he would not know how close it was nor how large was the ship that was coming to meet him. If he could keep alive for only twelve hours, he would be safe. The "if" was a somewhat considerable one.

K.15 looked moodily at his charts, wondering if it was worthwhile to burn the rest of his fuel in a final dash. But a dash to where? He would be completely helpless then, and the pursuing ship might still have enough in her tanks to catch him as he flashed outwards into the empty darkness, beyond all hope of rescue—passing his friends as they came sunwards at a relative speed so great that they could do nothing to save him.

With some people, the shorter the expectation of life, the more sluggish are the mental processes. They seem hypnotized by the approach of death, so resigned to their fate that they do nothing to avoid it. K.15, on the other hand, found that his mind worked better in such a desperate emergency. It began to work as it had seldom done before.

Commander Smith—the name will do as well as any other—of the cruiser *Doradus* was not unduly surprised when K.15 began to decelerate. He had half expected the spy to land on Mars, on the principle that internment was better than annihilation, but when the plotting room brought the news that the little scout ship was heading for Phobos, he felt completely baffled. The inner moon was nothing but a jumble of rock some twenty kilometers across and not even the economical Martians had ever found any use for it. K.15 must be pretty desperate if he thought it was going to be of greater value to him.

The tiny scout had almost come to rest when the radar operator lost it against the mass of Phobos. During the braking maneuver, K.15 had squandered most of his lead and the *Doradus* was now only minutes away—though she was now beginning to decelerate lest she overrun him. The cruiser was scarcely three thousand kilometers from Phobos when she came to a complete halt; but of K.15's ship, there was still no sign. It should be easily visible in the telescopes, but it was probably on the far side of the little moon.

It reappeared only a few minutes later, traveling under full thrust on a course directly away from the sun. It was accelerating at almost five gravities—and it had broken its radio silence. An automatic recorder was broadcasting over and over again this interesting message:

"I have landed on Phobos and am being attacked by a Z-class cruiser. Think I can hold out until you come, but hurry."

The message wasn't even in code, and it left Commander Smith a sorely puzzled man. The assumption that K.15 was still aboard the ship and that the whole thing was a ruse was just a little too naive. But it might be a double-bluff—the message had obviously been left in plain language so that he would receive it and be duly confused. He could afford neither the time nor the fuel to chase the scout if K.15 really had landed. It was clear that reinforcements were on the way, and the sooner he left the vicinity, the better. The phrase "Think I can hold out until you come" might be a piece of sheer impertinence, or it might mean that help was very near indeed.

Then K.15's ship stopped blasting. It had obviously exhausted its fuel, and was doing a little better than six kilometers a second away from the sun. K.15 *must* have landed, for his ship was now speeding helplessly out of the solar system. Commander Smith didn't like the message it was broadcasting, and guessed that it was running into the track of an approaching warship at some indefinite distance, but there was nothing to be done about that. The *Doradus* began to move toward Phobos, anxious to waste no time.

On the face of it, Commander Smith seemed the master of the situation. His ship was armed with a dozen heavy guided missiles and two turrets of electromagnetic guns. Against him was one man in a spacesuit, trapped on a moon only twenty kilometers across. It was not until Commander Smith had his first good look at Phobos, from a distance of less than a hundred kilometers, that he began to realize that, after all, K.15 might have a few cards up his sleeve.

To say that Phobos has a diameter of twenty kilometers, as the astronomy books invariably do, is highly misleading. The word "diameter" implies a degree of symmetry which Phobos most certainly lacks. Like those other lumps of cosmic slag, the asteroids, it is a shapeless mass of rock floating in space, with, of course, no hint of an atmosphere and not much more gravity. It turns on its axis once every seven hours thirty-nine minutes, thus keeping the same face always to Mars—which is so close that appreciably less than half the planet is visible, the Poles being below the curve of the horizon. Beyond this, there is very little more to be said about Phobos.

K.15 had no time to enjoy the beauty of the crescent world filling the sky above him. He threw all the equipment he could carry out of the air lock, set the controls, and jumped. As the little ship went flaming out towards the stars, he watched it go with feelings he did not care to analyze. He had burned his boats with a vengeance, and he could only hope that the oncoming battleship would intercept the radio message as the empty vessel went racing by into nothingness. There was also a faint possibility that the empty cruiser might go in pursuit, but that was rather too much to hope for.

He turned to examine his new home. The only light was the ochre radiance of Mars, since the sun was below the horizon, but that was quite sufficient for his purpose and he could see very well. He stood in the center of an irregular plain about two kilometers across, surrounded by low hills over which he could leap rather easily if he wished. There was a story he remembered reading long ago about a man who had accidentally jumped off Phobos; that wasn't quite possible—though it was on Deimos—as the escape velocity was still about ten meters a second. But unless he was careful, he might easily find himself at such a height that it would take hours to fall back to the surface—and that would be fatal. For K.15's plan was a simple one—he must remain as close to the surface of Phobos as possible *and diametrically opposite the cruiser*. The *Doradus* could then fire all her armament against the twenty kilometers of rock, and he wouldn't even feel the concussion. There were only two serious dangers, and one of these did not worry him greatly.

To the layman, knowing nothing of the finer details of astronautics, the plan would have seemed quite suicidal. The *Doradus* was armed with the latest in ultra-scientific weapons; moreover, the twenty kilometers which separated her from her prey represented less than a second's flight at maximum speed. But Commander Smith knew better, and was already feeling rather unhappy. He realized, only too well, that of all the machines of transport man has ever invented, a cruiser of space is far and away the least maneuverable. It was a simple fact that K.15 could make half a dozen circuits of his little world while her commander was persuading the *Doradus* to do even one.

There is no need to go into technical details, but those who are still unconvinced might like to consider these elementary facts. A rocket-driven spaceship can, obviously, only accelerate along its major axis—that is, "forwards." Any deviation from a straight course demands a physical turning of the ship, so that the motors can blast in another direction. Everyone knows that this is done by internal gyros or tangential steering jets—but very few people know just how long this simple maneuver takes. The average cruiser, fully fueled, has a mass of two or three thousand tons, which does not make for rapid footwork. But things are even worse than this, for it isn't the mass but the moment of inertia that matters here—and since a cruiser is a long, thin object, its moment of inertia is slightly colossal. The sad fact remains—though it is seldom mentioned by astronomical engineers—that it takes a good ten minutes to rotate a spaceship through one hundred eighty degrees, with gyros of any reasonable size. Control jets aren't much quicker, and in any case, their use is restricted because the rotation they produce is permanent and they are liable to leave the ship spinning like a slow-motion pinwheel, to the annoyance of all inside.

In the ordinary way, these disadvantages are not very grave. One has millions of kilometers and hundreds of hours in which to deal with such minor matters as a change in the ship's orientation. It is definitely against the rules to move in ten-kilometer-radius circles, and the commander of the *Doradus* felt distinctly aggrieved. K.15 wasn't playing fair.

At the same moment, that resourceful individual was taking stock of the situation, which might very well have been worse. He had reached the hills in three jumps and felt less naked than he had out in the open plain. The food and equipment he had taken from the ship he had hidden where he hoped he could find it again, but as his suit could keep him alive for over a day, that was the least of his worries. The small packet that was the cause of all the trouble was still with him, in one of those numerous hiding places a well-designed spacesuit affords.

There was an exhilarating loneliness about his mountain aerie, even though he was not quite as lonely as he would have wished. Forever fixed in his sky, Mars was waning almost visibly as Phobos swept above the night side of the planet. He could just make out the lights of some of the Martian cities, gleaming pin-points marking the junctions of the invisible canals. All else was stars and silence and a line of jagged peaks so close it seemed he could almost touch them. Of the *Doradus* there was still no sign. She was presumably carrying out a careful telescopic examination of the sunlit side of Phobos.

Mars was a very useful clock—when it was half full, the sun would rise and, very probably, so would the *Doradus*. But she might approach from some quite unexpected quarter; she might even—and this was the one real danger—have landed a search party.

This was the first possibility that had occurred to Commander Smith when he saw just what he was up against. Then he realized that the surface area of Phobos was over a thousand square kilometers and that he could not spare more than ten men from his crew to make a search of that jumbled wilderness. Also, K.15 would certainly be armed.

Considering the weapons which the *Doradus* carried, this last objection might seem singularly pointless. It was very far from being so. In the ordinary course of business, side arms and other portable weapons are as much use to a spacecruiser as are cutlasses and crossbows. The *Doradus* happened, quite by chance—and against regulations at that— to carry one automatic pistol and a hundred rounds of ammunition. Any search party would, therefore, consist of a group of unarmed men looking for a well-concealed and very desperate individual who could pick them off at his leisure. K.15 was breaking the rules again.

The terminator of Mars was now a perfectly straight line, and at almost the same moment the sun came up, not so much like thunder as like a salvo of atomic bombs. K.15 adjusted the filters of his visor and decided to move. It was safer to stay out of the sunlight, not only because he was less likely to be detected in the shadow but also because his eyes would be much more sensitive there. He had only a pair of binoculars to help him, whereas the *Doradus* would carry an electronic telescope of twenty centimeters' aperture at least.

It would be best, K.15 decided, to locate the cruiser if he could. It might be a rash thing to do, but he would feel much happier when he knew exactly where she was and could watch her movements. He could then keep just below the horizon, and the glare of the rockets would give him ample warning of any impending move. Cautiously launching himself along an almost horizontal trajectory, he began the circumnavigation of his world.

The narrowing crescent of Mars sank below the horizon until only one vast horn reared itself enigmatically against the stars. K.15 began to feel worried—there was still no sign of the *Doradus*. But this was hardly surprising, for she was painted black as night and might be a good hundred kilometers away in space. He stopped, wondering if he had done the right thing after all. Then he noticed that something quite large was eclipsing the stars almost vertically overhead, and was moving swiftly even as he watched. His heart stopped for a moment—then he was himself again, analyzing the situation and trying to discover how he had made so disastrous a mistake.

It was some time before he realized that the black shadow slipping across the sky was not the cruiser at all, but something almost equally deadly. It was far smaller, and far nearer, than he had at first thought. The *Doradus* had sent her television-homing guided missiles to look for him.

This was the second danger he had feared, and there was nothing he could do about it except to remain as inconspicuous as possible. The *Doradus* now had many eyes searching for him, but these auxiliaries had very severe limitations. They had been built to look for sunlit spaceships against a background of stars, not to search for a man hiding in a dark jungle of rock. The definition of their television systems was low, and they could see only in the forward direction.

There were rather more men on the chessboard now, and the game was a little deadlier, but his was still the advantage. The torpedo vanished into the night sky. As it was traveling on a nearly straight course in this low gravitational field, it would soon be leaving Phobos behind, and K.15 waited for what he knew must happen. A few minutes later, he saw a brief stabbing of rocket exhausts and guessed that the projectile was swinging slowly back on its course. At almost the same moment he saw another flare far away in the opposite quarter of the sky and wondered just how many of these infernal machines were in action. From what he knew of Z-class cruisers—which was a good deal more than he should—there were four missile-control channels, and they were probably all in use.

He was suddenly struck by an idea so brilliant that he was quite sure it couldn't possibly work. The radio on his suit was a tunable one, covering an unusually wide band, and somewhere not far away the *Doradus* was pumping out power on everything from a thousand megacycles upwards. He switched on the receiver and began to explore.

It came in quickly—the raucous whine of a pulse transmitter not far away. He was probably picking up only a subharmonic, but that was quite good enough. It D/F'ed sharply, and for the first time K.15 allowed himself to make long-range plans about the future. The *Doradus* had betrayed herself—as long as she operated her missiles, he would know exactly where she was.

He moved cautiously forward towards the transmitter. To his surprise the signal faded, then increased sharply again. This puzzled him until he realized that he must be moving through a diffraction zone. Its width might have told him something useful if he had been a good enough physicist, but he couldn't imagine what.

The *Doradus* was hanging about five kilometers above the surface, in full sunlight. Her "nonreflecting" paint was overdue for renewal, and K.15 could see her clearly. As he was still in darkness and the shadow line was moving away from him, he decided that he was as safe here as anywhere. He settled down comfortably so that he could just see the cruiser and waited, feeling fairly certain that none of the guided projectiles would come too near the ship. By now, he calculated, the commander of the *Doradus* must be getting pretty mad. He was perfectly correct.

After an hour, the cruiser began to heave herself round with all the grace of a bogged hippopotamus. K.15 guessed what was happening. Commander Smith was going to have a look at the antipodes, and was preparing for the perilous fifty-kilometer journey. He watched very carefully to see the orientation the ship was adopting, and when she came to rest again, was relieved to see that she was almost broadside on to him. Then, with a series of jerks that could not have been very enjoyable aboard, the cruiser began to move down to the horizon. K.15 followed her at a comfortable walking pace—if one could use the phrase—reflecting that this was a feat very few people had ever performed. He was particularly careful not to overtake her on one of his kilometer-long glides and kept a close watch for any missiles that might be coming up astern.

It took the *Doradus* nearly an hour to cover the fifty kilometers. This, as K.15 amused himself by calculating, represented considerably less than a thousandth of her normal speed. Once she found herself going off into space at a tangent, and rather than waste time turning end over end, again fired off a salvo of shells to reduce speed. But she made it at last, and K.15 settled down for another vigil, wedged between two rocks where he could just see the cruiser and he was quite sure she couldn't see him. It occurred to him that by this time Commander Smith might have grave doubts as to whether he really was on Phobos at all, and he felt like firing off a signal flare to reassure him. However, he resisted the temptation.

There would be little point in describing the events of the next ten hours, since they differed in no important detail from those that had gone before. The *Doradus* made three other moves, and K.15 stalked her with the care of a big-game hunter following the spoor of some elephantine beast. Once, when she would have led him out into full sunlight, he let her fall below the horizon until he could only just pick up her signals. But most of the time he kept her just visible, usually low down behind some convenient hill.

Once a torpedo exploded some kilometers away, and K.15 guessed that some exasperated operator had seen a shadow he didn't like— or else that a technician had forgotten to switch off a proximity fuse. Otherwise nothing happened to enliven the proceedings; in fact, the whole affair was becoming rather boring. He almost welcomed the sight of an occasional guided missile drifting inquisitively overhead, for he did not believe that they could see him if he remained motionless and in reasonable cover. If he could have stayed on the part of Phobos exactly opposite the cruiser, he would have been safe even from these, he realized, since the ship would have no control there in the moon's radio-shadow. But he could think of no reliable way in which he could be sure of staying in the safety zone if the cruiser moved again.

The end came very abruptly. There was a sudden blast of steering jets, and the cruiser's main drive burst forth in all its power and splendor. In seconds the *Doradus* was shrinking sunwards, free at last, thankful to leave, even in defeat, this miserable lump of rock that had so annoyingly balked her of her legitimate prey. K.15 knew what had happened, and a great sense of peace and relaxation swept over him. In the radar room of the cruiser, someone had seen an echo of disconcerting amplitude approaching with altogether excessive speed. K.15 now had only to switch on his suit beacon and to wait. He could even afford the luxury of a cigarette.

"Quite an interesting story," I said, "and I see now how it ties up with that squirrel. But it does raise one or two queries in my mind."

"Indeed?" said Rupert Kingman politely.

I always like to get to the bottom of things, and I knew that my host had played a part in the Jovian War, about which he very seldom spoke. I decided to risk a long shot in the dark.

"May I ask how you happened to know so much about this unorthodox military engagement? It isn't possible, is it, that *you* were K.15?"

There was an odd sort of strangling noise from Carson. Then Kingman said, quite calmly:

"No, I wasn't."

He got to his feet and started toward the gun room.

"If you'll excuse me a moment, I'm going to have another shot at that tree-rat. Maybe I'll get him this time." Then he was gone.

Carson looked at me as if to say: "This is another house you'll never be invited to again." When our host was out of earshot, he remarked in a coldly clinical tone:

"What did you have to say that for?"

"Well, it seemed a safe guess. How else could he have known all that?"

"As a matter of fact, I believe he met K.15 after the war; they must have had an interesting conversation together. But I thought you knew that Rupert was retired from the service with only the rank of lieutenant commander. The Court of Inquiry could never see his point of view. After all, it just wasn't reasonable that the commander of the fastest ship in the Fleet couldn't catch a man in a spacesuit."

THE MYTH OF A LIBERATION

by Truong Nhu Tang with Doan Van Toai

Editor's Introduction

The late Richard Weaver's best-known work is entitled *Ideas Have Consequences*. Weaver argued that Western intellectuals had a duty to be responsible in their thoughts and publications; that they should not hare off after every stray thought and whim, lest they discover they had created real monsters.

It is a lesson the U.S. intellectual community has not yet learned in either arts or sciences or political analysis. (For an exposition both insightful and hilarious on problems within the world of arts and letters, see Bryan F. Griffin's *Panic Among The Philistines*, Chicago, Regnery, 1983.)

To this day the U.S. academic community has not, as a body, understood what happened in Vietnam. This is not stupidity; it is a deliberate refusal to look at what happened there. One can sympathize, for the situation in Vietnam is grim; alas, it is a work made largely by American intellectuals. Having created the monster, they should be made to look upon their work.

The United States was invited to Vietnam by Ngo Dinh Diem, a French-educated official who ousted the puppet Emperor Bao Dai and proclaimed the ancient kingdom independent not only of France, but of the Tonkin (Hanoi) imperialists, who had always wanted control of Annam (central Vietnam, with capital in Hue) and Cochin China (the Delta).

A few years later the United States destroyed the Diem government and caused the massacre of Diem and his family. This was done largely on the advice of academic analysts who advised John F. Kennedy. They felt that the Diem regime was corrupt and unable to be reformed; a new revolutionary regime would be more tractable, more willing to listen to the advice of Harvard University.

The Diem government was certainly no model of democracy and freedom. There is no such model in Asia with the exception of Japan, whose democratic institutions were constructed under the tutelage of General of the Armies Douglas MacArthur and an American army of occupation. Perhaps Kennedy had in mind a similar project in Vietnam. Of course Vietnam was our ally, not a defeated and occupied country, but the nation-builders among Kennedy's whiz kids weren't going to let technical details stand in the way of their Great Work.

The Western intellectual community roundly condemned Ngo Dinh Diem for not bringing instant democracy and economic paradise to a newly liberated colony already torn by war. They were not alone, of course.

In addition to the North Vietnamese Communists and American intellectuals, there were some within South Vietnam who hated the Diem regime. The NLF, so beloved of Jane Fonda and other U.S. patriots, was formed.

One of the original founders of the NLF was Truong Nhu Tang. To quote from the original *New York Review of Books's* introduction, "There is no one whose revolutionary credentials are more secure, no one who worked harder to expel the U.S. from Vietnam and to establish a revolutionary government... He is a man beyond the charge of CIA complicity. His story is a simple human tragedy."

Truong Nhu Tang lives in Paris. His *Memoirs* have been written with, and translated by, his Vietnamese fellow exile Doan Van Toai, former Research Associate at the Fletcher School of Law and Diplomacy, now Director of the Institute for Southeast Asian Policy Analysis, Fresno, California.

Both long for the day when the intellectual community will wake up and assume its responsibilities.

———————————

On May 15, 1975, I was standing on the official dais reviewing the first Victory Day parade in Ho Chi Minh City (Saigon until several months earlier). The crowd marching by waved the flags of both the Democratic Republic of Vietnam (Hanoi) and the Provisional Revolutionary Government of the Republic of South Vietnam (Viet Cong). The troops, though, bore only the North's colors. I asked the four-star general standing next to me where were the famous Viet Cong Divisions 1, 5, 7, and 9. The general, Van Tien Dung, commander-in-chief of the North Vietnamese army, answered coldly that the armed forces were now "unified." At that moment I began to understand my fate and that of the NLF. In Vietnam we often said: "Take the juice of the lemon and throw away the peel." On that dais the years of communist promises and assurances revealed themselves for the propaganda they were. Victory Day celebrated no victory for the NLF, or for the South.

When I was a student in Paris in the late 1940s, I was tremendously attracted to Western liberal ideas. I studied the theory of democracy and saw at first hand something about how it worked. My own country had gone through such a different historical development: a thousand years of autocratic Chinese domination followed by an equally unenlightened French colonial regime. Ironically perhaps, I found I loved French culture and especially French political traditions. I wanted desperately for my own country nothing less than what France and other Western nations enjoyed: independence and a democratic political life. I felt elated and proud when Ho Chi Minh came to Paris to negotiate with the French, even more when the press hailed him as a hero of the Vietnamese people. I felt that I was touched by the glory reflected from this man. When I was invited to meet him, I was overwhelmed by happiness. An idealistic and innocent Vietnamese youth, I became at that meeting a devoted follower of Ho.

During the late 1950s, there were not many Vietnamese intellectuals who had studied at Western schools, and I was among the few who had graduated from a French university. When I returned to Saigon in 1958, I was the controller-general of a bank and then was appointed by the South Vietnamese government director of the national sugar refinery in 1964. With this appointment I began following the path of those fortunate intellectuals who had been educated in the West and moved automatically into high government positions with secure futures. Often they were promoted to the position of minister, which they enjoyed fully. They paid great attention to their own luxuries and careers and no attention at all to what I saw as the needs of the people.

In time I came to feel that scarcely any of the top South Vietnamese leaders was a patriot and that I could not serve the country together with such corrupt generals and officials. In particular, there was no political freedom as I had seen it in the West. I became preoccupied with thoughts of my countrymen who were suffering in prisons and in the jungles for independence and for the political ideals I shared. Secretly I made contacts with these revolutionaries. Together we decided that my contribution would be most effective if I kept my position in the sugar refinery and maintained clandestine contacts with my new associates. Thereafter I began secret biweekly meetings with an agent of Huynh Tan Phat, the future prime minister of the Provisional Revolutionary Government, and I kept up these meetings for the next two years. During this entire period President Ngo Dinh Diem's police never suspected my involvement with the Viet Cong.

In December 1960, at a memorable jungle meeting, my friends suggested that we form the Provisional Committee of the NLF. Subsequently a larger meeting was set up on a rubber plantation in Bien Hoa, twenty miles northeast of Saigon. Present were about twenty people, all of them Southerners and educated in France. Our first thought was to choose a president and Tran Kim Quan, a Saigon pharmacist, was proposed. Quan had been a leader of the 1954 peace movement and seemed the ideal candidate, but he refused. The second choice was a lawyer, Nguyen Huu Tho, who at that time was under house arrest in Qui Nhon. My comrades formed a commando unit to kidnap Tho, but on their first attempt they somehow managed to make off with the wrong man. Another raid was promptly organized and this time we succeeded. Shortly afterward, in February 1962, a second organizational meeting was held near Tay Ninh in the "Green Triangle" area near the Vietnam-Cambodia border. At this meeting we decided to form a Permanent Committee of the NLF and we officially elected the newly liberated Tho as president.

Throughout this period we had close support from the North Vietnamese communists. We were in fact dependent on them for weapons, communications, and especially for our propaganda network. But almost all of us were Southerners (along with a few Northerners who had moved south years earlier)—and many of us were not communists. Ours was not a communist movement and we believed that the North Vietnamese leaders, who had been fighting so resolutely against the French, would place the interests of the people and the nation above the interest of ideology.

The North Vietnamese on their part never indicated that they wanted to impose communism on the South. On the contrary, they knew, they said, that the South must have a different program altogether, one that embodied our aspirations not just for independence but also for internal political freedom. I believed, in addition, that the Northern leadership would have the wisdom to draw from the experiences—both good and bad—of other communist countries, and especially of North Vietnam, and that they could avoid the errors made elsewhere. North Vietnam was, as Ho Chi Minh often declared, a special situation in which nationalists and communists had combined their efforts. Clearly South Vietnam was no less special, and the newly constituted NLF Permanent Committee felt a certain amount of confidence in working with our Northern compatriots.

In 1964, I was arrested for the first time. I had been helping other Saigon intellectuals form the Self-Determination Movement of South

Vietnam, an organization opposed to the South Vietnamese regime. For this offense, I was imprisoned for two years. In a sense, though, it was only a warning because there was no evidence at that time of my Viet Cong contacts. Unfortunately, in 1967 a Viet Cong agent, who had been arrested and tortured, disclosed my NLF identity to the Thieu-Ky police. I was arrested again and this time my imprisonment was harsher. The police used many of their favorite techniques to torture me. They forced me to drink soapy water and ran 220-volt electric shocks through my body. For a month I was held in a tiny cell less than two meters square. They forced me to confess that I was a communist (although I was not), and to describe my underground activities.

I was still in prison when the 1968 Tet offensive swept the country. At one point the police told us that if the Viet Cong got into Saigon, we would all be killed. Shortly afterward the jailer ordered me to "take everything with you and follow me." The expression was ominous; I was sure I would be shot, along with other Viet Cong prisoners who I knew were being executed in the streets. Two other NLF members and I were thrown into a security truck and then transferred to an American Red Cross van. To my surprise and relief, there were two Americans in the van as well, and they brought us to a CIA safe house. Later I discovered that secret negotiations had been going on between the Americans and the NLF for a prisoner exchange and that I was to be traded for two American colonels.

Before I left the CIA safe house, I was given a letter for the NLF authorities and pressed to accept a radio as well, which I refused, believing it to contain an electronic bug. A helicopter flew me and two other exchanged prisoners to Trang Bang, a small district about fifty miles northwest of Saigon. We were released at a soccer field where the Viet Cong security chief for Loc Ninh province (a Viet Cong-controlled area) was waiting for us. From this rendezvous we were taken by motorized tricycle deep into the jungle toward the NLF's Central Office of South Vietnam, the famous COSVN headquarters from which the entire Viet Cong war effort was directed.

Traveling by night and sleeping by day to avoid ARVN hunters and American bombardments, we took almost two weeks to get there, even though COSVN was located on the Mimot plantation near the Cambodian border, only about one hundred miles from Saigon. COSVN's nerve center was a simple enclosure built ten meters underground to shield it from B-52 attacks, although any hit within 500 meters would have been devastating. The headquarters was guarded by a single regiment, and well armed though they were, I could not help wondering at the vulnerability of the place.

The war that COSVN directed was by that time being fought by large numbers of Northern troops along with the Viet Cong guerrillas. In the early sixties, before I was jailed, there had been quite a few North Vietnamese military cadres assisting us but not many soldiers. The great majority of our troops then were Southern resistance fighters, many of whom were veterans of the French colonial wars. Others were peasants who joined us when the NLF was formed. Almost all of this latter group still lived at home. During the day they were loyal citizens of South Vietnam; at night they became Viet Cong.

For the most part, these guerrillas cared nothing about Marxist-Leninism or any other ideology. But they despised the local officials who had been appointed over them by the Saigon dictatorship. Beyond this, joining the Viet Cong allowed them to stay clear of the ARVN draft and to remain near their families. They were treated as brothers by the NLF, and although Viet Cong pay was almost nonexistent, these peasant soldiers were loyal and determined fighters. Moreover, they had the support of much of the population: People in the countryside and even in the cities provided food and intelligence information and protected our cadres. Although South Vietnamese propaganda attacked us as communists and murderers, the peasants believed otherwise. To them we were not Marxist-Leninists but simply revolutionaries fighting against a hated dictatorship and foreign intervention.

Because it was a people's war, the Viet Cong cadres were trained carefully to exploit the peasants' sympathies. But our goals were in fact generally shared by the people. We were working for Southern self-determination and independence—from Hanoi as well as from Washington. While we in the Viet Cong were beholden to Hanoi for military supplies and diplomatic contacts, many of us still believed that the North Vietnamese leadership would respect and support the NLF political program, that it would be in their interest to do so.

As early as the 1968 Tet offensive, after I was released from Thieu's prisons, I protested to the communist leaders about the atrocities committed by North Vietnamese troops in Hue, where many innocent people were murdered and about a dozen American prisoners were shot. It was explained to me that these were political executions and also that a number of "errors" had been made. I managed to persuade myself then that no such "errors" would be necessary once the war was over.

Unfortunately the Tet offensive also proved catastrophic to our plans. It is a major irony of the Vietnamese war that our propaganda transformed this military debacle into a brilliant victory, giving us new leverage in our diplomatic efforts, inciting the American antiwar movement to even stronger and more optimistic resistance, and disheartening the Washington planners.

The truth was that Tet cost us half of our forces. Our losses were so immense that we were simply unable to replace them with new recruits. One consequence was that the Hanoi leadership began to move unprecedented numbers of troops into the South, giving them a new and much more dominant position in NLF deliberations. The Tet failure also retarded the organization of the Alliance of National, Democratic, and Peace Forces, an opposition coalition that had formed around thirty prominent South Vietnamese intellectuals and opinion makers. It wasn't until 1969 that we finally succeeded in bringing these disparate groups together under the leadership of Trinh Dinh Thao, a lawyer who had studied in France and had served as minister of justice for the French-backed government in the 1950s, and myself. Belatedly we began working on a broad political program and even on such details as choosing an anthem and designing a national flag.

In June 1969, in response to a request by the Communist Party, which was preparing to participate in the Paris peace conference, we formed the Provisional Revolutionary Government. At first I was proposed for the interior ministry, but because of my law degree, we finally concluded that I could function most effectively as minister of justice. I had about fifty officials at the Ministry of Justice in the jungle. Only a few of the PRO cabinet members were communists: Nguyen Huu Tho, president of the NLF; Huynh Tan Phat, prime minister of the PRO: General Tran Nam Trung, minister of defense; and Nguyen Thi Binh, minister of foreign affairs; and even these people were Southerners committed to the idea of a separate policy for South Vietnam. Almost all of the NLF leadership were of the same mind, as were most of our supporters from around the world.

The Hanoi leadership knew all this and orchestrated their position toward us accordingly. They accepted and supported the NLF platform at every point, and gave the firmest assurances of respect for the principle of South Vietnamese self-determination. Later, of course, we discovered that the North Vietnamese communists had engaged in a deliberate deception to achieve what had been their true goal from the start, the destruction of South Vietnam as a political or social entity in any way separate from the North. They succeeded in their deception by portraying themselves as brothers who had fought the same battles we were fighting and by exploiting our patriotism in the most cynical fashion. Nevertheless, the eventual denouement would not have taken place except for several wholly unpredictable developments.

After the Paris peace agreement was signed in 1973, most of us were preparing to create a neutralist government, balanced between Northern leftists and Southern rightists. We hoped that America and the other signers would play an active role in protecting the agreement. Certainly no one expected Watergate and Nixon's resignation. No one expected America's easy and startlingly rapid abandonment of the country. I myself, the soon-to-be minister of justice, was preparing a reconciliation policy that specifically excluded reprisals. But the sudden collapse of the South Vietnamese regime (caused partly by the hasty departure of many top Saigon leaders), together with abandonment by the Americans, left me and other "independent socialists" with no counterweight to the huge influx of Northern communists. It is important to note that our views were not based solely on naiveté. During the sixties neither the NLF leaders nor the Politburo ever hoped for total military victory against the Americans and their clients. Our entire strategy was formulated with the expectation that eventually we would be involved in some kind of coalition government. Such a government would have been immune to outright North Vietnamese domination and could have expected substantial international support.

The political climate was at that time a complex mix of three distinct factions: communist, non-communist, and anti-communist. The silent majority, if I can use that expression, were the non-communists. Le Due Tho, who negotiated the Paris peace agreement with Dr. Kissinger, in his news conference in Paris in 1972, said:

> *For our part we have said many times, since I returned to Paris, this is the fifth time we have declared clearly that the DRV government [Hanoi] and the PRO [Viet Cong] have never wished to force a Communist government on South Vietnam. We only want there to be in South Vietnam a National Reconciliation government having three segments, supporting peace, independence, neutrality and democracy. I can clarify for you what the three segments are: one segment belonging to patriots... people who don't like the US, but who also may not support the PRG and DRV; one segment belonging to the PRG; one belonging to the Saigon government. A government like this would reflect the real political situation in South Vietnam and would be a resolution in accord with the situation and with logic.*

Until March 1975, no one among us, including the Politburo members, imagined the Saigon regime's collapse and the abandon-

ment by the Americans. We were preparing for a coalition government.

Under these circumstances, a coalition government dedicated to con-
cord and reconciliation was (and still is) the most pragmatic as well as
the most humane means toward national unity. Such a government
would also be in accord with the strong Vietnamese moral tradition of
showing grace to the defeated and forgetting past hatred, a tradition
that historically marked Vietnamese conduct even toward the Mongol
and Chinese aggressors. The solemn communist promises of reconciliation without reprisals and with respect for Southern independence
that were so attractive to the West and to the South Vietnamese people
thus appeared to be built on a realistic assessment of the military situation, the internal political climate, and the Vietnamese character. It
was our assessment as well, and it shaped our strategy for the postwar
period.

Almost every Vietnamese family had ties with both communists and
anti-communists. A million North Vietnamese escaped to the South
in 1954, leaving millions of their relatives behind living under and
working for the communist regime. Many Viet Cong guerrillas had
relatives in the South Vietnamese army and throughout the war there
were innumerable defections, both overt and hidden, from one side
to the other. Family attachments, avarice, patriotism, and self-interest
caused sympathies to shift and evolve so that the line between loyalties
was rarely clear. (The three-star general Tran Van Trung, head of the
psychological warfare of the Thieu regime, hid in his house his sister-
in-law Mme. Duong Thi Chi, a Viet Cong cadre, who was head of
the people's uprising committee in Hue. She is now a member of the
National Assembly. A four-star general, Cao Van Vien, commander-
in-chief of the ARVN, hid in his villa one of his wife's nephews who
was the son of a communist army general. A three-star general, Hoang
Xuan Lam, hid in his house a communist commando colonel who was
his relative. General Lam was once commander of the first military
corps of South Vietnam.)

Unfortunately when the war did end, North Vietnamese vindictive-
ness and fanaticism blossomed into a ferocious exercise of power. Hundreds of thousands of former officials and army officers of the Saigon
regime were imprisoned in "re-education camps." Literally millions
of ordinary citizens were forced to leave their homes and settle in the
so-Called New Economic Zones. One month after the "re-education"
program was imposed, few of those arrested were released. I asked the
communist leaders why they didn't free the people in the camps as
promised. I was told that the authorities had said only that the former
officials and army officers of the Saigon regime should bring with them
food enough for a month. The government had never promised that
the term of "re-education" would last for a month!

A rigid authoritarianism settled down over the entire country, an
authoritarianism supported by the third largest army in the world,
although Vietnam is among the twenty poorest nations in the world.
And where in all this are the feelings of the common people? Members
of the former resistance, their sympathizers, and those who supported
the Viet Cong are now filled with bitterness. These innocent people
swear openly that had they another chance, their choice would be very
different. One often hears sentiments such as this one: "I wouldn't give
them even a grain of rice now. I would pull them out of their hiding
places and denounce them to the authorities." At the same time, the
myth of Ho Chi Minh, the great patriot, has dissolved to nothingness.

The radical and hidden nature of the Northern takeover resulted in
the displacement of virtually every moderate and neutralist element.
There was simply nothing to stop the most rapacious and destructive
communist plans from being carried out. Carpet-bagging Northern
officials fought each other, sometimes at gunpoint, for the best offices,
the most comfortable houses, the most lucrative positions.

Despite their misfortune, the people still kept their sense of humor:
They frequently ridiculed the Party's slogans. Formerly Ho Chi Minh
called on the population in the North to double and triple their efforts
to liberate their brothers and sisters of the South. Nowadays one hears
the same slogans, lightly changed as follows: "Everybody should double

his efforts to buy a radio and bike for the Party officials, and triple his production so that the officials can have a new house and a pretty girlfriend."

Throughout the country, the people have passively resisted forced collectivization. The Party for its part tries to ascribe economic failure to natural calamities and the destruction of war, but in fact the underlying causes are social and psychological. On the one hand there is widespread popular discontent and on the other hand the failures of a totalitarian regime. Behind the fagade of unanimity, the silence and resignation of the population, there is the threatening reality that the Party's daily Nhan Dan (Pravda of Vietnam) can no longer dissimulate: "Our plant and other equipment run at only 50 percent of their capacity." Theft of public goods and property is common. There is no close cooperation between the different bureaucracies and sometimes these clash. We know what will become of the regime if this situation persists. The cadres work less because they no longer believe in their communist leaders. In June 1981, Hoang Tung, Party theoretician and editor of *Nhan Dan*, in a desperate effort to save the situation, asked Moscow to grant a billion rubles to Vietnam to save the country from collapse, an indication of Hanoi's deep dependence on the Soviet Union. Moreover, Hanoi allowed the Soviets to build piers and other facilities to service nuclear submarines at the former U.S. supply base at Cam Ranh Bay.

Vietnam is now practically an instrument of Soviet expansionism in Southeast Asia. There are at least 10,000 Soviet advisers in Vietnam today. Since joining Comecon in June 1978, Vietnam has steadily become an integral part of the Soviet system, especially so because the leaders of Hanoi have transposed to Indochina the Soviet model of Eastern Europe. Le Duan, the secretary general of the Vietnamese Communist Party, told the Fourth Party Congress on December 26, 1976 that "the Vietnamese revolution is an integral part of the world revolution," and he firmly insisted that "the Vietnamese revolution is to fulfill the internationalist duty and the international obligation" it owes to the Soviet Union. In my talks with Party leaders, I told them:

"You can make a revolution without clothes but you cannot make a revolution by hunger, repression, and building gulags." I protested that they had cheaply sold Vietnam's independence to the USSR. The Vietnamese people hated the Soviets intensely, calling them "Americans without dollars"; many Western visitors have been attacked by the children and the people because they were mistaken for Russians.

Certainly the occupation of Cambodia does not mean the end of the regime's international ambitions. Because of its consistent military and ideological involvement in the revolutionary movements in the region, and the support and military power of the Soviet Union, Hanoi has the will and also the means of exporting the revolution beyond the borders of Indochina when conditions permit. Moreover, the Soviet Union's Communist Party has assigned its Vietnamese brothers the job of training not only Laotian and Cambodian communists, but also other communists in the region, particularly those of Thailand and Malaysia. This takes place in the Central School of Nationalities of Hoa Binh in North Vietnam and at the Nguyen Ai Quoc Institute (a familiar name of Ho Chi Minh), the training school of the Party leaders.

Not many people can believe these things, just as they could not believe in the past that the North would take over the South and set up a communist regime. But the truth is that for the first time in our history, people have risked their lives to leave Vietnam; large numbers of Vietnamese never tried to flee their country to escape French domination or the American intervention. The refugee exodus began in earnest as the active population was systematically drafted into the protracted war against Cambodia and occupied Laos. For the first time since 1945, when famine killed two million people, Vietnam has been facing grave and widespread food shortages because fanatical leaders have sacrificed their people in order to fulfill the obligations of "internationalism."

The developing catastrophe brought back to me the memory of my father visiting me in prison in 1967 and saying: "I can't understand why you abandoned everything—a good job, a bright future, a happy family—to join the communists. In return for your sacrifice they will never give you the smallest part of what you have now. Worse, they will betray you and persecute you all your life."

I answered that he would simply have to accept the fact that he was giving one of his six children to struggle for a free and independent Vietnam. In that jail cell I felt I was fulfilling my obligation to fight against the military dictatorship that was oppressing my country. And to me it was not just an obligation, it was an honor. In my fervor I believed Ho Chi Minh's protestations that nationalists and communists could coexist in a "special" Vietnamese form of socialism.

I was tragically wrong. Like many Western intellectuals, I believed that the Northern communists, who had made heroic sacrifices in their own struggle for independence, would never by choice become dependent on any superpower. With other liberals I shared the romantic notion that those who had fought so persistently against oppression would not themselves become oppressors. The truth, however, has nothing romantic about it. The North Vietnamese communists, survivors of protracted, blood-drenched campaigns against colonialism, interventionism, and human oppression, became in their turn colonialists, interventionists, and architects of one of the world's most rigid regimes, becoming at the same time dependent clients of the Soviets.

The golden opportunity to harness the energy of 55 million people to rebuild their shattered country came in April 1975 when foreign involvement ended. That was the moment to initiate a policy of national reconciliation without reprisals, to establish a representative government that would include a spectrum of political parties and pursue a foreign policy of nonalignment. That was the moment to foster a spirit of brotherhood and focus the country's attention on the task of national reconstruction.

The communists, however, chose aggrandizement rather than reconciliation. The moment of military victory was the moment they began to eliminate the NLF. Many of my friends lamented, "They buried the NLF without even a ceremony." At the simple farewell dinner we held to formally disband the NLF in 1976, neither the Party nor the government sent a representative. It was a gesture of scorn toward the nationalistic and democratic principles for which the Viet Cong had bled so copiously and which the international liberal community had sustained so faithfully.

In their incessant and predatory pursuit of concentrated power, the communists have divided Vietnam instead of healing it. Their strategy has been to dislocate as much of the social fabric as possible in order to preclude the formation of a coherent opposition. Even the Party itself has been kept off balance. One-third of the Central Committee was purged during the Fourth Congress in 1976. Soon after, the 1.5 million Party members of 1976 were reduced to 700,000. By 1980 new members were recruited to bring the membership to about 1.7 million. Under the pretext of eliminating pro-Chinese and corrupt elements, some 300,000 members were purged during the Fifth Party Congress of 1982. Also purged were thirty-three members of the Central Committee and six members of the Politburo, including General Vo Nguyen Giap, who defeated the French at Dien Bien Phu.

Political power is now being concentrated in the families of Le Duan, Ho Chi Minh's successor, and of Le Due Tho, Kissinger's Paris adversary. Le Hong, Le Duan's son, is chief of security for the Politburo. Le Anh, another son, commands the missile defenses for the entire country. Le Duan's son-in-law is head of the air force and his brother-in-law has charge of the Party propaganda apparatus. Le Due Tho's brother, Nguyen Due Thuan, has become secretary general of the trade unions while another brother, Mai Chi Tho, is mayor of Ho Chi Minh City and chief of security in the South. His cousin, Nguyen Due Tarn, has been promoted to the powerful position of chief of Party organization.

I was given the opportunity to work for this government. After the communists had eliminated the NLF and imprisoned most of those they considered potential enemies, they offered me the position of vice-minister of nutrition. I refused. I could not ally myself with a regime that had proved itself inhuman and that the people hated so passionately. During the 1960s, I gave up a good job to fight for certain ideals—which are still the ideals of the Vietnamese people: independence, democracy, and social welfare. I have now to acknowledge my responsibility for the disastrous state of my country.

After refusing the government's offer, I lived on a small farm outside Saigon to escape continual surveillance. But I still had two escorts, a car, and a high salary. Finally, though, in November 1979, I managed to deceive my escorts and flee the country on a boat loaded with forty refugees.

If anything, my obligation to my countrymen is greater now because the oppression they are suffering is unparalleled in Vietnam's history. The wars against the French and Americans, grim though they were, still had a dimension of humanity to them. Today the Vietnamese in particular and the Indochinese in general are fighting against the most obdurate and persistent imperialists of the century, the Soviets. And there are no antiwar movements in Moscow.

What is worse, public opinion in the free world is not yet ready to support resistance to the Vietnamese communists or their Russian patrons. There is still a confused feeling that those who are against communism must be reactionary while those who are progressive will necessarily support the socialist regimes of this world.

But the stark lesson of Vietnamese concentration camps and Vietnamese boat people should affect even this ingrained attitude. No previous regime in my country brought such numbers of people to such desperation. Not the military dictators, not the colonialists, not even the ancient Chinese overlords. It is a lesson that my compatriots and I learned through witnessing and through suffering in our own lives the fate of our countrymen. It is a lesson that must eventually move the conscience of the world.

PSI-REC: OF SWORD AND SITAR, THE WAR WITHOUT

by Peter Dillingham

Editor's Introduction

It is not always the poet's task to persuade. Sometimes the intention is something quite different. Peter Dillingham has perfected the skill of communicating images. Some of them can be quite disturbing.

———————————

Free companions of the Milky Way, we enter their arena, Sword and Sitar, enter this spotlit containment of Earth air paved with mirrors, as perhaps on some other alien world, Misha the Danseur and Aaraatuag the Eskimo Song Duelist, our brethren, lovers, tomorrow's enemy, mobilize Piseq and drum against Grand Jete, tour en l'air.

We enter this warzone, this theater, I Kensei, Sword Saint, sinister, he with the Sitar, dexter, Earth's martial elite, mercenaries, masters of Earth's most acclaimed art, most esteemed export—war—impeccable wars:

World Wars!
    Star Wars!
        Wars Waged Without Wrack Or Waste!

War more art than war. Wars arranged and hyped by Earth's dog-faced war brokers, holograds touting our skills, recommending combinations of combatants—such artistry, oh my beloved warlots:

VS

Shaman Sandpainter	The Mime Marcel
Mere magic	The sculpture of silence
Manilas de Plata	Miguelito the Matador
Malaguenas	Margaritas in a suit of lights

We their champions, what alien belligerents there in the swirling, caustic darkness? What sparked this call to arms? Dabbling dilettantes? Deadly serious? What matter! The contracts signed, earnests given, he for the right, I for the left, we will fight. We are warriors.

Happo Biraki, open on all eight sides, long sword and companion in hand, I wait, considering Mushashi's Five Rings, Way of the Warrior—Ground, Water, Fire, Wind, Void—I have learned, Master, the Five Attitudes, the Five Approaches. I have taught my body strategy, to hit the enemy in one timing. My sword my soul, I wait.

He begins. Raga, that which colors the mind. Alap, free flowing, without rhythm, ascending, descending like alien sword cuts, in rasa karuna. A trap this sentiment—pathetic, tearful, sad... Hypnotic, his intense singleness of mood. He would lure me with his loneliness, his longing. Jor.

Flowing Water Cut? Fire and Stones Cut? Red Leaves Cut? Kesagake, whiplike my sword slashes. One cut, calmly, to strike the King of Notes within the Lord of Melody's Court... Jhala, the chickari strings sound.

What match, Musashi, the spirit of one cut against Sitar's gentle curves, those minute, microtonic twinnings, shruti; what match to meend, that sliding, gliding note to note, winding whorls of detail, subtle ornament, intrinsicate... Sword snare that chain of melody, manrikigusari, with the power of ten thousand.

A primal scream torn from countless psi out there in the darkness sinister, the piercing agony of defeat. Visions of Hiroshima, forever etched deep in their souls. Poor, faceless fools to think our ritual combat, this supreme refinement of war, freed them of its horrors. And the victors? Scarred, tainted with their victory.

The sword sheathed, the sitar in its muslin bag, our road manager beckons us to our ship. We depart. Another world, another alien war awaits... this unconquerable lust.

SILENT LEGES

by Jerry Pournelle

Editor's Introduction

I wrote this story at a time when I was considerably less hopeful about the economic effects of technology, especially development of space resources, and considerably more hopeful about internal developments within the Soviet Union.

At that time I believed that the Soviet tyranny would evolve as tyrannies always have; that its leaders would become cynical; and that soon enough the Soviets would decide that, hate the U.S. as much as they would, it would be better to share the world with the U.S. than to admit any third party—such as China—to real power.

I also assumed that the U.S. might itself develop such a cynical view. This is not as unlikely as it seems. Certainly we have no lack of politicians who will sell out the real interests of the nation—as recognized by the politicians themselves—in order to win reelection. Take for example the California legislature, which cynically gerrymandered the state to insure the reelection of incumbents, this in the face of a statewide initiative demanding new redistricting. Take for example the spectacle of ever-mounting budget deficits while Congress continues to spend and spend and elect and elect and bombastically proclaim that the economy cannot withstand such terrible deficits. Take—but no need to break a butterfly on the wheel. Examples are all too easy to come by.

Given such trends in the U.S. and the Soviet Union, might they not agree to divide the world between them? If so, they might well set up a CoDominium government, in theory controlled by a Grand Senate but in practice dominated by the two superpowers. The CoDominium might have its own armed forces: Thus was born the stories of the CoDominium Fleet and CD Marines.

Could this happen in the real world? Probably not. The Union of Soviet Socialist Republics is governed by a troika: the Army, the Party and the KGB. Each has great power, but not sufficient to overcome the opposition of the other two. The Party has the fewest resources, but it controls promotions within the other two organizations; and it cannot share power with the West. Only the Army could do that, and it would do so only if it felt threatened from within.

After Stalin died in 1953, the Army and Party nearly destroyed the secret police. Then the Party discovered that it was unable to control the Army. There was, for a time, the possibility that the Soviet Empire would become yet another military despotism, subject to the usual factors that affect such despoties; a nation such as Ted Cogswell describes in the opening story of this volume.

Then the Party asked for help, and the KGB was reconstituted.

So long as the Party and the KGB prevail, the CoDominium is unlikely. It is not, however, impossible; and meanwhile, it gives birth to good stories.

Good soldiers do not make good butchers, and butchers seldom make good soldiers. There is an internal logic to any effective military force. Moreover, a small, powerful, volunteer military group, separated from and disliked by civilians, inevitably turns inward, receiving its rewards and taking its directions from its own traditions. The Legion is one such force. The United States Army in the period between the World Wars was another. Professional soldiers will often obey politicians, but they seldom respect them.

John Christian Falkenberg respects them not at all.

"Inter Armes, Silent Leges"
Legal Maxim

I

Eight thousand young bodies writhed to the maddening beat of an electronic bass. Some danced while others lay back on the grass and drank or smoked. None could ignore the music, although they were only barely aware of the nasal tenor whose voice was not strong enough to carry over the wild squeals of the theremin and the twang of a dozen steel-stringed guitars. Other musical groups waited their turn on the gray wooden platform erected among the twentieth-century Gothic buildings of Los Angeles University.

Some of the musicians were so anxious to begin that they pounded their instruments. This produced nothing audible because their amplifiers were turned off, but it allowed them to join in the frenzied spirit of the festival on the campus green.

The concert was a happy affair. Citizens from a nearby Welfare Island joined the students in the college park. Enterprising dealers hawked liquor and pot and borloi. Catering trucks brought food. The Daughters of Lilith played original works while Slime waited their turn, and after those would come even more famous groups. An air of peace and fellowship engulfed the crowd.

"Lumpen proletariat." The speaker was a young woman. She stood at a window in a classroom overlooking the common green and the mad scene below. "Lumpen," she said again.

"Aw, come off the bolshi talk. Communism's no answer. Look at the Sovworld—"

"Revolution betrayed! Betrayed!" the girl said. She faced her challenger. "There will be no peace and freedom until—"

"Can it." The meeting chairman banged his fist on the desk. "We've got work to do. This is no time for ideology."

"Without the proper revolutionary theory, nothing can be accomplished." This came from a bearded man in a leather jacket. He looked first at the chairman, then at the dozen others in the classroom. "First there must be a proper understanding of the problem. Then we can act!"

The chairman banged his fist again, but someone else spoke. "Deeds, not words. We came here to plan some action. What the hell's all the talking about? You goddamned theorists give me a pain in the ass! What we need is action. The Underground's done more for the Movement than you'll ever–"

"Balls." The man in the leather jacket snorted contempt. Then he stood. His voice projected well. "You act, all right. You shut down the L.A. transport system for three days. Real clever. And what did it accomplish? Made the taxpayers scared enough to fork over pay raises for the cops. You ended the goddamn pig strike, that's what you did!"

There was a general babble, and the Underground spokesman tried to answer, but the leather-jacketed man continued. "You started food riots in the Citizen areas. Big deal. It's results that count, and your result was the CoDominium Marines! You brought in the Marines, that's what you did!"

"Damned right! We exposed this regime for what it really is! The Revolution can't come until the people understand–"

"Revolution, my ass. Get it through your heads, technology's the only thing that's going to save us. Turn technology loose, free the scientists, and we'll be–"

He was shouted down by the others. There was more babble.

Mark Fuller sat at the student desk and drank it all in. The wild music outside. Talk of revolution. Plans for action, for making something happen, for making the Establishment notice them; it was all new, and he was here in this room, where the real power, of the university lay. God, how I love it! he thought. I've never had any kind of power before. Not even over my own life. And now we can show them all!

He felt more alive than he ever had in his twenty years. He looked at the girl next to him and smiled. She grinned and patted his thigh.

Tension rose in his loins until it was almost unbearable. He remembered their yesterdays and imagined their tomorrows. The quiet world of taxpayer country where he had grown up seemed very far away.

The others continued their argument. Mark listened, but his thoughts kept straying to Shirley: to the warmth of her hand on his thigh, to the places where her sweater was stretched out of shape, to the remembered feel of her knees against his back and her cries of passion. He knew he ought to listen more carefully to the discussion. He didn't really belong in this room at all. If Shirley hadn't brought him, he'd never have known the meeting was happening.

But I'll earn a place here, he thought. In my own right. Power. That's what they have, and I'll learn how to be part of it.

The jacketed technocracy man was speaking again. "You see too many devils," he said. "Get the CoDominium Intelligence people off the scientists' backs and it won't be twenty years before all of the earth's a paradise. All of it, not just taxpayer country."

"A polluted paradise! What do you want, to go back to the smog? Oil slicks, dead fish, animals exterminated, that's what—"

"Bullshit. Technology can get us out of—"

"That's what caused the problems in the first place!"

"Because we didn't go far enough! There hasn't been a new scientific idea since the goddamn space drive! You're so damned proud because there's no pollution. None here, anyway. But it's not because of conservation, it's because they ship people out, because of triage, because—"

"He's right, people starve while we—"

"Damn right! Free thoughts, freedom to think, to plan, to do research, to publish without censorship, that's what will liberate the world."

The arguments went on until the chairman tired of them. He banged his fist again. "We are here to do something," he said. "Not to settle the world's problems this afternoon. That was agreed."

The babble finally died away and the chairman spoke meaningfully. "This is our chance. A peaceful demonstration of power. Show what we think of their goddamned rules and their status cards. But we've got to be careful. It mustn't get out of hand."

Mark sprawled on the grass a dozen meters from the platform. He stretched luxuriantly in the California sun while Shirley stroked his back. Excitement poured in through all his senses. College had been like this in imagination. The boys at the expensive private school where his father had sent him used to whisper about festivals, demonstrations, and confrontations, but it hadn't been real. Now it was. He'd hardly ever mingled with Citizens before, and now they were all around him. They wore Welfare-issue clothing and talked in strange dialects that Mark only half understood. Everyone, Citizens and students, writhed to the music that washed across them.

Mark's father had wanted to send him to a college in taxpayer country, but there hadn't been enough money. He might have won a scholarship, but he hadn't. Mark told himself it was deliberate. Competition was no way to live. A lot of his friends had refused to compete in the rat race. None of them ended here, though; they'd had the money to get to Princeton or Yale.

More Citizens poured in. The festival was supposed to be open only to those with tickets, and Citizens weren't supposed to come on the campus in the first place, but the student group had opened the gates and cut the fences. It had all been planned in the meeting. Now the gate-control shack was on fire, and everyone who lived nearby could get in.

Shirley was ecstatic. "Look at them!" she shouted. "This is the way it used to be! Citizens should be able to go wherever they want to. Equality forever!"

Mark smiled. It was all new to him. He hadn't thought much about the division between Citizen and taxpayer, and had accepted his privileges without noticing them. He had learned a lot from Shirley and his new friends, but there was so much more that he didn't know. I'll find out, though, he thought. We know what we're doing. We can make the world so much better—we can do anything! Time for the stupid old bastards to move over and let some fresh ideas in.

Shirley passed him a pipe of borloi. That was another new thing for him; it was a Citizen habit, something Mark's father despised. Mark couldn't understand why. He inhaled deeply and relished the wave of contentment it brought. Then he reached for Shirley and held her in his warm bath of concern and love, knowing she was as happy as he was.

She smiled gently back at him, her hand resting on his thigh, and they writhed to the music, the beat thundering through them, faces glowing with anticipation of what would come, of what they would accomplish this day. The pipe came around again and Mark seized it eagerly.

"Pigs! The pigs are coming!" The cry went up from the fringes of the crowd.

Shirley turned to her followers. "Just stay here. Don't provoke the bastards. Make sure you don't do anything but sit tight."

There were murmurs of agreement. Mark felt a wave of excitement flash through him. This was it. And he was right there in front with the leaders; even if all his status did come from being Shirley's current boyfriend, he was one of the leaders, one of the people who make things happen...

The police were trying to get through the crowd so they could stop the festival. The university president was with them, and he was shouting something Mark couldn't understand. Over at the edge of the common green there was a lot of smoke. Was a building on fire? That didn't make sense. There weren't supposed to be any fires, nothing was to be harmed; just ignore the cops and the university people, show how Citizens and students could mingle in peace; show how stupid the damned rules were, and how needless–

There was a fire. Maybe more than one. Police and firemen tried to get through the crowd. Someone kicked a cop and the bluecoat went down. A dozen of his buddies waded into the group. Their sticks rose and fell.

The peaceful dream vanished. Mark stared in confusion. There was a man screaming somewhere, where was he? In the burning building? A group began chanting: *"Equality now! Equality now!"*

Another group was building a barricade across the green. "They aren't supposed to do that!" Mark shouted. Shirley grinned at him. Her eyes shone in excitement. More police came, then more, and a group headed toward Mark. They raised aluminum shields as rocks flew across the green. The police came closer. One of the cops raised his club.

He was going to hit Shirley! Mark grabbed at the nightstick and deflected it. Citizens and students clustered around. Some threw themselves at the cops. A big man, well-dressed, too old to be a student, kicked at the leading policeman. The cop went down.

Mark pulled Shirley away as a dozen black-jacketed Lampburners joined the melee. The Lampburners would deal with the cops, but Mark didn't want to watch. The boys in his school had talked contemptuously about pigs, but the only police Mark had ever met had been polite and deferential; this was ugly, and–

His head swam in confusion. One minute he'd been laying in Shirley's arms with music and fellowship and everything was wonderful. Now there were police, and groups shouting, "Kill the pigs!" and fires burning. The Lampburners were swarming everywhere. They hadn't been at the meeting. Most claimed to be wanted by the police. But they'd had a representative at the planning session, they'd agreed this would be a peaceful demonstration–

A man jumped off the roof of the burning building. There was no one below to catch him, and he sprawled on the steps like a broken doll. Blood poured from his mouth, a bright-red splash against the pink marble steps. Another building shot flames skyward. More police arrived and set up electrified barriers around the crowd.

A Civilian, his bright clothing a contrast with the dull police blue, got out of a cruiser and stood atop it as police held their shields in front of him. He began to shout through a bull horn:

"I READ YOU THE ACT OF 1991 AS AMENDED. WHEN-EVER THERE SHALL BE AN ASSEMBLY LIKELY TO ENDAN-GER PUBLIC OR PRIVATE PROPERTY OR THE LIVES OF

CITIZENS AND TAXPAYERS, THE LAWFUL MAGISTRATES SHALL COMMAND ALL PERSONS ASSEMBLED TO DIS-PERSE AND SHALL WARN THEM THAT FAILURE TO DIS-PERSE SHALL BE CONSIDERED A DECLARATION OF RE-BELLION THE MAGISTRATES SHALL GIVE SUFFICIENT TIME..."

Mark knew the act. He'd heard it discussed in school. It was time to get away. The local mayor would soon have more than enough authority to deal with this mad scene. He could even call on the military, US or CoDominium for help. The barriers were up around two sides of the green, but the cops hadn't closed off all the buildings. There was a doorway ahead, and Mark pulled Shirley toward it. "Come on!"

Shirley wouldn't come. She stood defiant, grinning wildly, shaking her fist at the police, shouting curses at them. Then she turned to Mark. "If you're scared, just go on, baby. Bug off."

Someone handed a bottle around. Shirley drank and gave it to Mark. He raised it to his lips but didn't drink any. His head pounded, and he was afraid. I should run, he thought. I should run like hell. The mayor's finished reading the act...

"EQUALITY NOW! EQUALITY NOW!" The chant was contagious. Half the crowd was shouting.

The police waited impassively. An officer glanced at his watch from time to time. Then the officer nodded, and the police advanced. Four technicians took hoses from one of the cruisers and directed streams of foam above the heads of the advancing blue line. The slimy liquid fell in a spray around Mark.

Mark fell. He tried to stand and couldn't. Everyone around him fell. Whatever the liquid touched became so slippery that no one could hold onto it. It didn't seem to affect the police.

Instant banana peel, Mark thought. He'd seen it used on tri-v. Everyone laughed when they saw it used on tri-v. Now it didn't seem so funny. A couple of attempts showed Mark that he couldn't get away;

he could barely crawl. The police moved rapidly toward him. Rocks and bottles clanged against their shields.

The black-jacketed Lampburners took spray cans from their pockets. They sprayed their shoes and hands and then got up. They began to move away through the helpless crowd, away from the police, toward an empty building.

The police line reached the group around Mark. The cops fondled their nightsticks. They spoke in low tones, too low to be heard any distance away. "Stick time," one said. "Yeah. Our turn," his partner answered.

"Does anyone here claim taxpayer status?" The cop eyed the group coldly. "Speak up."

"Yes. Here." One boy tried to get up. He fell again, but he held up his ID card. "Here." Mark reached for his own.

"Fink!" Shirley shouted. She threw something at the other boy. "Hypocrite! Pig! Fink!" Others were shouting as well. Mark saw Shirley's look of hatred and put his card back into his pocket. There'd be time later.

Two police grabbed him. One lifted his feet, the other lifted his shoulders. When he was a couple of feet off the ground, the one holding his shoulders let go. The last thing Mark heard as his head hit the pavement was the mocking laughter of the cop.

The bailiff was grotesque, with mustaches like Wyatt Earp and an enormous paunch that hung over his equipment belt. In a bored voice he read, "Case 457–984. People against Mark Fuller. Rebellion, aggravated assault, resisting arrest."

The judge looked down from the bench. "How do you plead?"

"Guilty, Your Honor," Mark's lawyer said. His name was Zower, and he wasn't expensive. Mark's father couldn't afford an expensive lawyer.

But I didn't, Mark thought. I didn't. When he'd said that earlier, though, the attorney had been contemptuous. "Shut up or you'll make it worse," the lawyer had said. "I had trouble enough getting the conspiracy charges dropped. Just stand there looking innocent and don't say a goddamn thing."

The judge nodded. "Have you anything to say in mitigation?"

Zower put his hand on Mark's shoulder. "My client throws himself on the mercy of the court," he said. "Mark has never been in trouble before. He acted under the influence of evil companions and intoxicants. There was no real intent to commit crimes. Just very bad judgment."

The judge didn't look impressed. "What have the people to say about this?"

"Your Honor," the prosecutor began. "The people have had more than enough of these student riots. This was no high-jinks stunt by young taxpayers. This was a deliberate rebellion, planned in advance.

"We have recordings of this hoodlum striking a police officer. That officer subsequently suffered a severe beating with three fractures, a ruptured kidney, and other personal injuries. It is a wonder the officer is alive. We can also show that after the mayor's proclamation, the accused made no attempt to leave. If the defense disputes these facts…"

"No, no." Zower spoke hastily. "We stipulate, Your Honor." He muttered to himself, just loud enough that Mark could hear. "Can't let them run those pix. That'd get the judge *really* upset."

Zower stood. "Your Honor, we stipulate Mark's bad judgment, but remember, he was intoxicated. He was with new friends, friends he didn't know very well. His father is a respected taxpayer, manager of General Foods in Santa Maria. Mark has never been arrested before. I'm sure he's learned a lesson from all this."

And where is Shirley? Mark wondered. Somehow her politician father had kept her from even being charged.

The judge was nodding. Zower smiled and whispered to Mark, "I stroked him pretty good in chambers. We'll get probation."

"Mister Fuller, what have you to say for yourself?" the judge demanded.

Mark stood eagerly. He wasn't sure what he was going to say.

Plead? Beg for mercy? Tell him to stick it? Not that. Mark breathed hard. I'm scared, he thought. He walked nervously toward the bench.

The judge's face exploded in a cloud of red. There was wild laughter in the court. Another balloon of red ink sailed across the courtroom to burst on the high bench. Mark laughed hysterically, completely out of control, as the spectators shouted.

"EQUALITY NOW!" Eight voices speaking in unison cut through the babble. "JUSTICE! EQUALITY! CITIZEN JUDGES, NOT TAXPAYERS! EQUALITY NOW! EQUALITY NOW! EQUALITY NOW! ALL POWER TO THE LIBERATION PARTY!"

The last stung like a blow. The judge's face turned even redder. He stood in fury. The fat bailiff and his companions moved decisively through the crowd. Two of the demonstrators escaped, but the bailiff was much faster than his bulk made him look. After a time the court was silent.

The judge stood, ink dripping from his face and robes. He was not smiling. "This amused you?" he demanded.

"NO," Mark said. "It was none of my doing!"

"I do not believe the outlawed Liberation Party would trouble itself for anyone not one of their own. Mark Fuller, you have pleaded guilty to serious crimes. We would normally send a taxpayer's son to rehabilitation school, but you and your friends have demanded equality. Very well. You shall have it.

"Mark Fuller, I sentence you to three years at hard labor. Since you have renounced your allegiance to the United States by participating in a deliberate act of rebellion, such participation stipulated by your attorney's admission that you made no move to depart after the reading of the act, you have no claim upon the United States. The United States therefore renounces you. It is hereby ordered that you be delivered to the CoDominium authorities to serve your sentence wherever they shall find convenient."

The gavel fell to the bench. It didn't sound very loud at all.

II

The low gravity of Luna Base was better than the endless nightmare of the flight up. He'd been trapped in a narrow compartment with berths so close together that the sagging bunk above his pressed against him at high acceleration. The ship had stunk with the putrid smell of vomit and stale wine.

Now he stood under glaring lights in a bare concrete room. The concrete was the gray-green color of moon rock. They hadn't been given an outside view, and except for gravity, he might have been in a basement on Earth. There were a thousand others standing with him under the glaring bright fluorescent lights. Most of them had the dull look of terror. A few glared defiantly, but they kept their opinions to themselves.

Gray-coveralled trusties with bell-mouthed sonic stunners patroled the room. It wouldn't have been worthwhile trying to take one of the weapons from the trusties, though; at each entrance was a knot of CoDominium Marines in blue and scarlet. The Marines leaned idly on weapons which were not harmless at all.

"Segregate us," Mark's companion said. "Divide and rule."

Mark nodded. Bill Halpern was the only person Mark knew. Halpern had been the technocrat spokesman in the meeting on campus.

"Divide and rule," Halpern said again. It was true enough. The prisoners had been sorted by sex, race, and language, so that everyone around Mark was white male and either North American or from some other English-speaking place. "What the hell are we waiting for?" Halpern wondered. There was no possible answer, and they stood for what seemed like hours.

Then the doors opened and a small group came in. Three CoDominium Navy petty officers, and a midshipman. The middie was no more than seventeen, younger than Mark. He used a bullhorn to speak to the assembled group. "Volunteers for the Navy?"

There were several shouts, and some of the prisoners stepped forward.

"Traitors," Halpern said.

Mark nodded agreement. Although he had meant it in a different way from Halpern, Mark's father had always said the same thing. "Traitors!" he'd thundered. "Dupes of the goddamn Soviets. One of these days that Navy will take over this country and hand us to the Kremlin."

Mark's teachers at school had different ideas. The Navy wasn't needed at all. Nor was the CD. Men no longer made war, at least not on Earth. Colony squabbles were of no interest to the people of Earth anyway. Military services, they'd told him, were a wasteful joke.

His new friends at college said the purpose of the CoDominium was to keep the United States and the Soviet Union rich while suppressing everyone else. Then they'd begun using the CD fleet and Marines to shore up their domestic governments. The whole CD was nothing more than a part of the machinery of oppression.

And yet—on tri-v the CD Navy was glamorous. It fought pirates (only Mark knew there were no real space pirates) and restored order in the colonies (only his college friends told him that wasn't restoring order, it was oppression of free people). The spacers wore uniforms and explored new planets.

The CD midshipman walked along the line of prisoners. Two older petty officers followed. They walked proudly—contemptuously, even. They saw the prisoners as another race, not as fellow humans at all.

A convict not far from Mark stepped out of line. "Mister Blaine," the man said. "Please, sir."

The midshipman stopped. "Yes?"

"Don't you know me, Mister Blaine? Able Spacer Johnson, sir. In Mister Leary's division in *Magog*."

The middie nodded with the gravity of a seventeen-year-old who has important duties and knows it. "I recall you, Johnson."

"Let me back in, sir. Six years I served, never up for defaulters."

The midshipman took papers from his clipboard and ran his finger down a list. "Drunk and disorderly, assault on a taxpayer, armed robbery, third conviction. Mandatory transportation. I shouldn't wonder that you prefer the Navy, Johnson."

"Not like that at all, sir. I shouldn't ever have took my musterin'-out pay. Shouldn't have left the Fleet, sir. Couldn't find my place with civilians, sir. God knows I drank too much, but I was never drunk on duty, sir, you look up my records—

"Kiss the middie's bum, you whining asshole," Halpern said.

One of the petty officers glanced up. "Silence in the ranks." He put his hand on his nightstick and glared at Halpern.

The midshipman thought for a moment. "All right, Johnson. You'll come in as ordinary. Have to work for the stripe."

"Yes, sir, sure thing, sir." Johnson strode toward the area reserved for recruits. His manner changed with each step he took. He began in a cringing walk, but by the time he reached the end of the room, he had straightened and walked tall.

The midshipman went on down the line. Twenty men volunteered, but he took only three.

An hour later a CoDominium Marine sergeant came looking for men. "No rebels and no degenerates!" he said. He took six young men sentenced for street rioting, arson, mayhem, resisting arrest, assault on police, and numerous other crimes.

"Street gang," Halpern said. "Perfect for Marines."

Eventually they were herded back into a detention pen and left to themselves. "You really hate the CD, don't you?" Mark asked his companion.

"I hate what they do."

Mark nodded, but Halpern only sneered. "You don't know anything at all," Halpern said. "Oppression? Shooting rioters? Sure, that's part of what the CD does, but it's not the worst part. Symptom, not cause. The cause is their goddamn so-called intelligence service. Suppression of scientific research. Censorship of technical journals. They've stopped even the pretense of basic research. When was the last time a licensed physicist had a decent idea?"

Mark shrugged. He knew nothing about physics.

Halpern grinned. There was no warmth in the expression. His voice had a bitter edge. "Keeping the peace, they say. Only discourage new weapons, new military technology. Bullshit, they've stopped everything for fear somebody somewhere will come up with–"

"Shut the fuck up." The man was big, hairy like a bear, with a big paunch jutting out over the belt of his coveralls. "If I hear that goddamn whining once more, I'll stomp your goddamn head in."

"Hey, easy," Halpern said. "We're all in this together. We have to join against the class enemy–"

The big men's hand swung up without warning. He hit Halpern on the mouth. Halpern staggered and fell. His head struck the concrete floor. "Told you to shut up." He turned to Mark. "You got anything to say?"

Mark was terrified. I ought to do something, he thought. Say something. Anything. He tried to speak, but no words came out.

The big man grinned at him, then deliberately kicked Halpern in the ribs. "Didn't think so. Hey, you're not bad lookin', kid. Six months we'll be on that goddamn ship, with no women. Want to be my bunkmate? I'll take good care of you. See nobody hurts you. You'll like that."

"Leave the kid alone." Mark couldn't see who spoke. "I said, let go of him."

"Who says so?" The hairy man shoved Mark against the wall and turned to the newcomer.

"I do." The newcomer didn't look like much, Mark thought. At least forty, and slim. Not thin though, Mark realized. The man stood with his hands thrust into the pockets of his coveralls. "Let him be, Karper."

Karper grinned and charged at the newcomer. As he rushed forward, his opponent pivoted and sent a kick to Karper's head. As Karper reeled back, two more kicks slammed his head against the wall. Then the newcomer moved forward and deliberately kneed Karper in the kidney. The big man went down and rolled beside Halpern.

"Come on, kid, it stinks over here." He grinned at Mark.

"But my buddy–"

"Forget him." The man pointed. Five trusties were coming into the pen. They lifted Halpern and Karper and carried them away. One of the trusties winked as they went past Mark and the other man. "See? Maybe you'll see your friend again, maybe not. They don't like troublemakers."

"Bill's not a troublemaker! That other man started it! It's not fair!"

"Kid, you better forget that word 'fair.' It could cause you no end of problems. Got any smokes?" He accepted Mark's cigarette with a glance at the label. "Thanks. Name?"

"Mark Fuller."

"Dugan. Call me Biff."

"Thanks, Biff. I guess I needed some help."

"That you did. Hell, it was fun. Karper was gettin' on my nerves anyway. How old are you, kid?"

"Twenty." And what does he want? Lord God, is he looking for a bunkmate too?

"You don't look twenty. Taxpayer, aren't you?"

"Yes—how did you know?"

"It shows. What's a taxpayer kid doing here?"

Mark told him. "It wasn't fair," he finished.

"There's that word again. You were in college, eh? Can you read?"

"Well, sure, everyone can read."

Dugan laughed. "I can't. Not very well. And I bet you're the only one in this pen who ever read a whole book. Where'd you learn?"

"Well—in school. Maybe a little at home."

Dugan blew a careful smoke ring. It hung in the air between them. "Me, I never saw a book until they dragged me off to school, and nobody gave a shit whether we looked at 'em or not. Had to pick up some of it, but—look, maybe you know things I don't. Want to stick with me a while?"

Mark eyed him suspiciously. Dugan laughed. "Hell, I don't bugger kids. Not until I've been locked up a lot longer than this, anyway. Man needs a buddy, though, and you just lost yours."

"Yeah. Okay. Want another cigarette?"

"We better save 'em. We'll need all you got."

A petty officer opened the door to the pen. "Classification," he shouted. "Move out this door."

"Got to it pretty fast," Dugan said. "Come on." They followed the others out and through a long corridor until they reached another large room. There were tables at the end, and trusties sat at each table. Eventually Mark and Dugan got to one.

The trusty barely looked at them. When they gave their names, he punched them into a console on the table. The printer made tiny clicking noises and two sheets of paper fell out. "Any choice?" the trusty asked.

"What's open, shipmate?" Dugan asked.

"I'm no shipmate of yours," the trusty sneered. "Tanith, Sparta, and Fulson's World."

Dugan shuddered. "Well, we sure don't want Fulson's World." He reached into Mark's pocket and took out the pack of cigarettes, then laid them on the table. They vanished into the trusty's coveralls.

"Not Fulson's," the trusty said. "Now, I hear they're lettin' the convicts run loose on Sparta." He said nothing more but looked at them closely.

Mark remembered that Sparta was founded by a group of intellectuals. They were trying some kind of social experiment. Unlike Tanith with its CoDominium governor, Sparta was more or less independent. They'd have a better chance there. "We'll take Sparta," Mark said.

"Sparta's pretty popular," the trusty said. He waited expectantly for a moment. "Well, too bad." He scrawled "Tanith" across their papers and handed them over. "Move along." A petty officer waved them through a door behind the table.

"But we wanted Sparta," Mark protested.

"Get your ass out of here," the CD petty officer said. "Move it." Then it was too late and they were through the door.

"Wish I'd had some credits," Dugan muttered. "We bought off Fulson's though. That's something."

"But—I have some money. I didn't know–"

Dugan gave him a curious look. "Kid, they didn't teach you much in that school of yours. Well, come on, we'll make out. But you better let me take care of that money."

CDSS Vladivostok hurtled toward the orbit of Jupiter. The converted assault troop carrier was crammed with thousands of men jammed into temporary berths welded into the troop bays. There were more men than bunks; many of the convicts had to trade off half the time.

Dugan took over a corner. Corners were desirable territory, and two men disputed his choice. After they were carried away, no one else thought it worth trying. Biff used Mark's money to finance a crap game in the area near their berths, and in a few days he had trebled their capital.

"Too bad," Dugan said. "If we'd had this much back on Luna, we'd be headed for Sparta. Anyway, we bought our way into this ship, and that's worth something." He grinned at Mark's lack of response. "Hey, kid, it could be worse. We could be with BuReloc. You think this Navy ship's bad, try a BuReloc hellhole."

Mark wondered how Bureau of Relocation ships could be worse, but he didn't want to find out. The newscasters back on Earth had documentary specials about BuReloc. They all said that conditions were tough but bearable. They also told of the glory: mankind settling other worlds circling other stars. Mark felt none of the glory now.

Back home Zower would be making an appeal. Or at least he'd be billing Mark's father for one. And so what? Mark thought. Nothing would come of it. But something might! Jason Fuller had some political favors coming. He might pull a few strings. Mark could be headed back home within a year…

He knew better, but he had no other hope. He lived in misery, brooding about the low spin gravity, starchy food, the constant stench of the other convicts; all that was bad, but the water was the worst thing. He knew it was recycled. Water on Earth was recycled too, but there you didn't think how it had been used to bathe the foul sores of the man two bays to starboard.

Sometimes a convict would rush screaming through the compartment, smashing at bunks and flinging his fellow prisoners about like matchsticks, until a dozen men would beat him to the deck. Eventually the guards would take him away. None ever came back.

The ship reached the orbit of Jupiter and took on fuel from the scoopship tankers that waited for her. Then she moved to the featureless point in space that marked the Alderson jump tramline. Alarms rang; then everything blurred. They sat on their bunks in confusion, unable to move or even think. That lasted long after the instantaneous Jump. The ship had covered light-years in a single instant; now they had to cross another star's gravity well to reach the next Jump point.

Two weeks later a petty officer entered the compartment. "Two men needed for cleanup in the crew area. Chance for Navy chow. Volunteers?"

"Sure," Dugan said. "My buddy and me. Anybody object?"

No one did. The petty officer grinned. "Looks like you're elected." He led them through corridors and passageways to the forward end of the ship, where they were put to scrubbing the bulkheads. A bored Marine watched idly.

"I thought you said never volunteer," Mark told Dugan.

"Good general rule. But what else we got to do? Gets us better chow. Always take a chance on something when it can't be no worse than what you've got."

The lunch was good and the work was not hard. Even the smell of disinfectant was a relief, and scrubbing off the bulkheads and decks got their hands clean for the first time since they'd been put aboard. In mid-afternoon a crewman came by. He stopped and stared at them for a moment.

"Dugan! Biff Dugan, by God!"

"Horrigan, you slut. When'd you join up?"

"Aw, you know how it is, Biff, they moved in on the racket and what could I do? I see they got you–"

"Clean got me. Sarah blew the whistle on me."

"Told you she wouldn't put up with you messing around. Who's your chum?"

"Name's Mark. He's learning. Hey, Goober, what can you do for me?"

"Funny you ask. Maybe I got something. Want to enlist?"

"Hell, they don't want me. I tried back on Luna. Too old."

Horrigan nodded. "Yeah, but the Purser's gang needs men. Freakie killed twenty crewmen yesterday. Recruits. This geek opened an air lock and nobody stopped him. That's why you're out here swabbing. Look. Biff, we're headed for a long patrol after we drop you guys on Tanith. Maybe I can fix it."

"No harm in trying. Mark, you lost anything on Tanith?"

"No." But I don't want to join the CD Navy, either. Only why not? He tried to copy his friend's easy indifference. "Can't be worse than where we are."

"Right," Horrigan said. "We'll go see the Purser's middie. That okay, mate?" he asked the Marine.

The Marine shrugged. "Okay by me."

Horrigan led the way forward. Mark felt sick excitement. Getting out of the prison compartment suddenly became the most important thing in his life.

Midshipman Greschin was not surprised to find two prisoners ready to join the Navy. He questioned them for a few minutes. Then he studied Dugan's records on the readout screen. "You have been in space before, but there is nothing on your record—

"I never said I've been out."

"No, but you have. Are you a deserter?"

"No," Dugan said.

Greschin shrugged. "If you are, we will find out. If not, we do not care. I see no reason why you cannot be enlisted. I will call Lieutenant Breslov."

Breslov was fifteen years older than his midshipman. He looked over Dugan's print-out. Then he examined Mark's. "I can take Dugan," he said. "Not you, Fuller."

"But why?" Mark asked.

Breslov shrugged. "You are a rebel, and you have high intelligence. So it says here. There are officers who will take the risk of recruiting those like you, but I am not one of them. We cannot use you in this ship."

"Oh." Mark turned to go.

"Wait a minute, kid." Dugan looked at the officer. "Thanks, Lieutenant, but maybe I better stick with my buddy–"

"No, don't do that," Mark said. He felt a wave of gratitude toward the older man. Dugan's offer seemed the finest thing anyone had ever tried to do for him.

"Who'll look out for ya? You'll get your throat cut."

"Maybe not. I've learned a lot."

Breslov stood. "Your sentiment for your friend is admirable, but you are wasting my time. Are you enlisting?"

"He is," Mark said. "Thank you, Lieutenant." He followed the Marine guard back to the corridor and began washing the bulkhead, scrubbing savagely, trying to forget his misery and despair. It was all so unfair!

III

Tanith was hot steaming jungle under a perpetual gray cloud cover. The gravity was too high and the humidity was almost unbearable. Yet it was a relief to be there after the crowded ship, and Mark waited to see what would happen to him. He was surprised to find that he cared.

He was herded through medical processing, immunization, identification, a meaningless classification interview, and both psychological and aptitude tests. They ran from one task to the next, then stood in long lines or simply waited around. On the fourth day he was taken from the detention pen to an empty adobe-walled room with rough wooden furniture. The guards left him there. The sensation of being alone was exhilarating.

He looked up warily when the door opened. "Biff!"

"Hi, kid. Got something for you." Dugan was dressed in the blue coveralls of the CD Navy. He glanced around guiltily. "You left this with me and I run it up a bit." He held out a fistful of CoDominium scrip. "Go on, take it, I can get more and you can't. Look, we're pullin' out pretty soon, and…"

"It's all right," Mark said. But it wasn't all right. He hadn't known how much friendship meant to him until he'd been separated from Dugan; now, seeing him in the Navy uniform and knowing that Dugan was headed away from this horrible place, Mark hated his former friend. "I'll get along."

"Damned right you will! Stop sniffing about how unfair everything is and wait your chance. You'll get one. Look, you're a young kid and everything seems like it's forever, but–" Dugan fell silent and shook his head ruefully. "Not that you need fatherly advice from me. Or that it'd do any good. But things end, Mark. The day ends. So do weeks and months."

"Yeah. Sure." They said more meaningless things, and Dugan left. Now I'm completely alone, Mark thought. It was a crushing thought. Some of the speeches he'd heard in his few days in college kept rising up to haunt him. "*Die Gedanken, Sie sind frei.*" Yeah. Sure. A man's thoughts were always free, and no one could enslave a free man, and the heaviest chains and darkest dungeons could never cage the spirit of man. Bullshit. I'm a slave. If I don't do what they tell me, they'll hurt me until I do. And I'm too damn scared of them. But something else he'd heard was more comforting. "Slaves have no rights, and thus have no obligations."

That, by God, fits, he thought. I don't owe anybody a thing. Nobody here, and none of those bastards on Earth. I do what I have to do and I look out for number-one and rape the rest of 'em.

There was no prison, or rather the entire planet was a prison; but the main CD building was intended only for classification and assignment. The prisoners were sold off to wealthy planters. There were a lot of rumors about the different places you might be sent to: big company farms run like factories, where it was said that few convicts ever lived to finish out their terms; industrial plants near big cities, which was supposed to be soft duty because as soon as you got trusty status, you could get passes into town; lonely plantations out in the sticks where owners could do anything they wanted and generally did.

The pen began to empty as the men were shipped out. Then came Mark's turn. He was escorted into an interview room and given a seat. It was the second time in months that he'd been alone, and he enjoyed the solitude. There were voices from the next room.

"Why do you not keep him, *hein*?"

"Immature. No reason to be loyal to the CD."

"Or to me."

"Or to you. And too smart to be a dumb cop. You might make a foreman out of him. The governor's interested in this one, Ludwig. He keeps track of all the high-IQ types. Look, you take this one, I owe you. I'll see you get good hands."

"Okay. *Ja*. Just remember that when you get in some with muscles and no brains, hein? Okay, we look at your genius."

Who the hell were they talking about? Mark wondered. Me? Compared to most of the others in the ship, I guess you could call me a genius, but—

The door opened. Mark stood quickly. The guards liked you to do that.

"Fuller," the captain said. "This is Herr Ewigfeuer. You'll work for him. His place is a country club."

The planter was heavy-set, with thick jowls. He needed a shave, and his shorts and khaki shirt were stained with sweat. "So you are the new convict I take to my nice farm." He eyed Mark coldly. "He will do, he will do. Okay, we go now, *ja*?"

"Now?" Mark said.

"Now, *ja*, you think all day I have? I can stay in Whiskeytown while my foreman lets the hands eat everything and lay around not working? Give me the papers, Captain."

The captain took a sheaf of papers from a folder. He scrawled across the bottom, then handed Mark a pen. "Sign here."

Mark started to read the documents. The captain laughed. "Sign it, goddamnit. We don't have all day."

Mark shrugged and scribbled his name. The captain handed Ewigfeuer two copies and indicated a door. They went through adobe corridors to a guardroom at the end. The planter handed the guards a copy of the contract and the door was opened.

The heat outside struck Mark like a physical blow. It had been hot enough inside, but the thick earthen walls had protected him from the worst; now it was almost unbearable. There was no sun, but the clouds were bright enough to hurt his eyes. Ewigfeuer put on dark glasses. He led the way to a shop across from the prison and bought Mark a pair. "Put these on," he commanded. "You are no use if you are blind. Now come."

They walked through busy streets. The sky hung dull orange, an eternal sunset. Sweat sprang from Mark's brow and trickled down inside his coveralls. He wished he had shorts. Nearly everyone in the town wore them.

They passed grimy shops and open stalls. There were sidewalk displays of goods for sale, nearly all crudely made or Navy surplus or black-market goods stolen from CD storerooms. Strange animals pulled carts through the streets and there were no automobiles at all.

A team of horses splashed mud on Ewigfeuer's legs. The fat planter shook his fist at the driver. The teamster ignored him. "Have you owned horses?" Ewigfeuer demanded.

"No," Mark said. "I hadn't expected to see any here."

"Horses make more horses. Tractors do not," the planter said. "Also with horses and jackasses you get mules. Better than tractors. Better than the damned stormand beasts. Stormands do not like men." He pointed to one of the unlikely animals. It looked like a cross between a mule and a moose, with wide, splayed feet and a sad look that turned vicious whenever anyone got near it. It was tied to a rail outside one of the shops.

There were more people than Mark had expected. They seemed to divide into three classes. There were those who tended the shops and stalls and who smiled unctuously when the planter passed; there were others who strode purposefully through the muddy streets; and there were those who wandered aimlessly or sat on the street corners staring vacantly.

"What are they waiting for?" Mark said. He hadn't meant to say it aloud, but Ewigfeuer heard him.

"They wait to die," the planter said. "*Ja,* they think something else will come to save them. They will find something to steal, maybe, so they live another week, another month, a year even; but they are waiting to die. And they are white men!" This seemed their ultimate crime to Ewigfeuer.

"You might expect this of the blacks," the planter said. "But no, the blacks work, or they go to the bush and live there—not like civilized men perhaps, but they live. Not these. They wait to die. It was a cruel day when their sentences ended."

"Yeah, sure," Mark said, but he made certain the planter had not heard him. There was another group sitting on benches near a small open square. They looked as if they had not moved since morning, since the day before, or ever; that when the orange sky fell dark, they would still be there, and when dawn came with its heat and humidity, they would be there yet. Mark mopped his brow with his sleeve. Heat lay across Whiskeytown so that it was an effort to move, but the planter hustled him along the street, his short legs moving rapidly through the mud patches.

"And what happens if I just run?" Mark asked.

Ewigfeuer laughed. "Go ahead. You think they will not catch you? Where will you go? You have no papers. Perhaps you buy some if you have money. Perhaps what you buy is not good enough. And when they catch you, it is not to my nice farm they send you. It will be to some awful place. Run, I will not chase you. I am too old and too fat."

Mark shrugged and walked along with Ewigfeuer. He noticed that for all his careless manner, the fat man did not let Mark get behind him.

They rounded a corner and came to a large empty space. A helicopter stood at the near edge. There were others in the lot. A man with a rifle sat under an umbrella watching them. Ewigfeuer threw the man some money and climbed into the nearest chopper. He gunned the engines twice, then let it lift them above the city.

Whiskeytown was an ugly sprawl across a plateau. The hill rose directly up from jungle. When they were higher, Mark could see that the plateau was part of a ridge on a peninsula; the sea around it was green with yellow streaks. The concrete CoDominium administration building was the largest structure in Whiskeytown. There was no other air traffic, and they flew across the town without making contact with any traffic controllers.

Beyond the town were brown hills rising above ugly green jungles. And hours later there was no change—jungle to the left and the green and yellow sea to the right. Mark had seen no roads and only a few houses; all of those were in clusters, low adobe buildings atop the brown hills. "Is the whole planet jungle?" he asked.

"*Ja*, jungles, marshes, bad stuff. People can live in the hills. Below is green hell, Weem's Beasts, killer things like tortoises, crocodiles so big you don't believe them and they run faster than you. Nobody runs far in that."

A perfect prison, Mark thought. He stared out at the sea. There were boats out there. Ewigfeuer followed his gaze and laughed.

"Some damn fools try to make a few credits fishing. Maybe smart at that, they get killed fast, they don't wait for tax farmers to take everything they make. You have heard of the Loch Ness monster? On Tanith we got something makes Nessie an earthworm."

They flew over another cluster of adobe buildings. Ewigfeuer used the radio to talk to the people below. They spoke a language Mark didn't know. It didn't seem like German, but he wasn't sure. Then they crossed another seemingly endless stretch of jungle. Finally a new group of buildings was in sight ahead.

The plantation was no different from the others they had seen. There was a cluster of brown adobe buildings around one larger whitewashed wooden house at the very top of the hill. Cultivated fields lay around that on smaller hills. The fields blended into jungle at the edges. Men were working in the fields.

It would be easy enough to run away, Mark thought. Too easy. It must be stupid to try, or there would be fences. Wait, he thought. Wait and learn. I owe nothing. To anyone. Wait for a chance–

—a chance for what? He pushed the thought away.

The foreman was tall and crudely handsome. He wore dirty white shorts and a sun helmet, and there was a pistol buckled on his belt.

"You look after this one, *ja*," Ewigfeuer said. "One of the governor's pets. They say he has brains enough to make supervisor. We will see. Mark Fuller, three years."

"Yes, sir. Come on, Mark Fuller, three years." The foreman turned and walked away. After a moment Mark followed. They went past rammed earth buildings and across a sea of mud. The buildings had been sprayed with some kind of plastic and shone dully. "You'll need boots," the foreman said. "And a new outfit. I'm Curt Morgan. Get along with me and you'll be happy. Cross me and you're in trouble. Got that?"

"Yes, sir."

"You don't call me sir unless I tell you to. Right now you call me Curt. If you need help, ask me. Maybe I can give you good advice. If it don't cost me anything, I will." They reached a rectangular one-story building like the others. "This'll be your bunkie."

The inside was a long room with places for thirty men. Each place had a bunk, a locker, and an area two meters by three of clear space. After the ship, it seemed palatial. The inside walls were sprayed with the same plastic material as the outside; it kept insects from living in the dirt walls. Some of the men had cheap pictures hung above their bunks: pinups, mostly, but in one corner area there were original charcoal sketches of men and women working, and an unfinished oil painting.

There were a dozen men in the room. Some were sprawled on their bunks. One was knitting something elaborate, and a small group at the end were playing cards. One of the card players, a small man, ferret-faced, left the game.

"Your new man," Curt said. "Mark Fuller, three years. Fuller, this is your bunkie leader. His name is Lewis. Lew, get the kid bunked and out of those prison slops."

"Sure, Curt." Lewis eyed Mark carefully. "About the right size for José's old outfit. The gear's all clean."

"Want to do that?" Curt asked. "Save you some money." Mark stared helplessly.

The two men laughed. "You better give him the word, Lew," Curt Morgan said. "Fuller, I'd take him up on the gear. Let me know what he charges you, right? He won't squeeze you too bad." There was laughter from the other men in the bunkie as the foreman left.

Lewis pointed out a bunk in the center. "José was there, kid. Left his whole outfit when he took the green way out. Give you the whole lot for, uh, fifty credits."

And now what? Mark wondered. Best not to show him I've got any money. "I don't have that much—"

"Hell, you sign a chit for it," Lewis said. "The old man pays a credit a day and found."

"Who do I get the chit from?"

"You get it from me." Lewis narrowed watery eyes. They looked enormous through his thick glasses. "You thinking about something, kid? You don't want to try it."

"I'm not trying anything. I just don't understand—"

"Sure. You just remember I'm in charge here. Anybody skips out, I get their gear. Me. Nobody else. José had a good outfit, worth fifty credits easy—"

"Bullshit," one of the cardplayers said. "Not worth more'n thirty and you know it."

"Shut up. Sure, you could do better in Whiskeytown, but not here. Look, Morgan said take care of you. I'll sell you the gear for thirty. Deal?"

"Sure."

Lewis gave him a broad smile. "You'll get by, kid. Here's your key." He handed Mark a magnokey and went back to the card game.

Mark wondered who had copies. It wasn't something you could duplicate without special equipment; the magnetic spots had to be in just the right places. Ewigfeuer would have one, of course. Who else? No use worrying about it. Mark tucked his money into the toe of a sock and threw the rest of his clothes on top of it, then locked the whole works into the locker. He wondered what to do with the money; he had nearly three hundred credits, ten months' wages at a credit a day—enough to be killed for.

It bothered him all the way to the shower, but after that, the unlimited water, new bar of soap, and a good razor were such pleasures that he didn't think about anything else.

IV

The borshite plant resembles an artichoke in appearance: tall, spiky leaves rising from a central crown, with one flowerbearing stalk jutting upward to a height of a meter and a half. It is propagated by bulbs; in spring the previous year's crop is dug up and the delicate bulbs carefully separated, then each replanted. Weeds grow in abundance and must be pulled out by hand. The jungle constantly grows inward to reclaim the high ground that men cultivate. Herbivores eat the crops unless the fields are patrolled.

Mark learned that and more within a week. The work was difficult and the weather was hot, but neither was unbearable. The rumors were true: Ewigfeuer's place was a country club. Convicts schemed to get there. Ewigfeuer demanded hard work, but he was fair.

That made it all the more depressing for Mark. If this was the easy way to do time, what horrors waited if he made a mistake? Ewigfeuer held transfer as his ultimate threat, and Mark found himself looking for ways to keep his master pleased. He disgusted himself—but there was nothing else to do.

He had never been more alone. He had nothing in common with the other men. His jokes were never funny. He had no interest in their stories. He learned to play poker so well that he was resented when he played. They didn't want a tight player who could take their money. Once he was accused of cheating, and although everyone knew he hadn't, he was beaten and his money taken. After that he avoided the games.

The work occupied only his hands, not his mind. There were no books to read. There was little to do but brood. I wanted power, he thought. We were playing at it. A game. But the police weren't playing, and now I've become a slave. When I get back, I'll know more of how this game is played. I'll show them. But he knew he wouldn't, not really. He was learning nothing here.

Some of the convicts spent their entire days and nights stoned into tranquility. Borshite plants are the source of borloi, and half the Citizens of the United States depended on borloi to get through each day; the government supplied it to them, and any government that failed in the shipments would not last long. It worked as well on Tanith, and Herr Ewigfeuer was generous with both pipes and borloi. Mark tried that route, but he did not like what it did to him. They were stealing three years of his life, but he wouldn't cooperate and make it easier.

His college friends had talked a lot about the dignity of labor. Mark didn't find it dignified at all. Why not get stoned and stay that way? he thought. What am I doing that's important? Why not go out of being and get it over? Let the routine wash over me, drown in it–

There were frequent fights. They had rules. If a man got hurt so that he couldn't work, both he and the man he fought with had to make up the lost work time. It tended to keep the injuries down and discouraged broken bones. Whenever there was a fight, everyone turned out to watch.

It gave Mark time to himself. He didn't like being alone, but he didn't like watching fights, especially since he might be drawn into one himself–

The men shouted encouragement to the fighters. Mark lay on his bunk. He had liquor but didn't want to drink. He kept thinking about taking a drink, just one, it will help me get to sleep—and you know what you're doing to yourself—and why not?

The man was small and elderly. Mark knew he lived in quarters near the big house. He came into the bunkie and glanced around. The lights had not been turned on, and he failed to see Mark. He looked furtively about again, then stooped to try locker lids, looking for one that was open. He reached Mark's locker, opened it, and felt inside. His hand found cigarettes and the bottle–

He felt or heard Mark and looked up. "Uh, good evening."

"Good evening." The man seemed cool enough, although he risked the usual punishments men mete out to thieves in barracks.

"Are you bent on calling your mates?" The watery eyes darted around looking for an escape. "I don't seem to have any defense."

"If you did have one, what would it be?"

"When you are as old as I am and in for life, you take what you can. I am an alcoholic, and I steal to buy drink."

"Why not smoke borloi?"

"It does little for me." The old man's hands were shaking. He looked lovingly at the bottle of gin that he'd taken from Mark's locker.

"Oh, hell, have a drink," Mark said.

"Thank you." He drank eagerly, in gulps.

Mark retrieved his bottle. "I don't see you in the fields."

"No. I work with the accounts. Herr Ewigfeuer has been kind enough to keep me, but not so kind as to pay enough to–"

"If you keep the work records, you could sell favors."

"Certainly. For a time. Until I was caught. And then what? It is not much of a life that I have, but I want to keep it." He stood in silence for a moment. "Surprising, isn't it? But I do."

"You talk rather strangely," Mark said.

"The stigmata of education. You see Richard Henry Tappinger, Ph.D., generally called Taps. Formerly holder of the Bates Chair of History and Sociology at Yale University."

"And why are you on Tanith?" Prisoners do not ask that question, but Mark could do as he liked. He held the man's life in his hands: a word, a call, and the others would amuse themselves with Tappinger. And why don't I call them? Mark asked himself. He shuddered at the thought that he could even consider it.

Tappinger didn't seem annoyed. "Liquor, young girls, their lovers, and an old fool are an explosive combination. You don't mind if I am not more specific? I spend a good part of my life being ashamed of myself. Could I have another drink?"

"I suppose."

"You have the stigmata about you as well. You were a student?"

"Not for long."

"But worthy of education. And generous as well. Your name is Fuller. I have the records, and I recall your case."

The fight outside ground to a close, and the men came back into the barracks. Lewis was carrying an unconscious man to the showers. He handed him over to others when he saw Tappinger.

"You sneaky bastard, I told you what'd happen if I found you in my bunkie! What'd he steal, Fuller?"

"Nothing. I gave him a drink."

"Yeah? Well, keep him out of here. You want to talk to him, you do it outside."

"Right." Mark took his bottle and followed Tappinger out. It was hot inside and the men were talking about the fight. Mark followed Tappinger across the quad. They stayed away from the women's barracks. Mark had no friends in there and couldn't afford any other kind of visit—at least not very often, and he was always disturbed afterwards. None of the women seemed attractive or to care about themselves.

"So. The two outcasts gather together," Tappinger said. "Two pink monkeys among the browns."

"Maybe I should resent that."

"Why? Do you have much in common with them? Or do you resent the implication that you have more in common with me?"

"I don't know. I don't know anything. I'm just passing time. Waiting until this is over."

"And what will you do then?"

They found a place to sit. The local insects didn't bother them; the taste was wrong. There was a faint breeze from the west. The jungle noises came with it, snorts and grunts and weird calls.

"What can I do?" Mark asked. "Get back to Earth and—"

"You will never get back to Earth," Tappinger said. "Or if you do, you will be one of the first ever. Unless you have someone to buy your passage?"

"That's expensive."

"Precisely."

"But they're supposed to take us back!" Mark felt all his carefully built defenses begin to crumble. He lived for the end of the three years—and now—

"The regulations say so, and the convicts talk about going home, but it does not happen. Earth does not want rebels. It would disturb the comfortable life most have. No, if you ship out, it will be to another colony. Unless you are very rich."

So I'm here forever. "So what else is there? What do ex-cons do here?"

Tappinger shrugged. "Sign up as laborers. Start their own plantations. Go into government service. You see Tanith as a slave world, which it is, but it will not always be that. Some of you, people like you, will build it into something else, something better or worse, but certainly different."

"Yeah. Sure. The Junior Pioneers have arrived."

"What do you think happens to involuntary colonists?" Tappinger asked. "Or did you never think of them? Most people on Earth don't look very hard at the price of keeping their wealth and their clean air and clean oceans. But the only difference between you and someone shipped by BuReloc is that you came in a slightly more comfortable ship, and you will put in three years here before they turn you out to fend for yourself. Yes, I definitely suggest the government services for you. You could rise quite high."

"Work for those slaving bastards? I'd rather starve!"

"No, you wouldn't. Nor would many others. It is easier to say that than to do it."

Mark stared into the darkness.

"Why so grim? There are opportunities here. The new governor is even trying to reform some of the abuses. Of course he is caught in the system just as we are. He must export his quota of borloi and miracle drugs, and pay the taxes demanded of him. He must keep up production. The Navy demands it."

"The Navy?"

Tappinger smiled in the dark. "You would be surprised at just how much of the CD Navy's operations are paid for by the profits from the Tanith drug trade."

"It doesn't surprise me at all. Thieves. Bastards. But it's stupid. A treadmill, with prisons to pay for themselves and the damned fleet–"

"Neither stupid nor new. The Soviets have done it for nearly two hundred years, with the proceeds of labor camps paying for the secret police. And our tax farming scheme is even older. It dates back to old Rome. Profits from some planets support BuReloc. Tanith supports the Navy."

"Damn the Navy."

"Ah, no, don't do that. Bless it instead. Without the CD Fleet, the Earth governments would be at each other's throats in a moment. They very nearly are now. And since they won't pay for the Navy, and the Navy is very much needed to keep peace on Earth, why, we must continue to work. See what a noble task we perform as we weed the borloi fields?"

Unbearably hot spring became intolerably hot summer, and the work decreased steadily. The borshite plants were nearly as high as a man's waist and were able to defend themselves against most weeds and predators. The fields needed watching but little else.

To compensate for the easier work, the weather was sticky hot, with warm fog rolling in from the coast. The skies turned from orange to dull gray. Mark had seen stars only twice since he arrived.

With summer came easy sex. Men and women could visit in the evenings, and with suitable financial arrangements with bunkie leaders, all night. The pressures of the barracks eased. Mark found the easier work more attractive than the women. When he couldn't stand it any longer, he'd pay for a few minutes of frantic relief, then try not to think about sex for as long as he could.

His duties were simple. Crownears, muskrat-sized animals that resembled large shrews, would eat unprotected borshite plants. They had to be driven away. They were stupid animals, and ravenous, but not very dangerous unless a swarm of them could catch a man mired down in the mud. A man with a spear could keep them out of the crops.

There were other animals to watch for. Weem's Beast, named for the first man to survive a meeting with one, was the worst. The crownears were its natural prey, but it would attack almost anything that moved. Weem's Beast looked vaguely like a mole but was over a meter long. Instead of a prehensile snout, Weem's Beast had a fully articulated grasping member with talons and pseudo-eyes. Men approached holes very carefully on Tanith; the Beast was fond of lying just below the surface and came out with astonishing speed.

It wouldn't usually leave the jungle to attack a man on high ground.

Mark patrolled the fields, and Curt Morgan made rounds on horseback. In the afternoons Morgan would sit with Mark and share his beer ration, and the cold beer and lack of work was almost enough to make life worth living again.

Sometimes there was a break in the weather, and a cooler breeze would blow across the fields. Mark sat with his back to a tree, enjoying the comparatively cool day, drinking his beer ration. Morgan sat next to him.

"Curt, what will you do when you finish your sentence?" Mark asked.

"Finished two years ago. Two Tanith, three Earth."

"Then why are you still here?"

Morgan shrugged. "What else do I know how to do? I'm saving some money; one day I'll have a place of my own." He shifted his position and fired his carbine toward the jungle. "I swear them things get more nerve every summer. This is all I know. I can't save enough to buy into the tax farming syndicate."

"Could you squeeze people that way?"

"If I had to. Them or me. Tax collectors get rich."

"Sure. Jesus, there's just no goddamn hope for anything, is there? The whole deck's stacked." Mark finished his beer.

"Where isn't it?" Morgan demanded. "You think it's tough now, you ought to have been here before the new governor came. Place they stuck me—my sweet lord, they worked us! Charged for everything we ate or wore, and you open your mouth, it's another month on your sentence. Enough to drive a man into the green."

"Uh, Curt—are there–?"

"Don't get ideas. I'd hate to take the dogs and come find you. Find your corpse, more likely. Yeah, there's men out in the green. Live like rats. I'd rather be under sentence again than live like the Free Staters."

The thought excited Mark. A Free State! It would have to be like the places Shirley and her friends had talked about, with equality, and there'd be no tax farmers in a free society. He thought of the needs of free men. They would live hard and be poor because they were fugitives, but they would be free! He built the Free State in his imagination until it was more real than Ewigfeuer's plantation.

The next day the crownears were very active, and Curt Morgan brought another worker to Mark's field. They rode up together on the big Percheron horses brought as frozen embryos from Earth and repeatedly bred for even wider feet to keep them above the eternal mud. The newcomer was a girl. Mark had seen her before, but never met her.

"Brought you a treat," Curt said. "This is Juanita. Juanny, if this clown gives you trouble, I'll break him in half. Be back in an hour. Got your trumpet?"

Mark indicated the instrument.

"Keep it handy. Them things are restless out there. I think there's a croc around. And pokers. Keep your eyes open." Curt rode off toward the next field.

Mark stood in embarrassed silence. The girl was younger than Mark, and sweaty. Her hair hung down in loose blonde strings. Her eyes had dark circles under them and her face was dirty. She was built more like a wiry boy than a girl. She was also the most beautiful girl he'd ever seen.

"Hi," Mark said. He cursed himself. Shyness went with civilization, not a prison!

"Hi yourself. You're in Lewis' bunkie."

"Yes. I haven't seen you before. Except at Mass." Each month a priest of the Ecumenical Catholic Church came to the plantation. Mark had never attended his services, but he'd watch idly from a distance.

"Usually work in the big house. Sure hot, isn't it?"

He agreed it was hot and was lost again. What should I say? "You're lovely" is obvious even if I do think it's true. "Let's go talk to your bunkie leader" isn't too good an idea even if it's what I want to say. Besides, if she lives in the big house, she won't have one. "How long do you have?"

"Another two. When I'm eighteen. They still run the sentences on Earth time. I'm eleven, really." There was more silence. "You don't talk much, do you?"

"I don't know what to say. I'm sorry–"

"It's okay. Most of the men jabber away like porshons. Trying to talk me into something, you know?"

"Oh."

"Yeah. But I never have. I'm a member of the church. Confirmed and everything." She looked at him and grinned impishly. "So that makes me a dumb hymn singer, and what's left to talk about?"

"I remember wishing I was you," Mark said. He laughed. "Not quite what I meant to say. I mean, I watched you at Masses. You looked happy. Like you had something to live for."

"Well, of course. We all have something to live for. Must have, people sure try hard to stay alive. When I get out of here, I'm going to ask the padre to let me help him. Be a nun, maybe."

"Don't you want to marry?"

"Who? A con? That's what my mother did, and look. I got 'apprenticed' until I was eighteen Earth years old because I was born to convicts. No kids of mine'll have that happen to 'em!"

"You could marry a free man."

"They're all pretty old by the time they finish. And not worth much. To themselves or anybody else. You proposin' to me?"

He laughed, and she laughed with him, and the afternoon was more pleasant than any he could remember since leaving Earth.

"I was lucky," she told him. "Old man Ewigfeuer traded for me. Place I was born on, the planter'd be selling tickets for me now." She stared at the dirt. "I've seen girls they did that with. They don't like themselves much after a while."

They heard the shrill trumpets in other fields. Mark scanned the jungle in front of him. Nothing moved. Juanita continued to talk. She asked him about Earth. "It's hard to think about that place," she said. "I hear people live all bunched up."

He told her about cities. "There are twenty million people in the city I came from." He also told her of the concrete Welfare Islands at the edges of the cities.

She shuddered. "I'd rather live on Tanith than like that. It's a wonder all the people on Earth don't burn it down and live in the swamps."

Evening came sooner than he expected. After supper he fell into an introspective mood. He hadn't wanted a day to last for a long time. It's silly to think this way, he told himself.

But he was twenty years old, and there wasn't anyone else to think about. That night he dreamed about her.

He saw her often as the summer wore on. She had no education, and Mark began teaching her to read. He scratched letters in the ground and used some of his money to buy lurid adventure stories—the only reading matter available in the barracks.

Juanita learned quickly. She seemed to enjoy Mark's company and often arranged to be assigned to the same field that he was. They talked about everything: Earth, and how it wasn't covered with swamps. He told her of blue skies, and sailing on the Pacific, and the island coves he'd explored. She thought he was making most of it up.

Their only quarrels came when he complained of how unfair life was. She laughed at him. "I was born with a sentence," she told him. "You lived in a fine house and had your own 'copter and a boat, and you went to school. If I'm not whinin', why should you, Mr. Taxpayer?"

He wanted to tell her she was unfair too, but stopped himself. Instead he told her of smog and polluted waters, and sprawling cities. "They've got the pollution licked, though," he said. "And the population's going down. What with the licensing, and BuReloc—"

She said nothing, and Mark couldn't finish the sentence. Juanita stared at the empty jungles. "Wish I could see a blue sky some day. I can't even imagine that, so you must be tellin' the truth."

He did not often see her in the evenings. She kept to herself or worked in the big house. Sometimes, though, she would walk with Curt Morgan or sit with him on the porch of the big house, and when she did, Mark would buy a bottle of gin and find Tappinger. It was no good being alone then.

The old man would deliver long lectures in a dry monotone that nearly put Mark to sleep, but then he'd ask questions that upset any view of the universe that Mark had ever had.

"You might make a passable sociologist some day," Tappinger said. "Ah, well, they say the best university is a log with a student at one end and a professor at the other. We have that, anyway."

"All I seem to learn is that things are rotten. Everything's set up wrong," Mark said.

Tappinger shook his head. "There has never been a society in which someone did not think there had to be a better deal—for himself. The trick is to see that those who want a better way enough to do something about it can either rise within the system or are rendered harmless by it. Which, of course, Earth does—warriors join the Navy. Malcontents are shipped to the colonies. The cycle is closed. Drugs for the citizens, privileges for the taxpayers, peace for all provided by the Fleet—and slavery for malcontents. Or death. The colonies use up men."

"I guess it's stable, then."

"Hardly. If Earth does not destroy herself—and from the rumors I hear, the nations are at each other's throats despite what the Navy can do—why, they have built a pressure cooker out here that will one day destroy the old home world. Look at what we have here. Fortune hunters, adventurers, criminals, rebels—and all selected for survival abilities. The lid cannot stay on."

They saw Juanita and Curt Morgan walking around the big house, and Mark winced. Juanita had grown during the summer. Now, with her hair combed and in clean clothes, she was so lovely that it hurt to look at her. Taps smiled. "I see my star pupil has found another interest. Cheer up, lad, when you finish here, you will find employment. You can have your pick of convict girls. Rent them, or buy one outright."

"I hate slavery!"

Taps shrugged. "As you should. Although you might be surprised what men who say that will do when given the chance. But calm yourself, I meant buy a wife, not a whore."

"But damn it, you don't buy wives! Women aren't things!"

Tappinger smiled softly. "I tend to forget just what a blow it is to you young people. You expect everything to be as it was on Earth. Yet you are here because you were not satisfied with your world."

"It was rotten."

"Possibly. But you had to search for the rot. Here you cannot avoid it."

On such nights it took Mark a long time to get to sleep.

V

The harvest season was approaching. The borshite plants stood in full flower, dull-red splashes against brown hills and green jungles, and the fields buzzed with insects. Nature had solved the problem of propagation without inbreeding on Tanith and fifty other worlds in the same way as on Earth.

The buzzing insects attracted insectivores, and predators chased those; close to harvest time there was little work, but the fields had to be watched constantly. Once again house and processing-shed workers joined the field hands, and Mark had many days with Juanita.

She was slowly driving him insane. He knew she couldn't be as naive as she pretended to be. She had to know how he felt and what he wanted to do, but she gave him no opportunities.

Sometimes he was sure that she was teasing him. "Why don't you ever come see me in the evenings?" she asked one day.

"You know why. Curt is always there."

"Well, sure, but he don't—doesn't own my contract. 'Course, if you're scared of him—"

"You're bloody right I'm scared of him. He could fold me up for glue. Not to mention what happens when the foreman's mad at a con. Besides, I thought you liked him."

"Sure. So what?"

"He told me he was going to marry you one day."

"He tells everybody that. He never told me, though."

Mark noted grimly that she'd stopped talking about becoming a nun.

"Of course, Curt's the only man who even says he's going to—Mark, look out!"

Mark saw a blur at the edge of his vision and whirled with his spear. Something was charging toward him. "Get behind me and run!" he shouted. "Keep me in line with it and get out of here."

She moved behind him and he heard her trumpet blare, but she wasn't running. Mark had no more time to think about her. The animal was nearly a meter and a half long, built square on thick legs and splayed feet. The snout resembled an earth warthog, with four upthrusting tusks, and it had a thin tail that lashed as it ran.

"Porker," Juanita said softly. She was just behind him. "Sometimes they'll charge a man. Like this. Don't get it excited, maybe it'll go away."

Mark was perfectly willing to let the thing alone. It looked as if it would weigh as much as he did. Its broad feet and small claws gave it better footing than hobnails would give a man. It circled them warily, about three meters away. Mark turned carefully to keep facing it. He held the spear pointed at its throat. "I told you to get out of here," Mark said.

"Sure. There's usually two of those things." She spoke very softly. "I'm scared to blow this trumpet again. Wish Curt would get here with his gun." As she spoke, there were gunshots. They sounded very far away.

"Mark," Juanita whispered urgently. "There is another one. I'm gettin' back to back with you."

"All right." He didn't dare look away from the beast in front of him. What did it want? It moved slowly toward him, halting just beyond the thrusting range of the spear. Then it dashed forward, screaming a sound that could never have come from an Earthly pig.

Mark jabbed at it with his spear. It flinched from the point and ran past. Mark turned to follow it and saw the other beast advancing on Juanita. She had slipped in the mud and was down, trying frantically to get to her feet, and the porker was running toward her.

Mark gave an animal scream of pure fury. He slid in the mud but kept his feet and charged forward, screaming again as he stabbed with the spear and felt it slip into the thick hide. The porker shoved against him, and Mark fell into the mud. He desperately held the spear, but the beast walked steadily forward. The point went through the hide on the back and came out again, the shaft sliding between skin and meat, and the impaled animal advanced inexorably up the shaft. The tusks neared his manhood. Mark heard himself whimper in fear. "I can't hold him!" he shouted. "Run!"

She didn't run. She got to her feet and shoved her spear down the snarling throat, then thrust downward, forcing the head toward the mud. Mark scrambled to his feet. He looked wildly around for the other animal. It was nowhere in sight, but the pinned porker snarled horribly.

"Mark, honey, take that spear of yours out of him while I hold him," Juanita shouted. "I can't hold long—quick, now."

Mark shook himself out of the trembling fear that paralyzed him. The tusks moved wickedly and he felt them even though they were nowhere near him, felt them tearing at his groin.

"Please, honey," Juanita said.

He tugged at the spear, but it wouldn't come free, so he thrust it forward, then ran behind the animal to pull the spear through the loose skin on the porker's back. The shaft came through bloody. His hands slipped but he held the spear and thrust it into the animal, thrust again and again, stabbing in insane fury and shouting, "Die, die, die!"

Morgan didn't come for another half an hour. When he galloped up, they were standing with their arms around each other.

Juanita moved slowly away from Mark when Morgan dismounted, but she looked possessively at him.

"That way now?" Morgan asked.

She didn't answer.

"There was a herd of those things in the next field over," Curt said. His voice was apologetic. "Killed three men and a woman. I came as quick as I could."

"Mark killed this one."

"She did. It would have had me–"

"Hold on," Curt said.

"It walked right up the spear," Mark said.

"I've seen 'em do that, all right." Morgan seemed to be choosing his words very carefully. "You two will have to stay on here for a while. We've lost four hands, and–"

"We'll be all right," Juanita said.

"Yeah." Morgan went back to his mount. "Yeah, I guess you will." He rode off quickly.

Tradition gave Mark and Juanita the carcass, and they feasted their friends that night. Afterwards Mark and Juanita walked away from the barracks area, and they were gone for a long time.

"Taps, what the hell am I going to do?" Mark demanded. They were outside, in the unexpected cool of a late summer evening. Mark had thought he would never be cool again; now it was almost harvest time. The fall and winter would be short, but Tanith was almost comfortable during those months.

"What is the problem?"

"She's pregnant."

"Hardly surprising. Nor the end of the world. There are many ways to—"

"No. She won't even talk about it. Says it's murder. It's that damned padre. Goddamn church, no wonder they bring that joker around. Makes the slaves contented."

"That is hardly the only activity of the church, but it does have that effect. Well, what is it to you? As you have often pointed out, you have no responsibilities. And certainly you have no legal obligations in this case."

"That's my kid! And she's my—I mean, damn it, I can't just—"

Tappinger smiled grimly. "I remind you that conscience and a sense of ethics are expensive luxuries. But if you are determined to burden yourself with them, let us review your alternatives.

"You can ask Ewigfeuer for permission to marry her. It is likely to be granted. The new governor has ended the mandatory so-called apprenticeship for children born to convicts. Your sentence is not all that long. When it ends, you will be free—"

"To do what? I saw the time-expired men in Whiskeytown."

"There are jobs. There is a whole planetary economy to be built."

"Yeah. Sure. Sweat my balls off for some storekeeper. Or work like Curt Morgan, sweating cons."

Tappinger shrugged. "There are alternatives. Civil service. Or learn the business yourself and become a planter. There is always financing available for those who can produce."

"I'd still be a slaver. I want out of the system. Out of the whole damned thing!"

Tappinger sighed and lifted the bottle to drink. He paused to say, "There are many things we all want. So what?" Then he drained the pint.

"There's another way," Mark said. "A way out of all this."

Tappinger looked up quickly. "Don't even think it! Mark, you believe the Free State to be some kind of dream world. That is what it is— a dream. In reality, there is nothing more than a gang of lawless men, living like animals off what they can steal. You cannot live without laws."

I can damned well live without the kind of laws they have here, Mark thought. And of course they steal. Why shouldn't they? How else can they live?

"And it is unlikely to last in any event. The governor has brought in a regiment of mercenaries to deal with the Free State."

About what I'd expect, Mark thought. "Why not CD Marines?"

Tappinger shrugged. "Budget. There are not enough CD forces to keep the peace. The Grand Senate will not pay for policing Tanith. So the planters are squeezed again, to pay for their protection."

And that's fine with me, Mark thought. "Mercenaries can't be much use. They'd rather lay around in barracks and collect their pay." His teachers had told him that.

"Have you ever known any?"

"No, of course not. Look, Taps, I'm tired. I think I better get to bed." He turned and left the old man. To hell with him, Mark thought. Old man, old woman, that's what he is. Not enough guts to get away from here and strike out on his own.

Well, that's fine for him. But I've got bigger things in mind.

The harvest began. The borshite pods formed and were cut, and the sticky sap collected. The sap was boiled, skimmed, boiled again until it was reduced to a tiny fraction of the bulky plants they had worked all summer to guard.

And Ewigfeuer collapsed on the steps of the big house. Morgan flew him to the Whiskeytown hospital. He came back with a young man: Ewigfeuer's son, on leave from his administrative post in the city.

"That old bastard wants to see you outside," Lewis said.

Mark sighed. He was tired from a long day in the fields. He was also tired of Tappinger's eternal lectures on the horrors of the Free State. Still, the man was his only friend. Mark took his bottle and went outside.

Tappinger seized the bottle eagerly. He downed several swallows. His hands shook. "Come with me," he whispered.

Mark followed in confusion. Taps led the way to the shadows near the big house. Juanita was there.

"Mark, honey, I'm scared."

Tappinger took another drink. "The Ewigfeuer boy is trying to raise money," he said. "He storms through the house complaining of all the useless people his father keeps on, and shouts that his father is ruining himself. The hospital bills are very high, it seems. And this place is heavily in debt. He has been selling contracts. One that he sold was hers. For nearly two thousand credits."

"Sale?" Mark said stupidly. "But she has less than two years to go!"

"Yes," Taps said. "There is only one way a planter could expect to make that much back from the purchase of a young and pretty girl."

"God damn them," Mark said. "All right. We've got to get out of here."

"No," Tappinger said. "I've told you why. No, I have a better way. I can forge the old man's signature to a permission form. You can marry Juanita. The forgery will be discovered, but by then—"

"No," Mark said. "Do you think I'll stay to be part of this system? A free society will need good people."

"Mark, please," Tappinger said. "Believe me, it is not what you think it is! How can you live in a place with no rules, you with your ideas of what is fair and what is—"

"Crap. From now on I take care of myself. And my woman and my child. We're wasting time." He moved toward the stables. Juanita followed.

"Mark, you do not understand," Tappinger protested.

"Shut up. I have to find the guard."

"He's right behind you." Morgan's voice was low and quiet. "Don't do anything funny, Mark."

"Where did you come from?"

"I've been watching you for ten minutes. Did you think you could get up to the big house without being seen? You damned fool. I ought to let you go into the green and get killed. But you can't go alone—no, you have to take Juanny with you. I thought you had more sense. We haven't used the whipping post here for a year, but a couple of dozen might wake you up to—" Morgan started to turn as something moved behind him. Then he crumpled. Juanita hit him again with a billet of wood. Morgan fell to the ground.

"I hope he'll be all right," Juanita said. "When he wakes up, Taps, please tell him why we had to run off."

"Yeah, take care of him," Mark said. He was busily stripping the weapons belt from Morgan. Mark noted the compass and grinned.

"You're a fool," Tappinger said. "Men like Curt Morgan take care of themselves. It's people like you that need help."

Tappinger was still talking, but Mark paid no attention. He broke the lock on the stable and then opened the storage room inside. He found canteens in the harness room. There was also a plastic can of kerosene. Mark and Juanita saddled two horses. They led them out to the edge of the compound. Tappinger stood by the broken stable door.

They looked back for a second, then waved and rode into the jungle. Before they were gone, Tappinger had finished the last of Mark's gin.

They fled southward in terror. Every sound seemed to be Morgan and a chase party following with dogs. Then there were the nameless sounds of the jungle. The horses were as frightened as they were.

In the morning they found a small clump of brown grass, a miniscule clearing of high ground. They did not dare make a fire, and they had only some biscuit and grain to eat. A Weem's Beast charged out of the small clump of trees near the top of the clearing, and Mark shot it, wasting ammunition by firing again and again until he was certain that it was dead. Then they were too afraid to stay and had to move on.

They kept southward. Mark had overheard convicts talking about the Free State. On an arm of the sea, south, in the jungle. It was all he had to direct him. A crocodile menaced them, but they rode past, Mark holding the pistol tightly, while the beast stared at them. It wasn't a real crocodile, of course; but it looked much like the Earthly variety. Parallel evolution, Mark thought. What shape would be better adapted to life in this jungle?

On the third day they came to a narrow inlet and followed it to the left, deeper into the jungle, the sea on their right and green hell to the left. It twisted its way along some forgotten river dried by geological shifts a long time before. Tiny streams had bored through the cliff faces on both sides and plunged a hundred meters across etched rock faces into the green froth at the bottom. Overhead the orange skies were misty with low cloud patches darting under the haze.

At dark they halted and Mark risked a fire. He shot a crownears and they roasted it. "The worst is over," Mark said. "We're free now. Free."

She crept into his arms. Her face was worried but contented, and it had lines that made her seem older than Mark. "You never asked me," she said.

He smiled. "Will you marry me?"

"Sure."

They laughed together. The jungle seemed very close and the horses were nickering in nervous fear. Mark built up the fire. "Free," he said. He held her tightly, and they were very happy.

VI

Mark awoke with a knife at his throat. A big, ugly man, burned dark and with scars crisscrossing his bare chest, squatted in front of them. He eyed Mark and Juanita. then grinned. "What have we got ourselves?" he said. "Couple of runaways?"

"I got everything, Art," someone said from behind them.

"Yeah. Okay, mates, up and at 'em. Move out, I ain't got all day."

Mark helped Juanita to her feet. One arm was asleep from holding her. As Mark stood, the ugly man expertly took the gun from Mark's belt. "Who are you?" Mark asked.

"Call me Art. Sergeant to the Boss. Come on, let's go."

There were five others, all mounted. Art led the way through the jungle. When Mark tried to say something to Juanita, Art turned. "I'm going to tell you once. Shut up. Say another word to anybody but me, and I kill you. Say anything to me that I don't want to hear, and I'll cut you. Got that?"

"Yes, sir," Mark said.

Art laughed. "Now you've got the idea."

They rode on in silence.

The Free State was mostly caves in hillsides above the sea. It held over five hundred men and women. There were other encampments of escapees out in the jungles, Art said. "But we've got the biggest. Been pretty careful—when we raid the planters, we can usually make it look like one of the other outfits did it. Governor don't have much army anyway. They won't follow us here."

Mark started to say something about the mercenaries that the governor was hiring. Then he thought better of it.

The Boss was a heavy man with long, colorless hair growing to below his shoulders. He had a handlebar mustache and staring blue eyes. He sat in the mouth of a cave on a big carved chair as if it were a throne, and he held a rifle across his knees. A big black man stood behind the chair, watching everyone, saying nothing.

"Escapees, eh?"

"Yes," Mark said.

"Yes, Boss. Don't forget that."

"Yes, Boss."

"What can you do? Can you fight?"

When Mark didn't answer, the Boss pointed to a smaller man in the crowd that had gathered around. "Take him, Choam."

The small man moved toward Mark. His foot lashed upward and hit Mark in the ribs. Then he moved closer. Mark tried to hit him, but the man dodged away and slapped Mark across the face. "Enough," the Boss said. "You can't fight. What can you do?"

"I–"

"Yeah." He looked backward over his shoulder to the black man. "You want him, George?"

"No."

"Right. Art, you found him. He's yours. I'll take the girl."

"But you can't!" Mark shouted.

"No!" Juanita said.

The other men looked at the Boss. They saw he was laughing. Then they all laughed. Art and two others took Mark's arms and began to drag him away. Two more led Juanita into the cave behind the Boss.

"But this isn't right!" Mark shouted.

There was more laughter. The Boss stood. "Maybe I'll give her back when I'm through. Unless Art wants her. Art?"

"I got a woman."

"Yeah." The Boss turned toward the cave. Then he turned back to Mark and the men holding him. "Leave the kid here, Art. I'd like to talk to him. Get the girl cleaned up," he shouted behind him. "And the rest of you get out of here."

The others left, all but the black man who had stood behind the Boss's throne. The black man went a few meters away and sat under a rock ledge. It looked cool in there. He took out a pipe and began stuffing it.

"Come here, kid. What's your name?"

"Fuller," Mark said. "Mark Fuller."

"Come over here. Sit down." The Boss indicated a flat rock bench just inside the cave mouth. The cave seemed to go a long way in; then it turned. There was no one in sight. Mark thought he could hear women talking. "Sit, I said. Tell me how you got here." The Boss's tone was conversational, almost friendly.

"I was in a student riot." Mark strained to hear, but there were no more sounds from inside the cave.

"Student, eh. Relax, Fuller. Nobody's hurting your girlfriend. Your concern is touching. Don't see much of that out here. Tell me about your riot. Where was it?"

The Boss was a good listener. When Mark fell silent, the man would ask questions—probing questions, as if he were interested in Mark's story. Sometimes he smiled.

Outside were work parties: wood details; a group incomprehensibly digging a ditch in the flinty ground out in front of the caves; women carrying water. None of them were interested in the Boss's conversation. Instead, they seemed almost afraid to look into the cave—all but the black man, who sat in his cool niche and never seemed to look away.

Bit by bit Mark told of his arrest and sentence, and of Ewigfeuer's plantation. The Boss nodded. "So you came looking for the Free States. And what did you expect to find?"

"Free men! Freedom, not–

"Not despotism." There was something like kindness in the words. The Boss chuckled. "You know, Fuller, it's remarkable how much your story is like mine. Except that I've always known how to fight. And how to make friends. Good friends." He tilted his head toward the black man. "George, there, for instance. Between us there's nothing we can't handle. You poor fool, what the hell did you think you'd do out here? What good are you? You can't fight, you whine about what's right and fair, you don't know how to take care of yourself, and you come off into the bush to find us. You knew who we were."

"But–"

"And now you're all broken up about your woman. I'm not going to take anything she hasn't got plenty of. It doesn't get used up." He stood and shouted to one of the men in the yard. "Send Art over."

"So you're going to rape Juanita." Mark looked around for a weapon, for anything. There was a rifle near the Boss's chair. His eyes flickered toward it.

The Boss laughed. "Try it. But you won't. Aw, hell, Fuller, you'll be all right. Maybe you'll even learn something. Now I've got a date."

"But—" If there was something I could say, Mark thought. "Why are you doing this?"

"Why not? Because I'll lose your valuable loyalty? Get something straight, Fuller. This is it. There's no place left to go. Live here and learn our ways, or go jump over the cliff there. Or take off into the green and see how far you get. You think you're pretty sharp. Maybe you are. We'll see. Maybe you'll learn to be some use to us. Maybe. Art, take the kid into your squad and see if he can fit in."

"Right, Boss. Come on." Art took Mark's arm. "Look, if you're going to try something, do it and get it over with. I don't want to have to watch you all the time."

Mark turned and followed the other man. Helpless. Damn fool, and helpless. He laughed.

"Yeah?" Art said. "What's funny?"

"The Free State. Freedom. Free men—"

"We're free," Art said. "More'n the losers in Whiskeytown. Maybe one day you will be. When we think we can trust you." He pointed to the cliff edge. The sea inlet was beyond it. "Anybody we can't trust goes over that. The fall don't always kill 'em, but I never saw anybody make it to shore."

Art found him a place in his cave. There were six other men and four women there. The others looked at Mark for a moment, then went back to whatever they had been doing. Mark sat staring at the cave floor and thought he heard, off toward the Boss's cave, a man laughing and a girl crying. For the first time since he was twelve, Mark tried to pray.

Pray for what? he asked himself. He didn't know. I hate them. All of them.

Just when, Mark Fuller, are you going to get some control over your life? But that doesn't just happen. I have to do it for myself. Somehow.

A week went past. It was a meaningless existence. He cooked for the squad, gathered wood and washed dishes, and listened to the sounds of the other men and their women at night. They never left him alone.

Then crying from the Boss's cave stopped, but he didn't see Juanita. When he gathered wood, there were sometimes women from the Boss's area, and he overheard them talking about what a relief it was that Chambliss—that seemed to be the Boss's name—had a new playmate. They did not seem at all jealous of the new arrival.

Play along with them, Mark thought. Play along until—until what? What can I do? Escape? Get back to the plantation? How? And what happens then? But I won't join them, I won't become part of this! I won't!

After a week they took Mark on hunting parties. He was unarmed— his job was to carry the game. They had to walk several kilometers away from the caves. Chambliss didn't permit hunting near the encampment.

Mark was paired with Art. The older man was neither friendly nor unfriendly; he treated Mark as a useful tool, someone to carry and do work.

"Is this all there is?" Mark asked. "Hunting, sitting around the camp, eating and–"

"–and a little screwing," Art said. "What the hell do you want us to do? Set up farms so the governor'll know where we are? We're doin' all right. Nobody tells us what to do."

"Except the Boss."

"Yeah. Except the Boss. But nobody hassles us. We can live for ourselves. Cheer up, kid, you'll feel better when you get your woman back. He'll get tired of her one of these days. Or maybe we'll get some more when we go raiding. Only thing is, you'll have to fight for a woman. You better do it better'n you did the other day."

"Doesn't she—don't the women have anything to say about who they pair up with?" Mark asked.

"Why should they?"

On the tenth day there was an alarm. Someone thought he heard a helicopter. The Boss ordered night guards.

Mark was paired with a man named Cal. They sat among rocks at the edge of the clearing. Cal had a rifle and a knife, but Mark was unarmed. The jungle was black dark, without even stars above.

Finally the smaller man took tobacco and paper from his pocket. "Smoke?"

"Thanks. I'd like one."

"Sure." He rolled two cigarettes. "Maybe you'll do, huh? Had my doubts about you when you first come. You know, it's a wonder the Boss didn't have you tossed over the side, the way you yelled at him like that. No woman's worth that, you know."

"Yeah."

"She mean much to you?" Cal asked.

"Some." Mark swallowed hard. His mouth tasted bitter. "'Course, they get the idea they own you, there's not much you can do."

Cal laughed. "Yeah. Had an old lady like that in Baltimore. Stabbed me one night for messing around with her sister. Where you from, kid?"

"Santa Maria. Part of San-San."

"I been there once. San-San, not where you come from. Here." He handed Mark the cigarette and struck a match to light both.

They smoked in silence. It wasn't all tobacco, Mark found; there was a good shot of burl in the cigarette. Mark avoided inhaling but spoke as if holding his breath. Cal sucked and packed.

"Good weed," Cal said. "You should have brought some when you run off."

"Had to get out fast."

"Yeah." They listened to the sounds of the jungle. "Hell of a life," Cal said. "Wish I could get back to Earth. Some Welfare Island, anyplace where it's not so damned hot. I'd live in Alaska. You ever been there?"

"No. Isn't there—don't you have any plans? Some way to make things better?"

"Well, the Boss talks about it, but nothing happens," Cal said. "Every now and then we go raid a place, get some new women. We got a still in not long ago, that's something."

Mark shuddered. "Cal?"

"Yah?"

"Got another cigarette?"

"You'll owe me for it."

"Sure."

"Okay." Cal took out paper and tobacco and rolled two more smokes. He handed one to Mark. "Been thinking. There ought to be something better'n this, but I sure don't see what it'll be." As Cal struck his match, Mark shut his eyes so he wouldn't be blinded. Then he lifted the rock he'd found in the darkness and brought it down hard onto Cal's head. The man slumped, but Mark hit him again. He felt something wet and sticky warming his fingers, and shuddered.

Then he was sick, but he had to work fast. He took Cal's rifle and knife, and his matches. There wasn't anything else useful.

Mark moved from the rocks onto the narrow strip of flinty ground. No one spoke. Mark ran into the jungle. He did not know where he was going. He tried to think. Hiding out until morning wouldn't help. They'd find Cal and come looking. And Juanita was back there. Mark ran through the squishy mud. Tears came and he fought them back, but then he was sobbing. Where am I going? Where? And why bother?

He ran on until he felt something moving beside him. He drew in a breath to cry out, but a hand clamped over his mouth. Another grasped his wrist. He felt a knifepoint at his throat. "One sound and you're dead," a voice whispered. "Got that?"

Mark nodded.

"Right. Just keep remembering it. Okay, Ardway, let's go."

"Roger," a voice answered.

He was half-carried through the jungle from the camp. There were several men. He did not know how many. They moved silently. "Ready to walk?" someone asked.

"Yes," Mark whispered. "Who are—"

"Shut up. One more sound and we cut your kidneys out. You'll take a week dying. Now follow the man ahead of you."

Mark made more noise than all the others combined, although he tried to walk silently. They went a long way, or so it seemed to be, through knee-deep water and thick mud, then over harder ground. He thought they were going slightly uphill. Then he no longer felt the loom of the trees. They were in a clearing.

The night was pitch black. How do they see? Mark wondered. And who? He thought he could make out a darker shape ahead of him. It was more a feeling than anything else, but then he touched it. It was soft. "Through that," someone said.

It was a curtain. Another was brought down behind him as he went through, and still another was lifted ahead of him. Light blinded him. He stood blinking.

He was inside a tent. Half a dozen uniformed men stood around a map table. At the end of the tent opposite Mark was a tall, thin man. Mark could not guess how old he was, but there were thin streaks of gray in his hair. His jungle camouflage uniform was neatly pressed. He looked at Mark without expression. "Well, Sergeant Major?"

"Strange, Colonel. This man was sitting guard with another guy. Neither one of them knew what he was doing. We watched them a couple of hours. Then this one beats the other one's brains out with a rock and runs right into the jungle."

Mercenaries, Mark thought. They've come to— "I need help," Mark said. "They've got my—my wife in there."

"Name?" the Colonel asked.

"Mark Fuller."

The Colonel looked to his right. Another officer had a small desk console. He punched Mark's name into it, and words flowed across the screen. The Colonel read for a moment. "Escaped convict. Juanita Corlee escaped with you. That is your wife?"

"Yes."

"And you had a falling-out with the Free Staters."

"No. It wasn't that way at all." Mark blurted out his story.

The Colonel looked back to the readout screen. "And you are surprised." He nodded to himself. "I knew the schools on Earth were of little use. It says here that you are an intelligent man, Fuller. So far you haven't shown many signs of it."

"No. Lord God, no. Who—who are you? Please."

"I am Colonel John Christian Falkenberg. This regiment has been retained by the Tanith governor to suppress these so-called Free States. You were captured by Sergeant Major Calvin, and these are my officers. Now, Fuller, what can you tell me about the camp layout? What weapons have they?"

"I don't know much," Mark said. "Sir." Now why did I say that?

"There are other female captives in that camp," Falkenberg said.

"Here," one of the other officers said. "Show us what you do know, Fuller. How good is this satellite photo map?"

"Christ, Rottermill," a third officer said. "Let the lad be for a moment."

"Major Savage, intelligence is my job."

"So is human compassion. Ian, do you think you can find this boy a drink?" Major Savage beckoned to Falkenberg and led him to the far corner of the tent. Another officer brought a package from under the table and took out a bottle. He handed the brandy to Mark.

Falkenberg listened to Savage. Then he nodded. "We can only try. Fuller, did you see any signs of power supplies in that camp?"

"No, sir. There was no electricity at all. Only flashlights."

"So it is unlikely that they have laser weapons. Rottermill, have any target seekers turned up missing from armories? What are the chances that they have any?"

"Slim, Colonel. Practically none. None stolen I know of."

"Jeremy, you may be right," Falkenberg said. "I believe we can use the helicopters as fighting vehicles."

There was a moment of silence; then the officer who'd given Mark the brandy said, "Colonel, that's damned risky. There's precious little armor on those things."

"Machines not much better than these were major fighting vehicles less than a hundred years ago, Captain Frazer." Falkenberg studied the map. "You see, Fuller, the hostages have always been our problem. Because of them we have kept Aviation Company back and brought in our troops on foot. We've not been able to carry heavy equipment or even much personal body armor across these swamps."

No, I don't expect you would, Mark thought. He tried to imagine a large group traveling silently through the swamps. It seemed impossible. What had they done when animals attacked? There had been no shots fired. Why would an armed man let himself be killed when he could shoot?

"I expect they will threaten their prisoners when they know we are here," Falkenberg said. "Of course we will refuse to deal with them. How long do you think it will take for them to act when they know that?"

"I don't know," Mark said. It was something he could not have imagined two years before: men who'd kill and torture, sometimes for no reason at all. No. Not men. Beasts.

"Well, you've precipitated the action," Falkenberg said. "They'll find your dead companion within hours. Captain Frazer."

"Sir."

"You have been studying this map. If you held this encampment, what defenses would you set up?"

"I'd dig in around this open area and hope someone was fool enough to come at us through it, Colonel."

"Yes. Sergeant Major."

"Sir!"

"Show me where they have placed their sentries." Falkenberg watched as Calvin sketched in outposts. Then he nodded. "It seems their Boss has some rudimentary military sense. Rings of sentries. In-depth defense. Can you infiltrate that, Sergeant Major?"

"Not likely, sir."

"Yes." Falkenberg stood for a moment. Then he turned to Captain Frazer. "Ian, you will take your scouts and half the infantry. Make preparations for an attack on the open area. We will code that Green A. This is no feint, Ian. I want you to try to punch through. However, I do not expect you to succeed, so conserve your men as best you can."

Frazer straightened to attention. "Sir."

"We won't abandon you, Ian. When the enemy is well committed there, we'll use the helicopters to take you out. Then we hit them in the flanks and roll them up." Falkenberg pointed to the map again. "This depression seems secure enough as a landing area. Code that Green A-One."

Major Jeremy Savage held a match over the bowl of his pipe and inhaled carefully. When he was satisfied with the light, he said, "Close timing needed, John Christian. Ian's in a spot of trouble if we lose the choppers."

"Have a better way, Jerry?" Falkenberg asked.

"No."

"Right. Fuller, can you navigate a helicopter?"

"Yes, sir. I can even fly one."

Falkenberg nodded again. "Yes. You are a taxpayer's son, aren't you? Fuller, you will go with Number 3 chopper. Sergeant Major, I want you to put a squad of headquarters assault guards, full body armor, into Number 3. Fuller will guide the pilot as close as possible to the cave where the Boss is holding the women. Number 2 with another assault squad will follow. Every effort will be made to secure the hostages alive. Understand, Sergeant Major?"

"Sir!"

"Fuller?"

"Yes, sir."

"Very good. When the troops are off, those choppers must move out fast. We'll need them to rescue Ian's lot."

"Colonel?" Mark said.

"Yes?"

"Not all the women are hostages. Some of them will fight, I think. I don't know how many. And not all the men are– not everybody wants to be in there. Some would run off if they could."

"And what do you expect me to do about it?"

"I don't know, sir."

"Neither do I. Sergeant Major, we will move this command post in one hour. Until then, Fuller, you can use that time to show Captain Rottermill everything you know about that camp."

It isn't going to work, Mark thought. I prayed for her to die. Only I don't know if she wants to die. And now she will. He took another pull from the bottle and felt it taken from his hand.

"Later," Rottermill said. "For now, tell me what you know about this lot."

VII

"They've found that dead guard." The radio sergeant adjusted his earphones. "Seem pretty stirred up about it."

Falkenberg looked at his watch. There was a good hour before sunrise. "Took them long enough."

"Pity Fuller couldn't guide that chopper in the dark," Jeremy Savage said.

"Yes. Sergeant Major, ask Captain Frazer to ready his men, and have your trail ambush party alerted."

"Sir."

"I have a good feeling about this one, John Christian." Savage tapped his pipe against the heel of his boot. "A good feeling."

"Hope you're right, Jeremy. Fuller doesn't believe it will work."

"No, but he seems to agree this is her best chance. He's steady enough now. Realistic assessment of probabilities. Holding up well, all things considered."

"For a married man." Married men make the kinds of promises no man can keep, Falkenberg thought. His lips twitched slightly at the memory, and for a moment Grace's smile loomed in the darkness of the jungle outside. "Sergeant Major, have the chopper teams get into their armor."

"Is it always like this?" Mark asked. He sat in the right hand seat of the helicopter. Body armor and helmet gave strange sensations. He sweated inside the thick clothing. The phones in his helmet crackled with commands meant for others. Outside the helmet there were sounds of firing. Captain Frazer's assault had started a quarter of an hour before; now there was a faint tinge of reddish gray in the eastern skies over the jungle.

Lieutenant Bates grinned and wriggled the control stick. "Usually it's worse. We'll get her out, Fuller. You just put us next to the right cave."

"I'll do that, but it won't work."

"Sure it will."

"You don't need to cheer me up, Bates."

"I don't?" Bates grinned again. He was not much older than Mark. "Maybe *I* need cheering up. I'm always scared about now."

"Really? You don't look it."

"All we're expected to do. Not look it." He thumbed the mike button. "Chief, everything set back there?"

"Aye-aye, sir."

The voice in Mark's helmet grew loud and stern. "ALL HELICOPTERS, START YOUR ENGINES. I SAY AGAIN, START ENGINES."

"That's us." Bates reached for the starting controls and the turbines whined. "Not very much light."

"HELICOPTERS, REPORT WHEN READY."

"Ready aye-aye," Bates said.

"Aye-aye?" Mark asked.

"We're an old CD Marine regiment," Bates said. "Lot of us, anyway. Stayed with the old man when the Senate disbanded his regiment."

"You don't look old enough."

"Me? Not hardly. This was Falkenberg's Mercenary Legion long before I came aboard."

"Why? Why join mercenaries?"

Bates shrugged. "I like being part of the regiment. Or don't you think the work's worth doing?"

"LIFT OFF. BEGIN HELICOPTER ASSAULT."

"Liftoff aye-aye." The turbine whine increased and the ship lifted in a rising, looping circle. Bates moved to the right of the three-craft formation.

Mark could dimly see the green below, with light increasing every minute. Now he could make out the shapes of small clearings among the endless green marshes.

"You take her," Bates said. His hands hovered over the controls, ready to take his darling away from this stranger.

Mark grasped the unfamiliar stick. It was different from the family machine he'd learned on, but the principles were the same. You never really forget, Mark thought. The chopper was not much more than a big airborne truck, and he'd driven one of those on a vacation in the Yukon. The Canadian lakes seemed endlessly far away, in time as well as in space.

Flying came back easily. He remembered the wild stunts he'd tried when he was first licensed. Once a group from his school had gone on a picnic to San Miguel Island and Mark had landed in a cove, dropping onto a narrow, inaccessible beach between high cliffs during a windstorm. It had been stupid, but wildly exciting. Good practice for this, he thought. And I'm scared stiff, and what do I do after this is over? Will Falkenberg turn me in?

There were hills ahead, dull brown in the early morning light. Men huddled in the rocky areas. The Catling in the compartment behind Mark crackled like frying bacon. The shots were impossibly close together, like a steady stream of noise, and the helicopter raked the Free State with its lash. The small slugs sent chips flying from the rocks. The other choppers opened up, and six tracer streams twisted in crazy patterns intertwining like some courtship dance.

Men and women died on that flinty ground. They lay in broken heaps, red blood staining the dirt around them, exactly like a scene on tri-v. Only it's not fake, Mark thought. They won't get up when the cameras go away. Did they deserve this? Does anyone?

Then he was too busy flying to think about anything else. The area in front of the cave was small, very small—was it large enough for the rotors to clear? A strong gust from the sea struck them, and the chopper rocked dangerously.

"Watch her–" Whatever Bates had intended to say, he never finished it. He slumped forward over the stick, held just above it by his shoulder straps. Something wet and sticky splashed across Mark's left hand and arm. Brains. A large slug had come angling upward to hit Bates in the jaw, then ricochet around in his helmet. The young lieutenant had almost no face. Get her down, Mark chanted, easy baby, down you go, level now, here's another gust, easy baby...

Men poured out of the descending chopper. Mark had time to be surprised: They jumped down and ran into the cave even as their friends fell around them. Then something stabbed Mark's left arm, and there were neat holes in the plexiglass windscreen in front of him. The men went on into the cave. They were faceless in their big helmets, identical robots moving forward or falling in heaps...

Lord God, they're magnificent. I've got to get this thing down! Suddenly that was the most important thing in his life. Get down and get out, go into the cave with those men. Find Juanita, yes, of course, but go with them, do something for myself because I want to do it–

"BATES, STOP WASTING TIME AND GET TO GREEN A-ONE URGENT."

God damn it! Mark fumbled with the communications gear. "Bates is dead. This is Fuller. I'm putting the chopper down."

The voice in the phones changed. Someone else spoke. "Are the troops still aboard?"

"No. They're off."

"Then take that craft to Green A-One immediately."

"My—my wife's in there!"

"The colonel is aware of that." Jeremy Savage's voice was calm. "That machine is required, and now."

"But—"

"Fuller, this regiment has risked a great deal for those hostages. The requirement is urgent. Or do you seriously suppose you would be much use inside?"

Oh, Christ! There was firing inside the cave, and someone was screaming. I want to kill him, Mark thought. Kill that blond-haired bastard. I want to watch him die. A babble filled the helmet phones. Crisp commands and reports were jumbled together as a background noise. Frazer's voice. "We're pinned. I'm sending them back to A-One as fast as I can."

There was more firing from inside the cave.

"Aye-aye," Mark said. He gunned the engine and lifted out in a whirling loop to confuse the ground fire. Someone was still aboard; the Gatling chattered and its bright stream raked the rocks around the open area below.

Where was Green A-One? Mark glanced at the map in front of the control stick. There was gray and white matter, and bright red blood, a long smear across the map. Mark had to lift Bates' head to get a bearing. More blood ran across his fingers.

Then the area was ahead, a clear depression surrounded by hills and rocks. Men lay around the top of the bowl. A mortar team worked mechanically, dropping the shells down the tube, leaning back, lifting, dropping another. There were bright flashes everywhere. Mark dropped into the bowl and the flashes vanished.

There were sounds: gunfire, and the whump! whump! of the mortar. A squad rushed over and began loading wounded men into the machine. Then the sergeant waved him off, and Mark raced for the rear area where the surgeon waited. Another helicopter passed, headed into the combat area.

The medics off-loaded the men.

"Stand by, Fuller, we'll get another pilot over there," Savage's calm voice said in the phones.

"No. I'll keep it. I know the way."

There was a pause. "Right. Get to it, then."

"Aye-aye, sir."

The entrance to the Boss's cave was cool, and the surgeon had moved the field hospital there. A steady stream of men came out of the depths of the cave: prisoners carrying their own dead, and Falkenberg's men carrying their comrades. The Free State dead were piled in heaps near the cliff edge. When they were identified, they were tossed over the side. The regiment's dead were carried to a cleared area, where they lay covered. Armed soldiers guarded the corpses.

Do the dead give a damn? Mark wondered. Why should they? What's the point of all the ceremony over dead mercenaries? He looked back at the still figure on the bed. She seemed small and helpless, and her breath rasped in her throat. An I.V. unit dripped endlessly.

"I expect she'll live."

Mark turned to see the regimental surgeon.

"We couldn't save the baby, but there's no reason she won't have more."

"What happened to her?" Mark demanded.

The surgeon shrugged. "Bullet in the lower abdomen. Ours, theirs, who knows? Jacketed slug, it didn't do a lot of damage. The colonel wants to see you, Fuller. And you can't do any good here." The surgeon took him by the elbow and ushered him out into the steaming daylight. "That way."

There were more work parties in the open space outside. Prisoners were still carrying away dead men. Insects buzzed around dark red stains on the flinty rocks. They look so dead, Mark thought. So damned dead. Somewhere a woman was crying.

Falkenberg sat with his officers under an open tent in the clearing. There was another man with them, a prisoner under guard. His face was hidden by the tent awning, but Mark knew him. "So they took you alive," Mark said.

"I seem to have survived." The Boss's lips curled in a sneer. "And you helped them. Fine way to thank us for taking you in."

"Taking us in! You raped–

"How do you know it was rape?" the Boss demanded. "Not that you were any great help, were you? You're no damned good, Fuller. Your help didn't make a damned bit of difference. Has anything you ever did made any difference?"

"That will do, Chambliss," Falkenberg said.

"Sure. You're in charge now, Colonel. Well, you beat us, so you give the orders. We're pretty much alike, you and me."

"Possibly," Falkenberg said. "Corporal, take Chambliss to the guard area. And make certain he does not escape."

"Sir." The troopers gestured with their rifles. The Boss walked ahead of them. He seemed to be leading them.

"What will happen to him?" Mark asked.

"We will turn him over to the governor. I expect he'll hang. The problem, Fuller, is what we do with you. You were of some help to us, and I don't like unpaid debts."

"What choices do I have?" Mark asked.

Falkenberg shrugged. "We could give you a mount and weapons. It is a long journey to the farmlands in the south, but once there, you could probably avoid recapture. Probably. If that is not attractive, I suppose we could put in a good word with the governor."

"Which would get me what?"

"It would depend on him. At the least he would agree to forget about your escape and persuade your patron not to prosecute for theft of animals and weapons."

"But I'd be back under sentence. A slave again. What happens to Juanita?"

"The regiment will take care of her."

"What the hell does that mean?" Mark demanded.

Falkenberg's expression did not change. Mark could not tell what the colonel was thinking. "I mean, Fuller, that it is unlikely that the troops would enjoy the prospect of turning her over to the governor. She can stay with us until her apprenticeship has expired."

"So you're no better than the Boss after all!"

"Watch it," one of the officers said.

"What Colonel Falkenberg means," Major Savage said, "is that she will be permitted to stay with us as long as she wishes. Certainly we lack for women; but there are some slight differences between us and your Free State. Colonel Falkenberg commands a regiment. He does not rule a mob."

"Sure. What if she wants to come with me?"

"Then we will see that she does. When she recovers," Savage said. "Now what is it you want to do? We don't have all day."

What do I want to do? Lord God. I want to go home, but that's not possible. Dirt farmer, fugitive forever. Or slave for at least two more years. "You haven't given me a very pleasant set of alternatives."

"You had fewer when you came here," Savage said.

A party of prisoners was herded toward the tent. They stood looking nervously at the seated officers, while their guards stood at ease with their weapons. Mark licked his lips. "I heard you were enlisting some of the Free Staters."

Falkenberg nodded. "A few. Not many."

"Could you use a helicopter pilot?"

Major Savage chuckled. "Told you he'd ask, John Christian."

"He was steady enough this morning," Captain Frazer said. "And we do need pilots."

"Do you know what you're getting into?" Falkenberg wanted to know. "Soldiers are not slaves, but they must obey orders. All of them."

"Slaves have to obey, too."

"It's five years," Major Savage said. "And we track down deserters."

"Yes, sir." Mark looked at each of the officers in turn. They sat impassively. They said nothing; they did not look at each other, but they belonged to each other. And to their men. Mark remembered the clubs that children in his neighborhood had formed. Belonging to them had been important, although he could never have said why. It was important to belong to something.

"You see the regiment as merely another unpleasant alternative," Falkenberg said. "If it is never more than that, it will not be enough."

"He came for us, Colonel," Frazer said. "When he didn't have to."

"Yes. I take it you are sponsoring him."

"Yes, sir."

"Very well," Falkenberg said. "Sergeant Major, is he acceptable to the men?"

"No objections, sir."

"Jeremy?"

"No objection, John Christian."

"Adjutant?"

"I've got his records, Colonel." Captain Fast indicated the console readout. "He'd make a terrible enlisted man."

"But not necessarily a terrible officer?"

"No, sir. He scores out high enough. But I've got my doubts about his motivations."

"Yes. But we do not generally worry about men's motives. We only require that they act like soldiers. Are you objecting, Amos?"

"No, Colonel."

"Then that's that. Fuller, you will be on trial. It will not be the easiest experience of your life. Men earn their way into this regiment."

"Yes, sir."

"You may go. There will be a formal swearing in when we return to our own camp. And doubtless Captain Fast will have forms for you to fill out. Dismissed."

"Yes, sir." Mark left the command tent. The times are out of joint, he thought. Is that the right line? Whatever. Does anyone control his own life? I wasn't able to. The police, the Marines, the Boss, now these mercenaries—they tell us all what to do. Who tells them?

Now I'm one of them. Mercenary soldier. It sounds ugly, but I don't have any choices at all. It's no career. Just a way out of slavery.

And yet…

He remembered the morning's combat and he felt guilt because of the memory. He had felt alive then. Men and women died all around him, but he'd felt more alive than he'd ever been.

He passed the graves area. The honor guard stood at rigid attention, ignoring the buzzing insects, ignoring everything around them as they stood over the flag-draped figures laid out in neat rows. A cool breeze came up from the sea. Winter was coming, and it would be pleasant on Tanith, but not for long.

AFTERWORD

Every generation since Hiroshima has grown up in the shadow of nuclear terror. The official policy of the United States was to remain helpless, to refuse to defend our land and people.

On March 23, 1983, the president made an historic speech proposing to change the defense strategy of the United States from Mutual Assured Destruction—MAD—to Assured Survival.

The instant reaction from much of the intellectual community was to speak of *Star Wars* and call the president "Darth Vader."

As months went by, the opposition did not decrease. In an editorial on October 23, 1983, the Los Angeles Times said:

"There is no guarantee that the system would shield the West from the missiles of the East. And if there were such a system, it would raise more terrifying questions. We cannot imagine the Soviet Union's responding with restraint if confronted with a system that jeopardized its side of the balance-of-terror equation.

"Pressed about the risks of a defensive arms race, the president replied: 'Well, would that be all bad? If you've got everybody building defense, then nobody's going to start a war.' An untested theory.

"The investment [in missile defenses] would again encourage dependence on technology at the expense of political ingenuity. The extraordinary research-and-development resources of the United States, as well as those of the Soviet Union, should be focused on the needs of a troubled world, not on new space weaponry."

The Times concluded that defending America would be "a terrible mistake."

That view seems to have been adopted by a large part of the media, with the support of a vocal group of academics and other intelligentsia.

I find it incomprehensible.

The first duty of any nation is to protect its citizens. The first duty of the United States of America is to "provide for the common defense." We speak of "entitlement" programs; are not the people of the United States entitled to defense?

No one disputes that we should focus our ample research and development capabilities on the needs of a troubled world. One of the principal needs of that world is peace.

Peace is more than the absence of smoke and armies. Communist Party theorists call the "socialist world"—which includes not only the Soviet Union but also Poland, Czechoslovakia, East Germany, Hungary, the late Baltic Republics and the rest of the satellite empire—"the Peace Zone"; but calling them that does not make them peaceful.

Certainly the Poles do not think they have peace merely because they have an absence of war.

Harold Lamb calls his history of the great nomads of Central Asia *The Earth Shakers*. Throughout history the West has trembled at the march of the barbarians, and with good reason: Ghengiz Khan made a pyramid of more than a million skulls and so reduced the city of Samarkand that "three times the Horde rode over the place where the city stood, and not a horse stumbled."

The last siege of Vienna by the Turks took place in 1683. In 1776 the great English historian Edward Gibbon could rejoice in the knowledge that cannon and stone fortresses had at last made Europe safe: The earth-shakers could no longer ride west to burn and slay.

The Poles, Czechs, Slovaks, Lithuanians, Latvians, Esthonians, Finns, Hungarians—all might disagree.

If we dare not defend ourselves now lest the Soviets fail to respond with restraint, what can we do when the Soviets have developed missile defenses? Have we already surrendered? Does nothing remain but to negotiate the terms of our slavery? But we have not come that far. We can, if we will, remain, for all our faults, the land of the free.

It would be simpler if by one supreme act of work and sacrifice, we could defend our land once and for all. Alas, we cannot do that. There is no perfect defense; there is no space-borne Maginot Line behind which we can hide. There is no single decisive, ultimate weapon that will save us forever.

Cannon and stone fortresses could not forever save Eastern Europe from the barbarians. Space weapons and ballistic-missile defenses cannot forever protect the West.

Technological war is dynamic warfare. It is silent and apparently peaceful, but it is nonetheless decisive. To refuse to engage in the Technological War would have exactly the same consequences as unilateral disarmament. History has taught that Appius Claudius the Blind spoke more truly than he knew: "If you would have peace, be then prepared for war."

In these perilous times, preparation for war is serious business, carrying us far beneath the seas and far beyond Earth.

Ideally, we should not need to do that. Ideally, we should explore the depths of the seas and the limits of our solar system for the peaceful benefit of all mankind. I know few who would not prefer that. Yet—is not preservation of freedom a benefit to mankind? Is not keeping part of the world free of the Gulag a goal worth treasure?

Historically, peace has been bought only by men of war. We may, in the future, be able to change that. It may be, as some say, that we have no choice. It may be that peace can and must be bought with some coin other than the blood of good soldiers; but there is no evidence that the day of jubilee has yet come.

Until that day comes, guard your peace, for there will be war.

CPSIA information can be obtained
at www.ICGtesting.com
Printed in the USA
BVHW070317280921
617648BV00004B/31

9 789527 303177